WHO WOULD BELIEVE A PRISONER?

WHO WOULD BELIEVE A PRISONER?

INDIANA WOMEN'S CARCERAL INSTITUTIONS, 1848–1920

Written by the scholars of the Indiana Women's Prison History Project—Michelle Daniel Jones, Anastazia Schmid, Kimberly Baldwin, Lara Campbell, Nicole Hayes, Rheann Kelly, Christina Kovats, Natalie Medley, Molly Whitted, and Michelle Williams

Edited by
Michelle Daniel Jones and
Elizabeth Nelson

THE
NEW
PRESS

NEW YORK
LONDON

Published in the United States by The New Press, New York, 2023
Distributed by Two Rivers Distribution

ISBN 978-1-62097-539-8 (hc)
ISBN 978-1-62097-540-4 (ebook)
CIP data is available

The New Press publishes books that promote and enrich public discussion and
understanding of the issues vital to our democracy and to a more equitable world.
These books are made possible by the enthusiasm of our readers; the support of a
committed group of donors, large and small; the collaboration of our many partners in
the independent media and the not-for-profit sector; booksellers, who often hand-sell
New Press books; librarians; and above all by our authors.

www.thenewpress.com

Composition by dix!
This book was set in Palatino Linotype

ART FOR
JUSTICE
FUND   This book was made possible, in part, by a generous grant from Art for Justice
Fund, a sponsored project of Rockefeller Philanthropy Advisors

Printed in the United States of America

10 9 8 7 6 5 4 3 2 1

We are proud of every scholar who had a hand in the work that follows:

Cynthia Averitte
Kim Baldwin
D'Antonette Burns
Susan Byrd
Lara Campbell
Michelle Daniel Jones
Shelley Dillman
Lori Fussner
Gracie Guerreo
Leslie Hauk
Nicole Hayes
Jennifer Hays
Lisa Hochstetler
Sonya Hulfachor
Chelsea Johnson

Rheann Kelly
Christina Kovats
Cynthia Long
Azizi McNeil
Natalie Medley
Carissa Miller
Beanca Newgent
Selina Porter
Lori Record
Anastazia Schmid
Lisa Van
Molly Whitted
Michelle Williams
Kelsie Wilt

Contents

Preface

Kelsey Kauffman

The Scarlet Letter, the great morality tale about seventeenth-century America, begins, quite literally, at "The Prison Door," through which Hester Prynne emerges, ostracized and condemned for the crime of adultery. Nathaniel Hawthorne's story of sin, psychological violence, and hypocrisy was an instant bestseller when it was published in 1850 and is still considered one of the finest early American novels.

Prisons remain a great American morality tale, perhaps the greatest, alongside slavery. More than 2 percent of Americans languish in prisons or jails today, more than all the enslaved people in the United States in 1830. Though only 5 percent of the world's population resides in the United States, U.S. carceral institutions hold a quarter of the world's imprisoned people and one-third of the world's imprisoned women.

"Like all that pertains to crime," Hawthorne wrote of Hester's prison, "it seemed never to have known a youthful era." Yet prisons as we know them today are barely out of their "youthful era," having been conceived by Americans not in Hester's day, nor in ancient Greece or ancient Rome millennia before, but rather in the aftermath of the American Revolutionary War, in part as a reaction to the many bloodthirsty punishments of the colonial era and in part as a response to the North's gradual abolition of slavery. No longer were prisons to be mere holding grounds for those like our fictional heroine Hester Prynne or for her real-life predecessors like Anne Boleyn or Saint Perpetua, for whom prisons and jails were where they awaited their real punishment. In the New World, prisons would *be* the punishment for crime.

As is fitting for a morality tale, the founders and chief proponents of the modern penitentiary were some of the greatest religious and moral leaders of the Revolutionary period, men like Benjamin Rush and Benjamin Franklin. The Quakers of Philadelphia were strong proponents, and their spiritual descendants in the twenty-first century are among the penitentiary's staunchest critics. By the time Hawthorne wrote *The Scarlet Letter*, six decades after the American Revolution, the ideal of the *penitentiary*, where prisoners, like monks, quietly contemplated their misdeeds in solitary cells, had already been displaced. Moneyed interests now saw prisoners as workers who could be treated as little more than slaves, while the arbiters of acceptable society used prisons as a means of banishing the unwanted and the offensive.

In Hester Prynne's day, indeed until after the U.S. Civil War, women and men were held together in prisons and jails, often in the same cells. Females were few in number, but the conditions for them were horrific. It was not until 1873 that the first state prison for women was opened in the United States—the Indiana Reformatory Institution for Women and Girls—and it was not until the 1950s that the last of the American states finally built separate prisons for women.

Like their male counterparts after the Revolutionary War, the founders of the first women's prisons in the United States were lionized (and continue to be) for their personal and civic virtue. Yet the stories of the Indiana Reformatory Institution for Women and Girls, and of the Catholic women's prisons that preceded it, are full of arrogance, cruelty, and, as one of the authors of this volume puts it, "counterfeit decency."

Rewriting the History

The Indiana Reformatory Institution for Women and Girls, now known simply as the Indiana Women's Prison (IWP), is the oldest continually operated women's prison in the United States, though it is now located a few miles from the original site. Historians, journalists, and civic leaders have long lauded the prison's founders for their character and vision in establishing the first women's prison, which still attracts visitors from around the nation and the world. A large portrait of the founding superintendent of the prison, Sarah Smith, holds a place of honor in the prison's administration building.

During the 1990s and the first decade of the 2000s, IWP was also praised for its progressive programming, including a well-regarded college program. Then in 2011, the Indiana General Assembly abruptly withdrew funding for the college program. As a member of the prison's Community Advisory Board, I proposed restarting the program with an entirely volunteer faculty and without government funding. The prison's superintendent, Steve McCauley, was skeptical but supportive, as were prison staff. The program grew quickly from eighteen students our first semester to more than one hundred students a year later, nearly 20 percent of the prison's population. Our annual budget, raised via GoFundMe campaigns, was just $5,000. Everything was strictly rationed, including paper and pencils, forcing students to forgo margins, and forcing faculty to decipher cramped writing as best they could. We had ten ancient computers, most still using floppy discs. (We joked that we were teaching the history of computers.) Yet, ironically, the blessing of a supportive administration and the absence of funding gave us far more freedom than most college programs allow, whether inside prisons or out, and gave us the unexpected advantage of an outstanding volunteer faculty, most of whom had retired from central Indiana's best colleges and universities.

On the downside, our students had no access to the internet, the prison's minuscule library contained mostly romance paperbacks, and interlibrary loans took months, if the books arrived at all. Students had none of the usual ways to learn how to do research. What we did have at IWP, though, were original documents pertaining to the founding of the prison, including all the original annual reports and a registry from the Indiana Archives and Records Administration that contained detailed information on every woman incarcerated at the prison from its founding in 1873 until 1900.

In the summer of 2013, I recruited some of our best students—twelve undergraduates and five "graduate" students who had completed their bachelor's degrees under the old college program—and told them we were going to spend the summer writing a history of the prison that we would then publish as a pamphlet. The students would learn how to do original research using primary documents, and prison officials would have a nice pamphlet to give to visitors.

We divided into teams that first semester. One group focused on life inside the prison: what the women ate (Carissa Miller), what books they read (Shelley Dillman), how life for the girls in the prison differed from life for the women (Jennifer Hays), and what the prison's annual expenditures were (Lori Record)—all topics richly described in the annual reports. Another group researched relevant histories that would provide important context and timelines for the nineteenth century: United States (Sonya Hulfachor), Indiana (Susan Byrd), women in the United States (Bianca Newgent), women reformers (Cynthia Averitte), Indiana men's prisons (Gracie Guerrero), and other "total institutions" (D'Antonette Burns).[1] Selina Porter was tasked with trying to visualize the physical prison—its layout, construction, and appearance—as no plans or photos exist. Lori Fussner was assigned the Quaker founders of the prison, Sarah Smith and Rhoda Coffin.

The five students who had already completed their bachelor's degrees at the prison had broader mandates: Rheann Kelly initially son ("norms, customs, habits, and social relations within the prison"). Kim Baldwin focused on female criminality in nineteenth-century America and the role prisons played in the U.S. economy at that time. Leslie Hauk, who descended from a line of Friends, wrote knowledgeably about nineteenth-century Quakers. Anastazia Schmid chose to research the mental and physical health of the imprisoned women, topics dear to her heart. Kimberly Jones, who had the best quantitative reasoning skills in the class, took on the task of digitizing and analyzing the prison's registries.

My original plan began to unravel at the beginning of our third week. Michelle memorably announced at the beginning of class, "Dr. K., we have a problem. There were no prostitutes in the prison in the nineteenth century and only one for any sex crime at all." We brainstormed how that could be. Indiana clearly wasn't libertarian at the time; indeed, a stated impetus for founding the prison was the inundation of prostitutes in Indianapolis after the Civil War. We found a handful in the city jail, but if news accounts were correct, the women made merry at the jail for a few days, paid a small fine, and were released.

"Where were the hos?" as Michelle so delicately and persistently put it at the start of every class. Stumped, we begged for help from the head reference librarian at the Indiana State Library, Monique Howell, who enlisted the assistance of her staff. After weeks of searching, they turned up a most confusing article—not from the mid-nineteenth century but from the mid-twentieth century— telling us that the Sisters of the Good Shepherd were leaving Indiana, having come *a century before to found the first women's prison in the state.* Yet we knew by then that not a single Catholic worked at the Indiana Women's Prison in the nineteenth century. Christina Kovats's chapter in this volume takes the story from there. Suffice it to say that the search for the prostitutes led to the discovery of a large network of women's prisons in the United States that preceded

IWP and were far more important than IWP and other early state prisons for women but that had been forgotten long since. That was the first but far from the only disruption of my original plans for that summer.

The second disruption concerned Theophilus Parvin, the prison's doctor for its first decade. Dr. Parvin has been justly celebrated by historians for his erudite annual reports documenting everything from eye surgeries, to his successful search for causes of a typhoid outbreak (one of the prison's wells), to efforts to vaccinate all the women, to his embrace of germ theory, which had only begun gaining traction in Europe but not yet in the United States. Indeed, while Parvin was at the prison, he was elected president of the American Medical Association and would go on to become the nation's most celebrated obstetrician-gynecologist of the late nineteenth century.

Anastazia, who had been tasked with writing about the mental and physical health of the women, took an instant dislike to Dr. Parvin. Why, she demanded to know, would such a high-caliber doctor be working at a women's prison in what was considered a backwater state at that time? I chided her for her skepticism but she persisted, until at last I searched for and found some of his scholarly publications written while he was at the prison and soon thereafter. The next morning, I went straight to the prison superintendent, Steve McCauley, to ask his permission to bring the articles into the prison. Why did I need to ask his permission? Because (as Steve quickly agreed) the articles were clearly pornographic, with Parvin's detailed, really quite gleeful, descriptions of digitally raping the women at the prison, and were deeply misogynistic and racist. Yet the articles had been written by the prison's own doctor and had been published in the leading gynecology journals of the day, so Steve (an amateur historian himself and a staunch supporter of our college program) gave his consent.

Parvin's articles didn't just expose a very fruitful and original line of inquiry, they, more important, paid tribute to Anastazia's skepticism and her fearlessness in asserting her own epistemic privilege, as someone who had lived experience of the prison world, over mainstream historians, regardless of their prestige, who had never been incarcerated. The scholars' epistemic privilege became critical to all that was to come, not least because it set in motion dynamic tensions between me (and later Elizabeth Nelson, Micol Seigel, and other outside scholars involved in the project) and the students, wherein they claimed insights based on their lived experience, and we demanded supporting evidence for their theories. This tension played out across many issues—from the character of the prison's founders, to the economic exploitation of the girls and women, to the possible trafficking in corpses (the last never proved)—and is felt everywhere in this book. It is why the book is scholarly in nature yet also deeply personal and accusatory in tone.

By the end of our first summer, we had many more questions than we had answers. So we pressed on during fall 2013, then spring 2014, until eventually the ever-transforming research project that led to this book became a year-round affair for close to a decade, first inside the prison, then eventually both inside and out. Membership was in constant flux. Some opted out after the first semester, but others (Azizi McNeil, Lisa Van, Amy Perman, and Cynthia Long) joined. Some who might have become core members, like Gracie Guerrera (our first expert on Jeffersonville) and Lori Fussner (a devoted fan of Rhoda Coffin), were released or transferred to other prisons. Still others were prevented from participating because of disciplinary actions that were often frustratingly petty. For example, we lost our best writer, Leslie Hauk, in the middle of the first semester when she was sent to solitary and then banned from the education building for eighteen months for the crime of writing "I ♥ Jenny" on the inside of the chapel's almost-inaccessible bell tower *after having volunteered well over a thousand hours to the chapel's renovation.*

We lost another excellent student, Lisa Hochstetler, when she was accused of kissing her friend on the cheek while out on the rec yard, a charge she denied and insisted that the surveillance cameras would prove she was right. She spent a month in solitary and was banished from our program for nearly two years, until the prison was finally ordered to view the video, and she was exonerated.

A more lasting loss occurred in the spring of 2016, when Kim Baldwin, one of the project's intellectual leaders, was exiled to remote Rockville Prison for being a perpetual thorn in the administration's side, a situation that had come to a head with Kim's determined efforts to expose the prison's culpability in the excruciating death of a young mother in Kim's cellblock, Tanya Moore.

But enough core members always remained, and new ones joined to sustain the project's focus and energy.

Ours might have remained an insular academic exercise had not my neighbor, an American history professor at DePauw University, suggested the students give a panel at the annual meeting of the Indiana Association of Historians (IAH). The IAH meeting is a modest affair, attended by a few dozen historians and their students, but it would provide a fairly safe challenge for the women, none of whom had ever been to, much less spoken at, an academic conference. Superintendent McCauley gave permission for the women to use the prison's antiquated videoconferencing system (normally reserved for remote parole hearings). The students spent an intense three months researching, writing, and practicing their presentations, including engaging in mock panels during which I and other faculty at the prison peppered them with the toughest questions we could think of—just in case.

When the day came, only six people showed up for our session. Four were undergraduates at the host university, who appeared to have wandered in. To our good fortune, the other two were Wendy Gamber and Eric Sandweiss, who were then, respectively, director of graduate studies and chair of the history department at Indiana University (IU). Likely because of them, we began to receive other invitations, including one from the American Historical Association asking for an article about our work for its magazine *Perspectives on History*, which Michelle wrote. Michelle and Lori Record, another excellent student who joined the project, also published the history project's first peer-reviewed article in the *Journal of the Indiana Academy of the Social Sciences*: "Magdalene Laundries: The First Prisons for Women in the United States." It was the journal's most-read article of the year and would go on to win an award for the best article published in 2014 by the JIASS.

In a little more than a year, the women in the project had moved from writing what I initially expected to be a glowing account of their own prison's founders to writing an increasingly sophisticated and well-received critique of the origins of women's prisons in the United States. Over the next six years, the students presented papers from the prison at dozens of conferences, including some of the top academic gatherings in the nation, such as the American Historical Association, the American Studies Association, and the Organization of American Historians. That they were able to do so was largely thanks to the dedication of Carol Foster, the director of educational programming at the prison, who volunteered dozens of times on her days off to supervise the presentations, and Gary Curto and Steve Egyhazi and their amazing tech team at Indiana University, who enabled us to connect to the rest of the world.

Our growing success, however, created problems. I had long struggled to keep up with requests for research materials to bring to the prison, especially given the demands of directing and teaching in the overall college program, of which the history project was just one part. As the history students got deeper into their own research topics, their requests increased not only in number but also in obscurity. Meg Galasso, a librarian who had once been a student of mine at DePauw University, and Sharon Maes, another DePauw student, were a great help, as were Monique Howell and her team at the Indiana State Library (Monique even came to the prison to meet with the students). Still, students often were forced to wait months for us to fill their requests, only to discover that what we had brought was not what they needed.

Then in March 2015, *Slate* magazine published a story about the project. The story was one of only two requests for media coverage that we agreed to in the early years of the project. (As a condition for access to any of our programs, we required that journalists agree ahead of time not to identify or to discuss the reasons the women were in prison. Most refused, which was fine with us. Much to our regret, we briefly dropped that policy in 2017 before reinstating it.) The *Slate* article generated offers of help from around the country. Perhaps none was more surprising or appreciated than that from an unhoused man in San Diego, California, who spent most of his days at a university library. For more than a month, he sent a torrent of relevant and helpful information, including Sarah Smith's British origins, the identities of wealthy funders of the Homes for Friendless Women in Indiana, and the "disposition of convicted prostitutes by the state of Indiana after the Civil War." I loved that incarcerated students in Indiana were being assisted in their quest to rewrite the history of prisons by a homeless scholar in San Diego. Then just as abruptly, his emails stopped, and we never heard from him again.

Fortunately, the students were beginning to acquire some outstanding intellectual mentors, none of whom was more important than Micol Seigel, a professor at Indiana University, who is both terrifyingly demanding of her students and utterly devoted to them. She agreed in fall 2014 to allow Michelle and Anastazia to join her graduate seminar via videoconferencing. By the time we received permission from everyone at the prison and the university, the IU tech team had figured out how to securely connect us, and I had acquired the books, the course was half over. Undaunted, Michelle and Anastazia secluded themselves in their cells over a long weekend, devoured the seven books the IU grad students had read over the past eight weeks, and emerged ready to engage as equals.

Their success in that course led us to establish a pseudo–graduate school program (i.e., one with many of the demands but with none of the credit of a real graduate program) at the prison, in which an amazing roster of scholars participated as faculty or mentors, including Alex Lichtenstein, Micol Seigel, Alex Tipei, John Dittmer, Mariam Kazanjian, Andrea Smith, Elizabeth Hinton, David Roediger, Talitha LeFlouria, Khalil Gibran Muhammad, Heather Thompson, Ougie Pak, Marlon Bailey, Caleb Smith, Pippa Holloway, Marcus Rediker, Lorna Rhodes, Emmalon Davis, and Charlene Fletcher Brown. (In addition to Anastazia and Michelle, students participating in the graduate program included Kim Baldwin, Lara Campbell, Leslie Hauk, Rheann Kelly, Natalie Medley, Nan Luckhart, Melinda Loveless, Sarah Pender, and Michelle Stancati.)

We were delighted when the students' work, individually and as a group, began to receive recognition. The Indiana Historical Society awarded us its Indiana History Outstanding Project for 2016, which was especially meaningful for us as 2016 was Indiana's bicentennial. That same year, Anastazia Schmid received the Gloria E. Anzaldúa Award from the American Studies Association for her outstanding work as an independent scholar. Meanwhile, three of our excellent undergraduates at the prison swept the annual Peggy Seigel awards for best undergraduate papers *in the state* on Indiana history. Christina's paper on Magdalene Laundries won first prize, and Molly Whitted and Michelle Williams's paper on the economic exploitation of the girls at the reformatory won honorable mention. (A later version of their paper was published by the *Midwest Social Sciences Journal*.) More recently, Michelle Daniel Jones received the

2020 Angela Y. Davis Prize, awarded annually to a scholar who has applied or used their scholarship for the public good.

While still at the prison, Anastazia and Michelle wrote a full-length play about Indianapolis's leading madam in the 1870s—known locally as the Duchess of Stringtown—and her relationships with key power players of the day, including the prison's founders and doctor. Much to our delight, Supt. McCauley approved two performances of *The Duchess of Stringtown*—as long as the playwrights deleted some of the racier scenes. With help from Bryan Fonseca, who was Indianapolis's leading independent theater director, and from beloved actor/director Gigi Jennewein, twenty of the women rehearsed all winter and spring of 2017. The first performance, held in the prison chapel, was for invited guests only, including a busload of historians from around the country who were attending the National Council on Public History conference in Indianapolis. The second performance was for the prison population itself—the best possible audience. Their delight in the performance was exceeded only by their pride that some of their own had written, directed, and performed such a play. I have never enjoyed a theater performance more![2]

Despite this triumph, the history project was already beginning to fracture as key students and key administrators left. As noted, in 2016, Kim was banished to rural Rockville Prison (and her papers and documents were lost, creating enormous headaches later as we tried to reconstruct footnotes for her chapters). In spring 2017, Anastazia was transferred—at her request—to another equally remote women's prison, in Madison, Indiana. Soon after, Christina Kovats was sent to a jail in the hills of tiny Dearborn County, and in August, Michelle Daniel Jones was released from prison to start work on her PhD at New York University. Meanwhile, two critical supporters of the project—Department of Correction (DOC) commissioner Bruce Lemmon and prison superintendent Steve

McCauley—retired and were replaced by far less supportive administrators. The very week Steve left, I moved to California to help raise my newborn grandchild.

By all rights, the history project should have died. That it did not is due primarily to Elizabeth Nelson, then a recent history PhD who took over my role as history project director in 2018. Unlike me, Elizabeth is a trained historian whose own academic expertise on psychiatric institutions fit well with the project. She inherited a strong group of remaining students, including grad students Lara Campbell, Natalie Medley, and Rheann Kelly, as well as undergraduates Molly Whitted and Michelle Williams, and brought in two new students, Nicole Hayes and Lisa Hochstetler. In some ways, the departure of Michelle, Anastazia, and Kim, who had focused on the origins of the Indiana Women's Prison, made space for equally important investigations of Indiana's Magdalene Laundry (Lara's, Natalie's, and Rheann's specialty) and for consideration of women and girls in contemporaneous institutions, such as the Fort Wayne School for Feeble-Minded Youth and the Indiana Girls' School.

Not long after Michelle Daniel Jones arrived in New York for her graduate studies, she met Ellen Adler, the publisher of The New Press, who took an immediate interest in the project. A few months later, the women in the program were offered a book contract. That posed some interesting dilemmas, the most critical being how royalties would be split were the book ever to turn a profit. So many women had been involved in the project that we could see no fair and accurate way to figure out what proportion of the final product each individual had contributed. Worse, we feared that if we tried to divide the contribution and profits, we would destroy the strong sense of sisterhood among the women. Thus, Michelle, Elizabeth, and I agreed that once the project's expenses had been covered, all profits would go to a fund to support similar projects benefiting women in prison nationally.

Before signing such a contract, of course, we needed the under-standing and the support of as many of the women as we could find, especially those who were still incarcerated. We sent a draft to the prison and to the Indiana DOC. With the consent of the new warden, I returned to IWP to meet with my former students. Our joyful reunion was cut short when a friend on staff at the prison— deeply embarrassed—informed me that a senior administrator in the Indiana DOC's central office had learned that I was at the prison and had ordered me escorted out immediately, because "offenders don't write books!" In that moment, the Prison History Project was transformed from one that was openly celebrated and facilitated by the prison system to one that was constantly threatened with being shut down.

Yet, under the steady leadership of Elizabeth Nelson, it survived and quietly thrived. Indeed, the Prison History Project grew be-yond the course at IWP to become a dynamic collective of incarcer-ated and formerly incarcerated scholars. Dividing her time among prisons and working with those who were out, Elizabeth inspired, enabled, cajoled, and reassured her authors, who eventually pro-duced the chapters of the book you have in hand. In doing so, she was ably assisted at various stages by undergraduate students at DePauw and Indiana University–Purdue University Indianapolis (IUPUI): Peper Langhout, Marlen Huesca, Jerome Bingham, and, especially, Monica Deck, who also played an important role in ed-iting chapters and providing the project with essential administra-tive support.

Of the ten named authors of this volume, five are now free: Anas-tazia Schmid, Michelle Daniel Jones, Nicole Hayes, Christina Ko-vats, and Molly Whitted. However, Kim Baldwin, Lara Campbell, Rheann Kelly, Natalie Medley, Michelle Williams, and dozens of other women who worked on the project remain caged.

My greatest hope in the publication of this book is that read-ers like you will come to see in a new light not only the origins of women's prisons in the United States but also the women who inhabit those prisons today, especially the authors of this volume. No good is served by their continued incarceration. I hope you will help us set them free.

Kelsey Kauffman
Greencastle, IN
June 2022

Methodology:
"We're Doing a New Thing"

Michelle Daniel Jones

Consider the plight of the incarcerated historian. At the Indiana Women's Prison, we did not have access to the internet; that is still true at the time of this writing. Our library was minuscule and was primarily stocked with romance novels. Interlibrary loan requests could take months to process, if they were completed at all. And we obviously could not visit archives or other repositories ourselves. We consistently faced challenges while researching this book, some of which were compounded by our unavoidable institutional restrictions.

We also had to place our research on Indiana's early carceral institutions for women in context. To begin, we studied the origins of prisons in the world, nineteenth-century U.S. history, and the contextual reasons that motivated the establishment of a separate prison and related facilities for women. We explored multiple additional fields of inquiry relevant to the various topics within the project, including historical definitions of crime, prison economies, and histories of medicine and public health.

Our professors and assistants invested countless hours searching for relevant material at the Indiana State Library, the Indiana State Archives, and across the internet. They spent hundreds of dollars photocopying material for us. Our research requests were always filtered through another person's understanding of what was needed for each topic. As our focus developed and shifted, following up on leads took weeks or even months; some students received more information than others did; sometimes, the sources found by our proxies weren't relevant or useful. While this was certainly a challenge, the consistent contact and engagement with these volunteer collaborators enabled us to grow and to develop expertise.

This improvised research process required asking pointed questions in order to expedite source discovery. For example, after we digitized and analyzed the prison registries and studied Indiana's history, we realized that women convicted of crimes of a sexual nature like prostitution weren't at the prison in its early years. Yet our reading of contemporary accounts of postbellum Indianapolis convinced us that women were indeed charged and convicted of sex crimes. We asked our professor and a state librarian to search county jail records for women convicted of prostitution, and when that failed to reveal the missing women they kept searching. It was this extensive search that led us to a critical article detailing the 1873 opening of a private facility for women prisoners, run by the Sisters of the Good Shepherd. Incidentally, this was the same year that the women's prison opened. This discovery sparked for us a new chapter of inquiry of historical Magdalene Laundries and their heretofore unknown role in the incarceration of women in Indiana.

We were also extremely challenged with access to technology. Our research team shared five old laptops dedicated for our use. When possible, we used the computers used by the undergraduates enrolled in college courses. Some of us whose work assignments provided access to computers negotiated with supervisors for more computer time.

These unusual methods, stemming from the difficulties inherent to the pursuit of academic research inside a prison, set in relief the riches of discovery, the expansion of ideas and viewpoints, and the development of a clearer view of history.

We Are Doing Something New

We are doing something new: our qualitative inquiry centers the captive and tells the truth in ways that counter dominant narratives that historically exclude and devalue captive voices. The standard methodological procedures and approaches to research served as our starting points. Ultimately, however, they proved inadequate to reflect the work we are doing as incarcerated and formerly incarcerated women scholars, and they did not take into consideration all that we have read and all that we have *lived*. Our work has three components: (1) researching women's carceral institutions in the state of Indiana, (2) excavating subjugated knowledge, and (3) critiquing the carceral state writ large. Formal shoes did not fit our feet; they were crafted by typically white, male, nonincarcerated academics who deem our feet unworthy. In this book and in all our work, we cobble our own shoes and we walk a new path: research conducted through the eyes of captive women.

Scholarly research rarely depicts incarcerated people as skillful, competent, and worthy human beings. Most research starts with criminality and assumes deviance. This research is never objective. As Linda Tuhiwai Smith writes, "Research is not an innocent or distant academic exercise, but an activity that has something at stake and that occurs in a set of political and social conditions."[1] Subjectivity is inherent in all research, especially in ethnography. Nicholas Wolfinger iterates that the ethnographer is actively shaping the data by what they choose to notice or not to notice, to record or not to record.[2] A critical yet often uncriticized aspect of research about incarcerated people conducted by nonincarcerated people is the message that we are unworthy human beings viewed exclusively as research subjects and as policy objects through the lens of "reform" and "rehabilitation."[3] The risks and consequences of research conducted on incarcerated and formerly incarcerated people are relatively unseen by investigators themselves and by readers of their research. The risks and consequences of such research are the burden of the captive.[4]

As incarcerated and formerly incarcerated scholars, we seek to privilege our experiences of incarceration so that "the past, our stories local and global, the present, our communities, cultures, languages and social practices" are not only "spaces of marginalization, but . . . also . . . spaces of resistance and hope."[5] Incarcerated scholars intimately understand and experience marginalization, secrecy, and subjection. We are also better able to comprehend through our own experiences the systematic subjugation of others. Unearthing human stories and the structures and formations that created their subjugated experiences is a vital strength we bring to our work.

Approaching an archive against the grain of traditional research methodologies and institutional formations is a bold decision that celebrates our humanity and our right to value ourselves fully. By researching and by writing history, we make the experiences of incarceration useful beyond notions of rehabilitation and reform.[6] We bring our whole selves to the work. Just as it is impossible to cut away one's race, gender, and class when approaching the archive, it is impossible to wall off the influence of our lived experience of incarceration and its afterlife from our research. In our experience, this reality is rich and fruitful. As Joy James explained in *Imprisoned Intellectuals*, the scholarship and "analyses of imprisoned intellectuals both deconstruct dominant ideologies and reconstruct new strategies for humanity. [Our] writings proffer reactive and proactive readings of struggle and freedom."[7] James's conclusions are concordant with our own experiences.

Patricia Hill Collins utilized the concept of the "outsider within" to describe the African American woman inside both the white master's house and the traditionally white academy. She privileges the orientation of the outsider, a stranger who is then possessed of a particular perspective as the "marginal intellectual" that "may reveal aspects of reality obscured by more orthodox approaches [to scholarship]."[8] This is also true for the incarcerated and the formerly incarcerated woman scholar.

Much like the stereotyped Black woman described by Black feminist scholars, incarcerated women, especially Black women and other women of color, carry the burden of stigma and derision expressed in the dominant social narratives informed by academic research.[9] In the Black feminist tradition of self-definition and self-valuation, we epistemically privilege our right to be knowers. We also privilege our right to use our background and our history with the criminal legal system, especially the prison, to be one lens through which we view the archive.

In *Decolonizing Methodologies*, Tuhiwai Smith demonstrates how research in the Western imperial and colonial context is the standard by which "proper" research is measured and in which Indigenous people historically are represented as Other. Conversely, many Indigenous people regard "proper" research by Westerners as forms of "amateur collecting, journalistic approaches, film making or other ways of 'taking' indigenous knowledge that has occurred so casually over the centuries."[10] Another word for this method of research is *extraction*. Smith situates Indigenous researchers in a place of primacy when conducting research with their own people and with other Indigenous populations. "Indigenous peoples across the world have other stories to tell, these stories not only question the assumed nature of those ideals and the practices they generate but also serve to tell an alternative story: the history of Western research through the eyes of the colonized."[11]

Within our work, our ability as incarcerated scholars to ask critical questions and to excavate subjugated knowledge is nurtured by the process of qualitative inquiry. Our research is not confined to quantitative measures, which criminologists critique as profoundly limiting what is possible to know about crime and punishment.[12] Qualitative inquiry, as opposed to statistical measurement, focuses on lived experiences and on the complexity of people's lives. It cares about the ephemeral processes of human endeavors. It is idiosyncratic. Qualitative methods recognize that subjugated knowledge may be delicate and fragmented and that it requires reconstruction using various sources. Qualitative inquiry requires a willingness to wrestle with the pieces and parcels of knowledge to complete a different historical picture of the dominant narratives. For example, the dominant narrative surrounding Rhoda Coffin and Sarah Smith, who in 1873 founded what is now called the Indiana Women's Prison, is about pioneering, benevolent prison reformers who fought to create a haven of reform for fallen and wayward women and girls.[13] This narrative presents the founding of the first state-run prison for women as progress. However, in sifting through the collections of knowledge from the women and girls themselves and in privileging their right to be knowers of their own experiences, a more complex picture of Rhoda and Sarah comes to fore. Most important, the process of qualitative inquiry allows for the excavation of subjugated knowledge. This process supports intellectual inquiries such as genealogies and critical histories of the present.[14] Genealogy as practice "is, then, a sort of attempt to de-subjugate historical knowledge, to set them free, or in other words to enable them to oppose and struggle against the coercion of a unitary, formal, and scientific theoretical discourse."[15] Genealogies throw into question institutionalized narratives, such as the perspective of nineteenth-century Indiana women reformers as selfless and benevolent, like we see in the portrait of Sarah Smith as presented by the authors of her 1900 memorial.[16] Through genealogy, we expose the imperialist, patriarchal underbelly of racial and cultural formations, such as the "cult of domesticity." We witness how Rhoda and Sarah sanctioned the use of ducking, sexualized physical abuse, and deprivations to control women's and girls' sexual expressions. And we discover how the prison doctor, Theophilus Parvin, boldly used incarcerated women and girls as subjects of experimentation and gynecological research. Research then becomes a viable collection of information that reveals the roots of problematic institutionalized practices and ideologies that plague the carceral state today.

In resurrecting subjugated knowledge, narratives are always incomplete. Michel Foucault suggested that subjugated knowledge is hidden *within* the dominant historical narratives and has to be desubjugated, excavated, and justified because it is disqualified by the powerful.[17] In our case, as incarcerated scholars in the Indiana Women's Prison History Project, we grappled with two forms of disqualification: the disqualification that comes with our incarcerated status and the disqualification of the perspectives of our historical subjects, incarcerated people.

What is at stake in this double disqualification? Failing to recognize that knowledge continues to be subjugated is an ongoing struggle. What knowledge is and whose stories are heard and believed remain fields for engagement. At stake is the potential loss of our collective stories and of our experiences as incarcerated people. At stake is the loss of our common humanity, our interconnectedness with one another. At stake is the perpetuation of penal policies that assault the personhood of the incarcerated and dehumanize and demean us all.

When incarcerated scholars privilege their experiences of incarceration as one lens through which to view the archive, we question the authority of the dominant scholars who write about the jailers and the jailed. We question through our actions whether those scholars can create an accurate and valid capture of history, knowledge, and experience. By so doing, incarcerated people, and incarcerated scholars in particular, defy and denounce the stereotypes and labels that superimpose false limitations on our intellectual reach and capacity. Just as Black feminist scholars "create their own standards for evaluating Afro-American womanhood and value their creations," we also create our own standards for evaluating the carceral archive of captive women in Indiana.[18] While I disagree with famed sociologist Erving Goffman on many things, I agree with his statement: "There's no way in which, if you're dealing with a lower group, you can start from a higher group, or be associated with a higher group."[19] I disparage the use of terminology like "lower" and "higher," but I agree that problems of understanding across perspectives exist when power imbalances persist.

What does it mean to imbue a viewpoint with epistemic privilege? This question should be considered in context with the force that operates in direct opposition to epistemic privilege: epistemic injustice. Prejudice regarding the incarcerated and formerly incarcerated is "linked to structural discrimination." It produces an indelible taint of criminality.[20] This prejudice is naturalized in society, floating in the background of minds and hearts as productive othering. Gayatri Spivak, in her work on the practices of silencing, uses the term *epistemic violence* to explain how this othering happens to the "lowest strata of the urban subproletetariat" in the United States.[21] Miranda Fricker's work on the believability of witness testimony in legal proceedings considers the ways race, gender, and class discrimination intersect with the right of the witness to be a "knower." In courtrooms, people of color, women, the poor, and the working class are denied the basic respect of knowing their own experiences. This is epistemic injustice.[22]

Epistemic injustice has a significant impact on the incarcerated and formerly incarcerated in this country. Our voices and contributions are devalued. In most cases, we are silenced.[23] Millions of people in the United States and in the world who have criminal records experience epistemic violence; we are defined and othered by the dominant group, who are not ensnared in the carceral state and who are not subject to the worst effects of the biographic mediation process.

Biographic mediation facilitates lasting discrimination. It affixes labels that justify stigma and exclusion. Institutional agents demand personal information as a requirement for access, including information that is directly linked to inherent and entrenched biases. For example, when a person has completed a sentence and has been released, a university admissions office can demand that the hopeful student produce officer arrest reports and court documents that narrate their conviction through the lens of criminality. From this vantage point, institutions create the frameworks within which we must tell our stories.[24] The institutionalization of organized prejudice and discrimination disadvantages the incarcerated and formerly incarcerated at our space of being and is thus a form of epistemic violence. Many acts of discrimination come fast and loose, attacking and exacting a cost not seen on the body but experienced in one's being, in one's ability to *be* and move about the world. It is disruptive and confusing and can cause targeted people to regress and not to progress.

We are not participant-observers. The very definition of *participant* forecloses this standard practice of ethnography from our usage. If we are using the lived experience of incarceration to inform our reading of the archive and incarcerated people cannot go home, then we are not participants, because the fact of doing research as incarcerated scholars is not voluntary. Anthropologist Hugh Gusterson argues that participant observation is not enough on its own and that "polymorphous engagement" offers opportunities for greater understanding and greater experience of a subject or topic.[25] A polymorphous engagement, in our case, is the fact of our involuntary confinement, coupled with our gender, race, class, sex, and academic work.

Participant action research (PAR) is oriented toward enacting social change through elevating the experiences of the participants in the design and implementation of research projects, using standard research methodologies, like participant observation and ethnography. PAR is designed also to inform the researcher, their processes, their findings, and ultimately their actions. Another

goal of PAR is the empowerment of the participants as contributors to social change, based on collection and analysis of data, which can inform the actions that a group could/should take: "PAR is not only research that is followed by action; it is action that is re-searched, changed, and researched within the research process by the participants."[26]

Critical participatory action research (CPAR) is realized in the work of Michelle Fine and Maria Elena Torre, who expand the reach of PAR to include and foreground social justice and change for marginalized people. They critique the extractive nature of traditional ethnography, particularly with regard to justice-involved people:[27] "CPAR is an approach to . . . research in which research collectives intentionally investigate these power differentials and inequities that hide under the banner of 'normality' as part of their methodological praxis."[28] PAR and CPAR are powerful and extremely valuable methodologies for research conducted about, on, and for incarcerated people. In a similar fashion, our method elevates the experience of the incarcerated researcher as an individual and carceral expert. However, while PAR and CPAR do not entirely foreclose the possibility of investigating conditions of confinement through historical archival research, they also don't require centering the condition of confinement as a unique key component in conducting historical research on captive populations, as our methodology does.

Historians contend with which sources to use, the accuracy of those sources, and how to credit them. Historically, the voices of women and girls in Indiana's carceral institutions have frequently gone unrecorded. Our methodology acknowledges the voices of women and girls and privileges their accounts.

Our methodology considers the reality and the everyday consequences of living in prison. At no point would facility staff and the Indiana Department of Correction (DOC) permit us to research our *current* living conditions and experiences as incarcerated women in the same way we researched the living conditions of women and girls in the nineteenth and early twentieth centuries. They would have shut us down if we had set out to expose abuse perpetrated by currently employed prison officials. The choice to focus on a historical time period is therefore a key aspect of our methodology. Researching, writing, and publishing about the facility's nineteenth-century origins proved to be a "safe" project—at least in the eyes of facility authorities and the DOC. Bringing primary source data to the facility and analyzing a supposedly distant past did not seem to pose a threat. To many administrators, it seemed safe enough for us to present our research at local, state, and national conferences, using the facility's videoconferencing equipment. The chronological distancing afforded by history is essential to our methodology. By researching incarcerated women of the past using primary source documents, we could revive and tell their stories while slyly critiquing the current carceral state. Lastly, additional courses offered us rich continuing education experiences that fed directly into our reading of the archive and into the development of the methodology we used in writing our book.

As we researched and wrote based on our unique perspective, our faculty looked for opportunities for us to publish and to present at local, state, national, and international conferences, and we followed up on all opportunities. Our forty-plus conference papers often served as the starting point for publications, which helped several of us to pursue higher education post-incarceration. Creating opportunities for incarcerated scholars' professional development is germane to this methodology.

There is a precedent in Indiana history for aspects of this methodology. Harrie J. Banka (real name, Harry Youngman) was incarcerated at the Jeffersonville men's prison from August 12, 1868, to May 20, 1871. He proclaimed at the start of his book *State Prison Life: By One Who Has Been There*: "A true narrative of State Prison Life can be written only by a convict, in a convict's cell; for he, and he alone, knows that life in all its phases."[29] Banka wrote to reveal the horrors happening inside the Jeffersonville prison because he understood that the "outside world" knew very little about the "inner workings of a prison."[30] He believed that he owed it to himself, to his fellow incarcerated men and women, and to humanity to tell the story. He argued that his viewpoint is critical and necessary to counter the "nicety" narratives and the reports of "House, Senate, and select committee" officials. Banka promised that he "shall write truth. And if it is stranger than fiction, it is truth, still."[31] His writing countered that of a person "with a contented mind, benevolent fancy, and flowing pen," who sought to "smooth away the sufferings of prison life. . . . What I write, I shall be able to prove."[32] Most important for this work, Banka's account includes firsthand observation of the women who were incarcerated at Jeffersonville prior to the founding of the separate prison for women. In particular, he recounts the horrible experiences these women faced at the hands of the warden and guards.[33] Our methodology has much in common with Banka's, such as humanizing the incarcerated, countering dominant narratives, privileging the narratives of the incarcerated, and critiquing the ideology and practices of the carceral state.

Access and audience are also key elements of the methodology we have built. Because prisons are cordoned, secretive spaces and because the people in them are often forgotten or ignored, we knew that our work had to reach more than just those in academia. Funneling our research into public-facing projects has been important to us, to ensure that more people can engage with our work and can experience this new understanding of incarceration. Included in this book is an excerpt from the original play by Anastazia Schmid, which brings new life to characters and key historical moments in our research through script and storytelling. Schmid also wrote a play about Mary Schweitzer, one of the women in prison, and the illegal operations performed on her by Dr. Parvin. We have made a point to present our work to as many diverse groups as possible, engaging with feminists, historians, undergraduates, activists, researchers, and teachers. We even have challenged our own faculty and program administrators in legitimizing the artistic production of our research. Converting our traditionally trained historians to our cause and gaining their support required them to see research as art. Our 2017 production of *The Duchess of Stringtown*, performed at the prison for the National Council on Public History conference, is evidence that art and research work together to shift narratives and open opportunity. Our goal is to transcend traditional disciplinary and stylistic boundaries to share our methods and knowledge widely.

What then is epistemic privilege in the context of academic research performed within conditions of confinement? For us, it has a specific meaning: the recognition and the validation of the voices of incarcerated and formerly incarcerated people through time. From the very beginning, our work on this project has sought to privilege, elevate, and center our lived experiences with the criminal legal system, and with the prison in particular, and to use our experiences as a lens through which we analyze the archive. As C. Wright Mills said, "The most admirable things within the scholarly community . . . do not split their work from their lives. They seem to take both too seriously to allow such dissociation, and they want to use each for the enrichment of the other." [34]

Our methodology is not quite participant observation as seen in standard ethnography because it is embodied in forced captivity. And it is not quite participatory action research because it reaches through time to better understand the origins of the present moment. We offer a new terminology: the *embodied observer*, one who views the archive from the position of the captive, from the inside of their experience. For example, as embodied observers, each one of us took seriously the allegations of sexual and gendered violence reported by the women and girls incarcerated in the Indiana

Reformatory Institution for Women and Girls from the moment it opened. No other scholar captured the investigations of abuse perpetrated by the two prominent Quaker reformers who founded the reformatory. No other scholar recognized that the histories and stories of those imprisoned women and girls are likely factual and need to be told. We, as incarcerated scholars and thus embodied observers, know the truth of the conditions of confinement, the realities of carceral trauma, and the presence of gendered and sexual violence in our personal prison experiences. All this informs our examination of the archive: we captured the voices and the experiences of those women and girls, captives like us. Presenting these narratives alongside the stories of the prison reformers provides a more complex, nuanced, and accurate history of these spaces in this period.

The concept of an embodied observer captures the difference between the body under literal confinement and that same body subjected to the taint of criminality, a type of confinement postincarceration. The embodied observer, however, is not limited to the experience of incarceration or the physical prison. Carceral geographic spaces writ large are key for the inscription of confinement that remains on the body, and therefore this methodology could apply to other carceral spaces, like asylums, orphanages, hospitals, mother-baby homes, Magdalene Laundries, juvenile homes and schools, and jails. Indeed, as our research expanded, we considered the histories of related Indianapolis institutions, such as private, religiously affiliated homes for "fallen women" and the state facility devoted to the care of the "feeble-minded."

We maximized our position as new researchers, as embodied observers, and we embraced the difficult answers and complexities of understanding that came from our pursuits. Others have written histories of the Indiana Women's Prison and its related carceral institutions, but we have uncovered much that previously has been omitted or unknown. We are committed to the pursuit of true contextual insight from our primary sources, and we engage with our secondary sources to form strong and compelling arguments. There is great power in incarcerated women writing these histories because we know which questions to ask. We are here to counter the dominant narratives, to expand the canon of knowers and knowledge, and to rewrite history justly.

WHO WOULD BELIEVE A PRISONER?

PART I

Indiana's First Prisons, Homes, and Reformatories for Women

1

Sallie and Eva at Indiana's First Prison, Jeffersonville

Michelle Daniel Jones

Sallie, likely Sarah Martin, was incarcerated at the Indiana State Prison South from 1865 to 1867.[1] She was a woman in crisis. Prison officials had sexually assaulted her numerous times by the time she spoke with Harrie J. Banka, an incarcerated man who in 1871 would publish an exposé on the conditions at the prison.[2] She told Banka that prison officials would regularly summon her to the warden's office or guards' quarters to be raped.

> Well, the worst of those brutes F——r, (the deputy warden), has ordered me to be prepared to receive nightly visits from him,

A portion of this chapter was presented via videoconferencing by Michelle Jones (Daniel), "Rhoda Coffin and the Fallout of the Cult of Domesticity in Indiana's Gilded Age," presented at the Indiana Women's Bicentennial History Conference, Hoosier Women at Work, Indianapolis, Indiana, March 26, 2016; Michelle Jones (Daniel), "Failing the Fallen: Sexual and Gendered Violence on Incarcerated Women in the Gilded Age," the American Historical Association Annual Conference, Atlanta, Georgia, January 7, 2016; Michelle Jones (Daniel), "Origins of the Indiana Women's Prison and the Criminalized Sexuality of Incarcerated Women," American Correctional Association Annual Conference, Indianapolis, Indiana, August 14, 2015; and "Sexual Violence Is an Old Hat: Criminalized Sexuality of Incarcerated Women in Indiana in the Gilded Age," presented via videoconferencing by Michelle Jones (Daniel) to Women and Gender Historians of the Midwest Annual Conference, June 12, 2015. I would like to thank everyone at those early conferences and institutions that gave us the opportunity to present our research via videoconferencing.

and he is coming this very night! Oh, it was bad enough before, to be called to the warden's office, or waylaid when about my work in the guard's quarters, and outraged by the chief devil of this State hell! You know very well, Mrs. B. (the matron), that there is not a day passes but I or some other girl is insulted by Col. Merriweather. But that is enough. This devil-dog must now come and bid me entertain him by night! . . . Oh, if I were out of here, I would kill him if he touched me; here, he *will* kill me if I oppose him; he told me so. . . . Next will come the guards; then we poor girls, instead of being mistress to two men, must act mistress to twenty.[3] (Emphasis added.)

If not for Banka reporting what he saw and what Sallie and other women said to him, the voices of these victimized women from Jeffersonville would be lost to history. Personal narratives are one of the most potent forms of resistance. They tell any reader or listener that control of one's story won't reside solely with one's oppressor. Fortunately, Sallie's voice echoes across time, and her anguish and anger foment from the loss of control of her own body. Her voice scathingly condemns the designing men, lawmakers, executors of the law, and grasping brothel-owning women who took advantage of her and her body and, in turn, labeled her deviant and consigned her to prison. While Sallie spoke for herself, she also spoke for the other women who suffered alongside her:

Before, I prayed for night, now I shall pray for death; for night and day will be hell alike. And they convict *us* of crime, and send us *here* to reform! We, who have fallen through misfortunes and temptations that *they* have never known; we, who have been led step by step astray, until obliged to commit crime to save us from starvation or shield us from cold! First death or some unseen calamity throws us upon the world. Do men reach out a strong hand to guide us in the straight course that leads to respectability? Do our own sex throw over us the protecting mantle of sisterly love? *No!* Sleek, smooth-tongued villains—the very men, perhaps, who help to make our criminal code—with glitter of gold and protestations of love, tempt us to ruin, rob us of our virtue and self-respect, crush the last spark of womanly love from our hearts, and then fling us from them as a thing to be despised. Female devils stand ready—the law licenses them to trade in our shame. When we have fallen so low that none will traffic with us, we are arrested, tried by the very law that aided in our ruin, sent to prison by the law, outraged by the executors of the law, who fight each other like devils to see who shall insult us first. Did I ever commit a crime so bad as will be done in this cell-house today? Mrs. B. (the matron), there is no use—no use! I wish I could die and end it all.[4]

Although Sallie often used the pronoun "we," if we read deeply into her speech, we can hear her personal story. Harrie Banka, in telling Sallie's story using titillating Victorian prose, aimed to capture the reader. His sensational style of writing was common for the era. Nevertheless, we can hear Sallie's anguish and can extract the meat of her story.

Sallie had been pursued by a man holding a political, possibly judiciary, position of some power and influence: he helped "make our criminal code." This man was affluent, "glitter of gold," and approached her with "protestations of love." She believed in him and was willing to lose her "virtue," most likely with the belief that marriage would shortly follow. Her tone was bitter because she probably loved this affluent, law-enforcing, respectable man, and he broke her heart. He robbed her of "self-respect and crush[ed] the last spark of womanly love" from her heart. Discarded by her lover and left with a ruined reputation, Sallie became a sex worker to feed and provide for herself. She lamented that no respectable man would marry her now.

Sallie's story is not unusual; many "ruined" women were left with few options, as many employers would not hire them.[5] In her story as told to Banka, she was taken advantage of by brothel owners, "female devils" who failed to offer her the "mantle of sisterly love" and to help her rise above her desperate circumstances. Sallie found herself degraded, sunk "so low that none [would] traffic" with her. Sallie was likely imprisoned for petty larceny; it was the most common charge women received in Indiana in this period.[6] Sallie expected the prison to be a place of reform. To her horror, she discovered a warden, a deputy warden, and guards who threatened, violated, and exploited her, in a place where "night and day would be hell alike." Her story takes us deep inside the blurred lines between sex workers and unfortunate women "ruined" by men, according to the societal standards of the day. Prison reformers like Sarah Smith, who would found Indiana's separate prison for women in 1873, believed they could draw a line between the two, saving unfortunate women while condemning prostitutes. The reality was more convoluted and complex.

Sallie was not even able to find peace, to find rest, in her cell. The inebriated deputy warden forced her to have sex with him repeatedly and strangled her into silence, promising to twist her "infernal neck off" if she alerted anyone.[7] Sallie was made to perform degrading sexual acts, beaten with a cat-o'-nine-tails, and raped repeatedly for three months straight.[8] She couldn't fathom how the deputy warden could justify sexually abusing her along with the use of the "cat." She cried, "Oh, you brutish dog, you ravish me one minute and whip me the next."[9] This particular beating occurred after the deputy warden accused Sallie of having sex with someone else. Sallie's story gives us a glimpse of women's experiences in prison in the 1860s.

The state of Indiana opened its first prison in 1822, just six years after achieving statehood. When it opened, the prison housed a single man.[10] From the beginning, the prison operated under a convict lease system, meaning that a private contractor leased the physical prison as a whole and the incarcerated men within it.[11] A cost-effective way to pay for a prison, the convict lease system disregarded decent living standards for the incarcerated.[12] In 1846, famed prison reformer Dorothea Dix visited the Indiana prison and reported in a local newspaper that "the lodging cells are worse beyond all comparison than any cells I ever saw allotted to human creatures. They are *horribly disgusting, filthy, and wretched.*"[13] She made other observations about poor ventilation and the failure of the administration to keep a punishment record. Dix suggested that the prison be abandoned. In 1847, it was.

The state prison moved to Clarksville, Indiana, located just outside Jeffersonville, but most people continued to erroneously call the prison "Jeffersonville."[14]

Moving the location of the prison did little to change the conditions for the men incarcerated there. The convict lease system subjected the men to a private contractor whose primary goal was to extract as much labor and make as much profit from the men as possible. As Banka explained in *State Prison Life*, the needs of the men were only marginally accommodated.[15] They worked long, arduous hours at brickyards and lumberyards, farms, docks, railroad stations, and the prison. Some were skilled tradesmen and worked as blacksmiths, shoe makers, carpenters, and coopers (makers of casks and barrels).[16] The lessee in charge when Dix visited the prison was Samuel Patterson, who won his first contract in 1836.[17] Some legislators and governors argued that the lease system in Indiana was exploitative, but nothing was done about it until 1846, when the Indiana General Assembly learned about Patterson's abusive methods: "It was his aim to get the last stroke of work out of the men with just as little outlay as possible."[18] According to Banka, the prison's first warden, William Lee, actually reduced the abuse the men experienced. However, after 1849, the warden

The administration building at the Indiana Reformatory Institution for Women and Girls in the 1890s

Colonel Lemuel Ford permitted wide use of the cat-o'-nine-tails. Officers swung the weapon and "cut and slashed to suit their own ideas." [19] Eventually, the revelation of abuse, and even torture, at Jeffersonville led the state legislature to appoint a warden to oversee "the government of the prison," and the legislature later appointed a board of directors as well. In 1856, Patterson's lease expired. He fought to renew it, but a report from the new board of directors to the assembly sunk his bid:

> We beg leave to the state, that at the time we took charge of the prison it was in a very dirty and filthy condition, and very much out of repair. The bedding was miserable, being nearly worn out, and dirty beyond conception, and entirely unfit for a human being to sleep upon. The clothing of the prisoners was

very shabby, and a number of them were suffering from an attack of scurvy, superinduced, no doubt, by bad diet and loathsome bedding; and their general appearance indicated a mode of treatment most assuredly not contemplated by the laws of the State.[20]

Convict lease practices did not end, however. They spiked during the Civil War. The state of Indiana ran the prison as cheaply as possible and allowed the warden and board to lease individuals for labor, even though a smallpox epidemic removed several men from the contract rolls.[21]

In 1865, a turnover of Jeffersonville staff took place. Many of the new officials and guards were Civil War veterans. As Banka described them, "men whose sensibilities had been blunted by camp-life, and whose consciences had been seared by years of debauchery in the lowest haunts of our worst cities."[22] In the wake of the war, the conduct of the staff prompted Governor Conrad Baker to enlist the help of Rhoda and Charles Coffin to investigate the northern and southern Indiana state penitentiaries.[23]

Affluent Quaker leaders and a true power couple of their time, the Coffins were known for their reform efforts throughout the state, including establishing the House of Refuge, a reformatory for juvenile boys, in Plainfield, Indiana.[24] When they visited the prison in 1868 on the request of Baker, several incarcerated men told the Coffins about the widespread violence against the women held there. At that time, there were about twenty women confined at the Jeffersonville Prison, in a building designated for them. Here is one report from an incarcerated man, as recounted in Rhoda Coffin's memoir:

A number of the guards had keys to the women's prison and entered when they wished to gratify their lusts. If the women could be bought up, they gave them trinkets or goods out of the government stores, if they did not yield, they were reported as incorrigible and stripped and whipped in the presence of as many as wished to look on.[25]

Prison officials also made up cruel, sexually exploitative games for their own entertainment. In one such game, a group of women were stripped naked and made to race one another along the prison grounds:

> In the court of the prison there was a large reservoir where the men prisoners were obliged to bathe once a week. On Sabbath afternoons, the women prisoners were brought out and compelled to strip, and thus exposed, required to run from the opposite side of the court and jump into the water, the guards using, if necessary, their lashes to drive them out to the howling amusement of the guards and their friends who were permitted to be present; keeping it up as long as they pleased.[26]

Coffin saw that rape and sexual violations were easy and frequent at Jeffersonville and that the all-male staff worked together to tyrannize and silence the women. Twenty-six women were incarcerated there between 1823 (the year the first matron, Mary A. Johnson, was hired) and 1859. The matron locked the women in the female department at night, but she did not reside on the grounds, and was therefore unable to protect the women in her charge.

Colonel J.B. Merriweather, the prison's warden from 1865 to 1868, was abusive, often inebriated, and just as culpable as his subordinates. He instituted the practice of keeping a mistress in the female department, a practice that the officers and guards quickly imitated.[27] As a result, women lived under the constant threat of violation and violence. Harrie Banka, incarcerated at Jeffersonville from 1868 to 1871, described how Merriweather commanded a young woman working in his residence to sing for him.[28] When she refused, the outraged warden left to retrieve the cat-o'-nine-tails. It was only the intervention of the warden's wife that prevented the assault.[29] According to Banka, Merriweather shamelessly charged prison officials $10 a month for open-ended use of the women in the female department. One prison official who took advantage of Merriweather's offer was the hospital steward, Jo Vanoy. In addition, when a staff member discovered Merriweather sexually assaulting a woman in her cell, the employee received a sudden promotion, ensuring his silence.[30] Allegations in the local news that the warden practiced concubinage in the facility recast the prison into a "vast bawdy house."[31]

In 1866, a young woman named Eva Green entered Jeffersonville and was immediately set on by the hospital steward, Jo Vanoy. Banka described Eva as a "very beautiful girl." Vanoy took advantage of Merriweather's open season and coerced and then blackmailed Eva into frequent sexual intercourse with him in the doctor's office. To Eva's horror, he infected her with a sexually transmitted disease, most likely syphilis. The disease caused lesions and scarring of her face and body.[32] Once Eva was infected, Vanoy discarded her. Before Eva's release in 1868, "covered with the eternal marks of her disgrace, and smarting from the keenest of anguish," she sat and wrote a complete account of Vanoy's abuses and demanded an investigation, with her physical body as evidence. She was not denied.[33] At the trial, Eva presented her case. Standing before the prison directors, she revealed that Vanoy infected her with a "loathsome disease, which festered and covered almost her entire person with putrid sores," and she was no longer "beautiful."[34] Several other Jeffersonville women testified about Vanoy's deeds and stood with Eva for justice. According to Banka, the women convinced the prison's board of directors of the hospital steward's guilt.[35] Vanoy reportedly hung his head between his legs as Eva bared her disfigured face and pointed at him. Eviscer-ated with guilt from "her simple but truthful tale," Vanoy asked to leave. Yet he was cleared by the directors. This is not surprising. Col. Merriweather was Vanoy's counsel in the presentation before the board of directors, and two of the directors were also lawyers. Merriweather summed up Vanoy's argument against Eva with a resounding imperative: "You can't believe that woman; caught her in a thousand lies."[36] The gavel sounded to deny justice for Eva. It echoes through time as the carceral system continues to strip con-fined women of their personhood, to deny them justice, and to in-validate of their experiences.

The prominent Quaker couple mentioned earlier, Rhoda and Charles Coffin, visited the prison in 1868 to investigate allegations of abuse and corruption. They published their findings the next year in their *Report of the Committee on Prison, Together with the Ev-idence of the Officers and Others before the Committee at the Southern Prison (Jeffersonville)*. They noted that "very grave charges were presented to the committee against officers and guards formerly in charge of the prison, of drunkenness, and treatment of prisoners, prostitution of female convicts, and demoralization generally."[37] The Coffins' report triggered a legislative investigation.[38]

Col. Merriweather and the guards presented a fit and decent prison to the investigating committee. Some incarcerated men were paid to play along, and the warden kept the committee tied up in long conversations with the men in the shops and dorms.[39] The leg-islative committee's report after visiting Jeffersonville was glowing. The brutish warden and his conspirators evaded exposure.[40]

Banka recorded all this arrogance, Merriweather's certainty that he would never be taken down, and certainly not by an inmate of the prison. After all, as Banka wrote, "Guard's word is always taken in preference to the prisoner's."[41] Yet Banka refused to let such fla-grant abuses of power go unaddressed. In his 1871 exposé, he ad-dressed the corrupt Jeffersonville guards directly:

You think you are safe from exposition, because the frowning walls of a prison shut out the world . . . and you think a prisoner dare not raise his voice or pen against "us!" "Besides," you argue, "who would believe a prisoner?" Well, we shall see. I expect to live, please God! to see you work your own ruin.[42]

The title of this book comes from Banka's exposition about the prison officials. Banka was keenly aware of the epistemic injustice that protected violent state employees while discrediting the testimonies of people like himself who had experienced incarceration. He still asserted the power and validity of his own narrative, writing and publishing to raise public awareness about the horrors at the prison. Banka was not the only person concerned for the well-being of the women at Jeffersonville. The Coffins' 1869 report took their informants' claims of widespread and systematic sexual violence seriously, with additional evidence likely presented by the number of children born to women incarcerated longer than nine months.

After the failed investigation of 1868, Jo Vanoy and another prison employee went on a thirty-day debauchery spree in the town of Jeffersonville. The citizens demanded their immediate dismissal, and Col. Merriweather bowed to the public pressure.[43] Vanoy pressured the warden for his job back. When the reinstatement wasn't forthcoming, Vanoy decided to tell the prison's board of directors everything he knew about what Col. Merriweather allowed to occur inside the prison. Much of it was reported in newspapers.[44] Vanoy charged that Merriweather was a "murderer, adulterer, abortionist, swindler, cruel tyrant, and father of the prisoner-woman's babe, and a monster guilty of every crime that it had been possible for him to commit."[45]

Col. Merriweather came before the prison's board of directors. After hearing the evidence presented by Vanoy, they suggested Merriweather resign to avoid prosecution.[46] Before he went, Merriweather had the young pregnant woman swear the child on Vanoy, which ensured Vanoy wouldn't be rehired. This failing of the state

Illustration in Harrie J. Banka's *Last of M_R.*

of Indiana in prison management found its way to the *New York Times* in 1869:

> The legislative report in which all of these outrages are related abounds with such sickening details that the conclusions at which the members of the Committee who framed the report arrived appear exceedingly tame; and the honor of the State requires most imperatively that the villains who perpetrated these atrocities should not be permitted to escape the punishment due to their crimes by merely resigning their offices.[47]

Unfortunately, none of the villains were prosecuted. But Banka rejoiced: "Col. Merriweather has resigned." The removal of the warden was enough for him. Considering that children were born into what was essentially a state-operated sex trafficking ring, it is no wonder Banka was relieved. The *Greencastle Press* reported these scandals, adding that the guards provided incarcerated women with whiskey, tobacco, and opium, such that "the women in the prison wing . . . led lives not a whit better than before their imprisonment. Such a thing as reform was never heard of." [48]

Upon Merriweather's resignation, he, like Vanoy, began to tell about his experience in the prison. He sent a letter to the Senate Committee, and a second investigation was launched in 1869.[49] Col. Merriweather came before this committee and readily admitted that he had sex with the women, was drunk on the job, allowed guards to board at his mansion, and made use of state supplies, but he denied that he beat or allowed a man to be beaten to death.[50]

Merriweather alleged that two members of the prison's board of directors, F.M. Meredith and M.P. McGhee, extorted money from him regularly, essentially making him pay for the privilege of being warden. "They frequently wrote me for money, and I sent it to them," Merriweather claimed.[51] He alleged that these two board members made contractors pay for the privilege to "exercise of their official authority" and that Meredith was compensated by an incarcerated man, Jon L. Mathews, to obtain a pardon on his behalf.[52] Feeling unable to keep up with Meredith and McGhee's demands for funds, Merriweather started asking employees to help him pay. Was this the moment in which Merriweather began charging the guards $10 a month for open access to the women? Of course, Meredith and McGhee refuted Merriweather's testimony, and with a new warden, Colonel Lawrence S. Shuler, officials expected changes for the better.[53]

Col. Shuler, like Merriweather, was a former military commander. At the outset of the Civil War, Shuler recruited a company of soldiers and quickly earned a captain's commission. After being injured in battle, he returned home, entered politics, and was promptly elected auditor of Hendricks County, Indiana. When Col. Merriweather resigned in 1868, Col. Shuler applied for the position and was appointed warden of Jeffersonville. His arrival offered a reprieve from Merriweather's cruel and exploitative regime.[54] Banka reported that Shuler got rid of the indiscriminate use of the "cat," and put on notice the guards who had served under the previous warden to change their behavior or be dismissed.[55] Banka offered a glowing tribute to Shuler, describing him as wise and decent to the incarcerated men. In praising Shuler's reformation in the management of the prison, Banka included snippets of dialogue between Shuler and the guards who were resistant to reducing corporal punishments and testimony from newspaper clippings presenting the findings of the first legislative committee.[56]

By 1871, however, Col. Shuler was himself under investigation.[57] Like Merriweather, Shuler had a problem with the women held in the prison. The matron charged that Shuler used inappropriate language with the women, allowed incarcerated husbands to visit their incarcerated wives in their cells, acquired a pardon for one woman who became pregnant, and maintained an inappropriate relationship with Nancy Clem, a "notorious murderess."[58] Many formerly incarcerated men, Jeffersonville businessmen, local officials, and guards and other prison staff testified that Shuler used incarcerated men to work outside the prison (essentially reinstituting convict leasing) and enhanced his private property using state equipment and incarcerated labor. In contrast to the testimonies against Merriweather, the testimonies against Shuler were that he failed to provide the discipline of the cat-o'-nine-tails to make the men work, he allowed several men to escape on his watch, and he permitted Harry Youngman (Harrie Banka) to write a book.[59]

Regarding Harrie Banka's book specifically, the chaplain stated the following:

> I know the book spoken of; the book was written by Youngman, a convict; he commenced writing the book before Shuler became warden. Soon after Col. Shuler took charge of the prison he [Youngman] was appointed as my assistant in the Library; he brought all his manuscript with him and had perfect liberty to write when not engaged in his duties of distributing books

to the prison. . . . I did not assist him in writing the book—not one word; and so far as reference is made to acts done while I was there, they are true; I mean so far as the printed book conformed to the manuscript. . . . Youngman got access to the records of the prison by the consent of the Warden.[60]

An investigation into Shuler's tenure, published in 1875, showed gross fraud and misappropriation of state funds, not only in contractual obligations to the lessee but also in the conversion of his private house and grounds into a luxurious estate.[61]

Merriweather's and Shuler's prison leadership proved ineffective, dangerous, and corrupt. The effects of their leadership, or lack of leadership, touched everyone in Jeffersonville, especially the incarcerated women. In the 1869 congressional session, Governor Conrad Baker implored legislators to create a separate prison for women:

I therefore urgently recommend that a separate prison for female convicts be established with the least practicable delay, and that there be connected with it on the same grounds and under the same direction and management, but in different buildings, a reformatory for girls. . . . I commend the subject to your careful consideration, with the expression of the hope that the result of your deliberations will show that the cause of these unfortunate women has not been presented in vain.[62]

Col. Shuler, the deputy warden, the director, and the moral instructor were all dismissed in the wake of the investigation. By then, just over 160 women had been incarcerated in the chaotic and corrupt environment at Jeffersonville since its opening. In 1873, in preparation for the transfer of women to the new reformatory, approximately 13 women were discharged or pardoned.[63] Interestingly, approximately 5 women were incarcerated at Jeffersonville after the reformatory opened, but all the women were gone from there by 1877.

From what we can surmise from the existing records, Sallie and Eva Green were not transferred to the new women's prison. One hopes they were able to heal from the trauma they experienced in the Indiana State Prison South, aka Jeffersonville.

2

Rhoda and Sarah—Toward the Home for Friendless Women

Michelle Daniel Jones

Sarah Smith, a Quaker minister from England, believed God called her to save "fallen" women and girls. Relying heavily on her Quaker faith to change the women in her charge at the new Indiana prison, she said, in 1874, "I can thankfully record that in both departments (Penal and Reformatory), I am assisted by earnest Christian workers who labor faithfully for the temporal and spiritual improvement of those under their charge."[1] Smith's birth name was Sarah J. Willan, and she was born on October 31, 1814, in Dewsbury, England.[2] Her father recorded her birth in his diary: "A little daughter born this morning. I dedicate her to the Lord and to His service."[3] There is no accounting of what happened to her mother, but Sarah grew up in the Friends boarding school, Ackworth, and later in a Quaker home. "Friends" is a term used to describe members of a Quaker congregation and is synonymous with the word "church." The Society of Friends is in essence a Quaker church. It is likely that Sarah remained at Ackworth through her teens. At eighteen, she heard Joseph John Gurney speak and was inspired. Gurney was a minister of the Religious Society of Friends, a branch of Quakerism that espoused evangelical Christian doctrines concerning Jesus Christ, atonement, and the Bible. Sarah began to feel a divine calling to reform women and girls living sinful lives. She and James Smith, a fellow Quaker and Sheffield native, were married in 1836, when Sarah was twenty-two. Together, they had three children: Eliza, Maria, and John. Smith applied herself to temperance work, ridding her community of the abuse of alcohol, and formed "Mothers' Meetings to aid and instruct those needing help and sympathy."[4] Citing concerns for her health, Sarah emigrated in 1849 from Manchester, England, to America with her husband and children.[5] They settled in Wayne County, Indiana, on a farm in the town of Milton. They lived there with the Mclaughlin family, which at the time of the 1850 census comprised nine members.[6] The Smith family joined the Indiana Yearly Meeting, where they met Rhoda and Charles Coffin.

In addition to raising her children, Sarah Smith visited public institutions, including prisons, and traveled with Elizabeth Comstock, a Quaker minister, abolitionist, and social reformer, to Cincinnati, Louisville, Jeffersonville, and other cities.[7] Sarah preached to the sick and dying, and many sought the salvation she described in her talks. Sarah's service during the Civil War included working with freedmen and soldiers, distributing clothing, helping the sick, and holding religious meetings. As a part of the Committee on Freedmen, she went to Louisiana and Mississippi to work with newly freed African Americans and taught "the then very ignorant class how to use their freedom."[8] Smith, and likely Rhoda Coffin, was spurred to action by watching Angelina Grimké and her sister lecture across the country about the evils of slavery, the need to reform the spiritual and moral character of America, and the way women were uniquely fit to meet said challenges.[9] By all accounts, Smith was a devoted Quaker minister who took very seriously her work serving and teaching the poor and unfortunate.

Rhoda Coffin, a preeminent Quaker prison reformer, speaking at the National Prison Congress in 1885, after twenty years of working

Portrait of Sarah J. Smith.

with "fallen" women and "wayward" girls, communicated her in-grained beliefs about incarcerated women and elite white men:

Men cannot reform debased women. It is an impossibility. Most women who have descended so low as to be incarcerated in a prison under sentence, have lost self-respect and the finer sensibilities of her character.[10]

For Coffin, the "debased" woman was beyond reformation if left in the hands of men. Smith echoed the statement:

Woman is competent to govern the depraved and desperate of her own sex by womanly measures and appliances, with-out a resort to the rigorous means which are generally means supposed to be necessary in prisons governed by men, and in-tended wholly or chiefly for male convicts.[11]

Rhoda Coffin was born on February 1, 1826. Raised in an affluent Quaker home and instilled with strict religious values, she had a firm sense of herself and of her place in the world.[12] She married into another upper-middle-class Quaker family; her husband, Charles Coffin, was a leading Quaker and citizen of the Richmond, Indiana, community. Rhoda was a homemaker, devoted and faithful to her husband, and followed his lead. She bore six children: five boys, and one girl who died young. By her own account, Rhoda raised her children to be studious followers of the gospel. She presented the perfect home, proudly capturing in her memoir the many prominent Friends and others she received in her home and fondly reflecting on placing family first and above all things.[13]

From the outset, Rhoda desired to be visible in the public sphere.[14] In the space between having pride in the perfect home and desiring to be visible in the public sphere is a tension that Rhoda didn't address explicitly. She was bored in the role of homemaker and decided to step out of that sphere, declaring, "I must be about

Portrait of Rhoda Coffin.

my Father's business."[15] She expanded the Victorian dictates of the female sphere and the "cult of domesticity" to include activity for women in the public sphere with a "reliance on spiritual justification, domestic skills and volunteer labor."[16] Women activists worked within the bounds of womanhood to accomplish their goals, even as they forged these pathways into the public sphere.[17] Charles Coffin's career advancements, as president of the Richmond National Bank and as clerk of the Indiana Yearly Meeting, afforded the employment of domestic workers in their home by the 1860s.[18] At that point, Rhoda Coffin was free to seek her own interests.[19]

From the start, she focused on benevolence. Rhoda's early benevolent activities involved serving on a board of visitors and inspectors for a public high school and assisting in the establishment of the Marion Street Sabbath School in Richmond in 1865, which served poor families of all faiths suffering in the aftermath of the Civil War.[20] She and Charles positioned themselves to serve in the various reform efforts within the Quaker community.[21] In their travels throughout the state of Indiana and the wider United States, Rhoda and Charles shared their faith, preached the gospel, and made a point to visit jails, the poor, and other Quakers.[22] Rhoda became known to many as she and Charles gained notoriety, both nationally and internationally, as leading experts in prison reform through prison visitation and frequent communion with other leading prison reformers in the United States and in Europe.

The benevolence that Sarah Smith and Rhoda Coffin pursued in Indiana built on the work of antebellum women reformers from all faiths and races that started in Pennsylvania. Women from Protestant, Quaker, and Catholic backgrounds organized themselves around the care and concern for humanity. African American women started the first organization, the Female Benevolent Society of St. Thomas, at an African American church in Philadelphia that focused on benevolent work, in 1793.[23] Free African American women (and men) created their own organizations, rather than

dealing with "the inconsistencies and condescension of white paternalism," particularly in areas where the population of African
Americans was highest (Philadelphia, Providence, Newport, Boston, and New York City) and where the free outnumbered the
enslaved.[24] In 1795, white women established the first benevolent
institution independent of a church body, called the Female Society
of Philadelphia, and dozens more were established in the twenty
years that followed. Women in cities such as New York and Boston gathered and created independent civic organizations, which
proved to be "an extraordinary historical step, one that forever al-
tered the social field in which women could undertake collective
religious, political, ideological, and economic activities."[25] In their
work of organizing, "women in the new nation formed associations
to achieve personal and group goals, and in the process shaped
new experiences, representations, and expectations of womanhood" and saw their work grow from small-scale neighborhood benevolent work to large-scale movements.[26]

   White, Black, and Indigenous women's lives of the antebellum
era were typically subject to the will of men, and even women's
organizations privileged masculine and patriarchal ideas.[27] Yet
women were not completely without choices.[28] For example, while
women could not enter into contract without the permission of a
man and could not vote, they could exercise agency within the
home and through the elements that flowed from the home: sometimes commodities, but mostly culture, ideologies, and beliefs.[29]
The late eighteenth and early nineteenth centuries therefore saw
not only the growth of cities and industrial processes but also the
growth of women's organizations, which developed from private
coffee table meetings to public actions and movements. Quaker
women like Angelina and Sarah Grimké exemplified that shift.[30]
Their work represented a link between the abolitionism and
women's rights organizing, two movements that did not always
work in tandem.[31]

From the late 1830s, the Grimké sisters spoke publicly in cities across the country against the ills of slavery, moving women into the public sphere and forging a path to the development of women's rights and organized women's groups. Raised in Charleston, North Carolina, a southern city with sixty thousand slaves and twenty thousand whites, where slavery was ubiquitous, the Grimké sisters' abolitionist and evangelical work helped open the way for other women to publicly engage in politics in their own farming, rural, and anti-revivalist communities.[32]

Religion played a key role in the Grimké sisters' activism.[33] The Second Great Awakening (1800–1860) emphasized the "sacred power of individual will," which protected the abolitionists in their fight against the rule of law, or the social order.[34] This awakening empowered a new middle class to seek salvation and to empower themselves to be "free of sin."[35] Sarah, and then Angelina, came to Quakerism largely because of its opposition to slavery and because of the lack of abolitionist activism in their own Episcopal church. By 1835, the sisters were members of the Anti-Slavery Society.[36] The two sisters would go on breaking tradition by speaking in public, preaching the abolition of slavery, and publicly asserting that women were the spiritual and moral equals of men, even as fellow abolitionists began to complain that the issue of women's rights clouded the arguments for abolition.

The Grimké sisters left the Anti-Slavery Society in 1838, and the group splintered over the issue of combining the cause of women's rights with the abolition movement. Lucretia Mott and Elizabeth Cady Stanton organized the first convention of women's rights in Seneca Falls, New York, and saved the women's rights movement from fracturing the antislavery movement.[37] By the 1850s, the women's rights movement attracted temperance organizers and members of the moral reform movement, as well as those who advocated for marriage and property rights for women, effectively changing "the lives of most middle-class white women."[38]

Unfortunately, in the women's rights movement, those interests did not have large support for including African American women.[39] In the years following the Civil War, the women's rights movement split completely over the issue of race and the interpretation of the Fifteenth Amendment, which included race but not gender in the language of who could vote.[40] African American women fought to keep themselves in the conversation and in the legal fight, as leading African American men like Frederick Douglass absorbed "Black woman" into "Black people" and white women leaders like Cady Stanton opposed African American men from getting the right to vote before women got it. Ultimately, African American women abolitionists like Frances Harper and Sojourner Truth, famed speakers of African American and women's rights, remained on the fringes of the two major white women's suffrage organizations that never fully embraced them. After the Civil War, African American women like Ida B. Wells, a gifted educator, lecturer, and writer, formed separate suffrage organizations.

The Victorian cult of domesticity developed amid the rise of capitalism and supported the capitalist infrastructure.[41] The 1820s and 1830s saw the proliferation of periodicals published to educate young girls, young women, and mothers on how to live the "right" kind of life. Such texts were written by both women and men, with a focus on reinforcing a woman's place in the domestic sphere through religious ideologies that fashioned "the world" in stark contrast to "the home."[42] As the industrialization of the European and American economies led to increasing numbers of men working away from the home, women were left in charge of creating a "proper" home and raising children. These duties reinforced contemporary notions of a woman's proper state as pious, clean, chaste, obedient, and childlike. For Rhoda Coffin and Sarah Smith, a woman's proper state included teaching the gospel and living a godly life.[43] The home—the female sphere—was the counterpart to the competitive and treacherous world of capitalism, and the home demarcated the boundary of women's influence.[44] Married Victorian women were devoid of legal personhood, owned little to no property, and rarely labored outside the home.[45] These conditions reinforced the cult of domesticity. Indoctrinated into this cult, Coffin and Smith learned to embody the ideal American woman and wife through religious piety, purity, submissiveness, and domesticity.[46] Coffin and Smith did not challenge the social precepts emphasizing domesticity, marriage, and children; to their best ability, they upheld them as aligning with Quaker beliefs and life.[47]

The female sphere, particularly after the 1830s, became less about subservience and the inferiority of women and more about definitive and inherent difference of place. Within this domestic sphere, "influence" (the ability to persuade others because of one's race and class status) shaped "virtue" (moral standing, holiness, purity) and "implied a more rigid difference between men and women, depicting women as more naturally suited for benevolent work."[48] It was in this space that women publicly sought education, sisterhood, personal strength, and power—and even openly displayed opposition to men.[49] Ironically, the primary reason Coffin and Smith could venture into the public sphere was that their husbands were wealthy enough to hire help to perform domestic duties. A wife was considered successful if she could produce these outcomes in her home. Failure to maintain a proper home supported arguments that women like Coffin and Smith, who dabbled in the public sphere, were "out of place"; so hiring domestic help was of the utmost importance. Therefore, the two women found that female domestic workers were imperative to creating the "proper" home as they crossed out of the home and into the public sphere.

Both women sought to expand the Victorian dictates of the feminine ideal and its cult of domesticity to include activity for women like themselves in the public sphere. Donning the mantle of religious morality, Smith and Coffin "reconnected [the female] sphere with the well-being of society."[50] Armed with this declaration of purpose, these women countered the correlation of the "public woman" to the prostitute and crafted a public presence that overtook the masculine "legitimacy of civil virtue."[51]

The cult of domesticity created hierarchical roles based on gender, race, class, religion, and even marital status. Only married, white, affluent women like Coffin and Smith saw themselves commanding leadership roles in the public sphere. Conversely, African American, immigrant, undocumented, and criminalized women dealt with systemic racism and pervasive discrimination, which constrained their efforts to reach beyond the female sphere in the same way.

This highlights an important point about the variable agency afforded to women in the late nineteenth century. Quaker women's middle-class status led them to believe they were distinctly equipped to reform the "fallen" and "wayward" women and girls of lower social classes and to put them on a path of their (the Quaker women's) ideological making. Only women with Smith's and Coffin's social privilege could even imagine expanding the female sphere *and* creating institutions in the public sphere that they themselves would control and lead, which contained women of all races.

Indiana in the time after the Civil War was particularly challenging for women. While William Robeson Holloway, a chronicler of Indianapolis, reported that businessmen and the state of Indiana reaped great economic gains from opportunities stemming from the Civil War, women for the most part lost. Many women had lost their income-producing fathers, husbands, and sons, creating precarious lifeways for them. Even though many women had worked the family farms and plantations, they were enmeshed in marginalized economic and political positions and remained so after the war. Many "Indiana Democrats remained convinced the white man must stand above black men and all women."[52] In addition, women had few opportunities to earn a living wage, and those who were working (typically domestic jobs) earned definitively less than men did.[53] Even though some women used their homes to take in board-ers, most women were powerless in a system they did not control. Sex work, theft, and fraud became, in many cases, the only alterna-tive to destitution and death.[54]

Sex workers were the bane of Indianapolis society after the Civil War. Commentators proclaimed that they were everywhere. In 1870, one observed that among the worst evils the war brought was the inundation of prostitutes:

> They flaunted their gay shame in every public place. They crowded decency, in its own defense, out of sight. Their ba-gnios (brothels) polluted every street. The military camps were not always, with all the vigilance of sentries and rigidity of dis-cipline, safe from their noisome intrusion. The jail was nightly filled with them and their drunken victims. And the remuner-ation of their vice was so ample and constant that a fine was a trifle. Even if it could not be paid, the alternative of a few days' confinement only restored them in better health, with strong allurements and appetites, to their occupation.[55]

In hegemonic spaces of power and control, there will be resis-tance. In lieu of "decent" jobs, these women flouted convention to exercise their sexual agency, constituting material survival strate-gies in the scarcity and lack after the war. The mayor felt compelled to find someplace for them to go. Land was donated "just beyond the southern suburbs," "just beyond the city limits" for county courts to send sex workers. The message: keep the deviant influ-ence of prostitution far from our city of "good" and "pure" women. State officials were to send sex workers to a "prison for the vicious and intractable—as a home for the more mild and teachable."[56]

In Christian doctrine, women stood responsible for prostitution, as Eve stood at fault for Adam's fall. Eve was the tempter, the seduc-tress, who caused Adam to sin. Many believed that "without the check of reason over her emotion and instincts, woman was always in danger of going astray, and that check has come from white men, using the Bible, force, coercion and the language of purity and righteousness and the fear of falling to control and subdue the female body."[57] Instituting patriarchal control of women and their bodies can be seen as emerging directly from Christianity, and in Indiana, the Coffins often led in those efforts.

By Quaker standards, the Coffins and the Smiths were progressive in their ecumenical reform efforts, and they bonded over the importance of engaging the world at large with the gospel and reform.[58] They visited prisons, asylums, and institutional homes. The Coffins' and the Smiths' interests stood in opposition to the strict Quaker tenets of isolation, quietism, and reserved dress. The Coffins and the Smiths stood against the rigidity and the repression of orthodox Quakerism, a battle that fell largely along generational lines, with the elders dominating the meetings and the various aspects of Quaker life.[59]

The younger generation tended to follow the branch of Quakerism founded by George Fox. Fox "rejected absolute male hierarchy," which reinforced that "being a wife and mother was not the only approved role for a Quaker woman."[60] Popular women's culture and feminism itself identified and highlighted the root of conflict between men and women as an imbalance of power, which in Fox's Quakerism did not manifest itself in the same way.[61] The tension between Quakerism, evangelical Protestantism, and notions of traditional gender roles is present in Rhoda's voice when she said,

> I never could follow closely in a groove laid out by another. I tried hard to do so, for I realized my position: was an important one. . . . I was in a position to exert some influence, and it was important that I should act so as to exert an influence which should not close the way or in any way hinder the

service of either my husband or myself. . . . I honestly tried to walk as they directed, . . . but it was all an utter failure.[62]

Coffin tried to adhere to the strict tenets as much as possible for her own sake, and for the sake of her husband's position, but, as stated, she broke most determinedly from them all. Sarah Smith and her husband followed the Coffins in this shift.

Encouraged by Quaker friends and imbued with a revolutionary spirit, the Coffins made room for major changes in the Quaker faith. These changes included singing and speaking in the meetings, encouraging evangelism, and advocating for ecumenical benevolent work and social reform. The Coffins also encouraged the promotion of Quaker values and precepts through the mass production of religious tracts and pamphlets, which increased the visibility of Quakers and their faith. "The Richmond Preparative Meeting was organized in the first month of 1865. It was an offshoot of a prayer meeting [that] commenced [in the private house] of Charles and Rhoda Coffin"; "the Richmond Preparative Meeting established Sabbath schools, Bible classes, Reading circles, which met at different homes, Tracts and Tract Readings, Cottage Prayer Meetings, etc."[63]

The Coffins also developed the Friends' Foreign Mission Association and traveled to various nations ministering the gospel. Sarah and James Smith were extremely active in this work alongside the Coffins. In Rhoda Coffin's memoir, she conveyed that the purpose of the new meetings was not to cause division but to expand the church's reach and to make their faith more palatable and accessible.[64]

Their moral superiority underscored their gendered and elite perspective and was informed by their religious backgrounds and the political climate of their time. How did Rhoda Coffin and Sarah Smith arrive at the conclusion that "debased" and "depraved"

women—women who are devalued and deemed "lower" in character and class—could not be helped or rehabilitated by men? What
ideas and opportunities informed their understanding of the differ-
ences between women convicted of crimes and women like themselves? Sarah and Rhoda's beliefs about women's activism and how
and why these two took on the reformation of women and girls in
Indiana become clearer when these benevolent prison reformers
are explored within the historical context of the Victorian era and
when the dominant narrative of these women as purely benevolent
is disrupted and the human complexity of their motivations and
their work is revealed.

A Sabbath school is a religious school wherein Bible study, discussion, outreach, and fellowship are key components. Once the Marion Sabbath School was up and running, Rhoda Coffin shifted her
focus to the creation of the Home Mission Association of Women of
the Yearly Meeting (HMAW) in 1866. As the association's first president and key founder, Coffin desired to give Quaker women the
freedom to organize and to play active evangelical and missionary
roles in the church.[65] Working with her husband and other Friends
couples, she observed the lack of women's input in the church administration. The HMAW was a platform for young Friends, including men and husbands, to participate in church missionary work
in a time of much religious revival and conversion.[66] The HMAW
represents a major benchmark for Rhoda Coffin. She took matters
into her own hands and communicated to the Quaker meeting her
desire to create a women's organization that would generate other
organizations led by women, continuing the legacy of the women
reformers before her.[67]

Traditionally, Quaker membership in Indiana remained largely
white. There is no evidence that Smith and Coffin formed alliances
with freed African American women before, during, or after the

Civil War in various movements organized for alleviating social ills, even though Smith served African American families during the Civil War. Contrasted against the abolitionist and women's rights movements in New York and Philadelphia that included freed African American women, the organizations formed by Smith and Coffin were led by decidedly white, middle-class, Protestant, and Quaker members.[68] Within the available archive, there is no evidence to support that Quaker women's benevolent organizations in Indiana reached across the racial line as the many women's benevolent groups along the East Coast did.[69] The white women and African American women in these areas created their own separate benevolent organizations, to flee from the "inconsistencies and condescension of white paternalism" in antislavery, poverty organizations, and the like.[70] In Indiana, these activist women maintained race and class distinctions, established themselves independent of men, led and directed the work, and "situated themselves in positions where poor men, women, children, white, black, native-born, recent immigrants, became their dependents."[71]

The HMAW operated successfully for six years without men before Rhoda advocated for inviting men to participate and incorporated the organization into the church body.[72] After the creation of the HMAW, Smith and Coffin were then integral to the creation of the House of Refuge, a reformatory home for boys, and a home for women.

The HMAW established the Indianapolis Home for Friendless Women (HFFW) in 1867 as a home for sex workers, which introduced Coffin and Smith to state and local lawmakers.[73]

One of many similar institutions in the country, the HFFW brought the domestic roles typically performed in the home— preparing food, providing alms, and promoting family values— into public organizations and facilities.[74] It is likely that Rhoda Coffin and Sarah Smith heard the clarion call of Elizabeth Fry, who

Indianapolis Home for Friendless Women, located at what was Tennessee and Ninth Streets.

in 1827 stated, "May the time quickly arrive, when there shall not exist, in this realm, a single public institution [where women] . . . shall not enjoy the *efficacious superintendence* of the pious and benevolent of THEIR OWN SEX!"[75] At eighteen years of age, Smith had learned about Joseph John Gurney, the English Quaker minister whose beliefs led to a schism in the faith, and his sister, Elizabeth Fry, an English prison reformer, philanthropist, and Quaker, and sought to imitate Elizabeth.[76] Taking their cue from Fry and others, Coffin and Smith were convinced that any unfortunate woman or girl could be helped only by institutions organized and operated by women, like the HFFW.

Lawmakers in the state sought Rhoda Coffin as the best candidate to manage the Indianapolis Home for Friendless Women because she was the president of the HMAW, and the HFFW Richmond location was well managed. According to Coffin, however, because of all her other work, she herself could not run the home, so she handpicked Sarah Smith to run the new facility in Indianapolis. It began receiving women in 1867.[77] Smith managed the home for six years, until the new prison for women opened.[78]

A second institution, the Richmond Home for Friendless Women, opened in 1868, and it served as a home for convicted women, "helpless women with children, friendless girls, strangers passing through the city . . . and diseased, deformed, and illegitimate children."[79] The home was one of the first brick buildings in the city and included forty beds, a chapel, a laundry, a nursery, and eighteen chambers.[80]

Because of the appalling conditions women faced at the men's state prison in Jeffersonville, and impressed with the Indianapolis HFFW, county commissioners, authorized by new legislation, incorporated the Richmond HFFW as a city prison, and Rhoda Coffin and Sarah Smith were made deputy sheriffs.[81] The deputization of Coffin and Smith is unusual, as no other carceral institution in this book had women administrators empowered to "arrest and transport" convicted women. What was it about Smith and Coffin and the conditions of Indiana's criminal justice system that allowed this to occur? Desperation? Lack of interest? Respect for Smith and Coffin's work?

A woman, likely a white woman, charged with theft drove the push for county commissioners to approve the costs for outfitting a room at the HFFW as a prison.[82] In fact, the completion of the prison occurred in anticipation of her conviction. Upon her plea of guilty, the woman was taken into custody by Smith and Coffin, acting as deputy sheriffs, and placed "in our County Prison for women" in Richmond.[83] Coffin proudly related the woman's religious conversion to Quakerism and her eventual Friends' marriage. Thus begins Smith and Coffin's entrance into penal administration and reform.

While Rhoda's husband, Charles, and other elite Quakers lobbied state legislators at the government center, Rhoda and Sarah went to the nearby Bates Hotel to convince the governor to create a separate facility to reform young boys. Neither woman allowed her gender to deter them from their goal. The board of the Indiana House of Refuge was organized in the spring of 1867, and Charles Coffin was elected as its president.[84] By the following year, the facility began receiving boys. Lobbying for the House of Refuge and orchestrating the opening of both Homes for Friendless Women represent Coffin and Smith's entrance into Indiana political activism, a space in which they were quite successful.

With the influence gained from Sarah's missionary work and the two women's positions in the Quaker community, Rhoda and Sarah were able to shape greater Indiana. Their efforts were noticed by Indiana city officials, and in addition to becoming a sheriff, Sarah was named "City Missionary" of Indianapolis.[85] Sarah and Rhoda became a part of the very fabric of the political infrastructure that governed the state. They plainly felt that power should belong to them, and others like them, in the administration of public facilities, especially those involving women.[86] According to historian Lori Ginzberg, antebellum New York politicians' support for women's moral reform organizations rested on the fact that "by granting assistance to women's benevolent organizations, local politicians implicitly acknowledged that the women's efforts directly relieved governments of much of the responsibility for poor or aged citizen."[87] I suggest that this was likely true for Indiana politicians in the 1860s as well. In helping Coffin and Smith, Indiana politicians would not need to bother with women and girls who were abandoned, had "fallen," or were convicted of crimes. Therefore, with the state's support, Coffin and Smith's efforts surpassed visiting children, the sick, and the poor to encompass building carceral institutions. These two women envisioned a path out of the separate female sphere and into the public sphere.

Once plans for the reformatory were under way, the Coffins went on an expedition in the United States and around the world and attended the International Prison Congress in London in 1872. They visited prisons, jails, and houses of ill repute and in general surveyed reform efforts at home and abroad. The couple made influential connections everywhere, advancing their cause and growing in recognition. In acquirement of their position, Rhoda related that they traveled with "official documents given to us by our own governor with the noble seal upon it," which gave them access to closed prison doors internationally.[88]

After the Civil War, Indianapolis had its hands full with sex workers. Many of those women were sent to the HFFW. Unfortunately, a fire on September 23, 1870, reduced the building, except for a few outer walls, to ashes. And yet the number of sex workers arrested, charged, and convicted by county courts continued to rise. After the HFFW burned, what happened to these women who were forced or consented to engage in sexual promiscuity, and thus were considered "fallen" by the standard of the day? By all accounts, survival strategies of fallen women were particularly constrained. To quote historian Estelle Freedman:

Arrest, conviction, or imprisonment for offenses against chastity, decency, or public order carried a unique penalty for the nineteenth-century female criminal—the label of "fallen woman." No longer the perpetrator of a single immoral act, those who crossed the boundary of chastity gained a lifetime identity as a "fallen woman."

A nineteenth-century fallen woman experienced a greater stigma than did contemporary male criminals or than had women criminals in the past. Many women and men refused to associate with or employ even a suspected fallen woman. Thus outcast, the first offender often entered a vicious cycle which led her directly into the criminal class, often as a prostitute, as case histories illustrate.[89]

In 1897, a journalist for the *Fort Wayne News* put it succinctly:

In the minds of legislators and public men generally, a woman fallen is down forever. That an unfortunate or criminal woman or girl is so much worse than a criminal man or boy, that there is no hope for her reformation.[90]

3

Belle at the Home for Friendless Women

Kim Baldwin

On November 26, 1873, Belle Ward, an unwed pregnant white woman from Lawrenceburg, Indiana, died after giving birth at the Home for Friendless Women (HFFW) in Indianapolis. For a brief moment in time, her unnamed, unclaimed body had profound implications for some of the most powerful and influential women in Indianapolis. Then she was forgotten. Belle's story reveals a great deal about prevailing class and gender conventions after the Civil War and forces us to revise the prevailing historical view of late nineteenth-century social reformers.

Belle, born in 1840, was the youngest of three girls from Lawrenceburgh (now Lawrenceburg), Indiana, a waterfront town on the Ohio River frequented by flatboats and sailing ships. Growing up, she would have seen people bought and sold. Perhaps she even saw people freed through the underground railroad that ran through the area. She survived the hardships of the Civil War only

An earlier version of this chapter was presented as "The Plight of Poor Women in the Affluent Nineteenth Century: The Belle Ward Story, A Case of Deliberate Indifference," via videoconferencing by Kim Baldwin to Hoosier Women at Work, an Indiana Bicentennial conference held at the Indiana State Library, Indianapolis, Indiana, on March 26, 2016. We would like to thank the organizers of the conference for including our panel of incarcerated scholars speaking live from the Indiana Women's Prison.

to die mercilessly on a cold, rainy November day at the Indianapolis HFFW, a benevolent institution dedicated to the rescue and reform of fallen women.

By 1873, Belle and her two sisters were "orphans, the mother having died some years ago, the father having been killed by a train."[1] The country was in the early stages of what would come to be known historically as the Long Depression, wherein currency was devalued, small banks failed, and public infrastructure collapsed. Amid this economic insecurity, Belle's two older sisters traveled to Indianapolis in search of work. Both were fortunate to find jobs as seamstresses for prominent families.[2] Meanwhile back in Lawrenceburgh, Belle found herself the victim of a cruel deception. Her fiancé wanted her and her sisters to sell the small house they inherited from their parents and to give the money to him. The house was worth only about $400, but it was all they had of value. Not willing to part with it, they refused his offer and he in turn broke off the engagement. Pregnant, with nowhere else to turn, Belle fled to her sisters' tiny boardinghouse room in Indianapolis, where together they came up with a temporary solution: the Home for Friendless Women.[3]

The HFFW was around three years old when, on November 1, 1873, Miss Mary E. Brower replaced the inimitable Sarah Smith as the home's matron.[4] Among Mary's first actions was to meet with Ettie Ward, one of Belle's sisters, and to make arrangements for Belle. For $40 a month,[5] Belle, under the alias "Smith," would occupy one of the home's forty-nine rooms.[6] Belle was thirty-three years old when she arrived at the three-story brick building that sat just outside the city limits, on North Tennessee Street.[7] She stayed there until she died three weeks later.

Like any other expectant mother, Belle would have been dreaming about her baby, choosing a name, planning a future. Ultimately, she would labor in great distress and deliver her baby without a doctor present. After giving birth, Belle began convulsing, and she

Richmond Home for Friendless Women.

died two days later. The assistant matron and "three other inmates" were present, but again, no doctor was in attendance.[8] Matron Brower tried to ship Belle's corpse via railway back to Lawrenceburgh, but without a death certificate verifying that the body was clear of transmittable disease it was forbidden, and health officers were alerted.[9] Out of options, Brower summoned the undertaker and asked him how long the body of the dead woman would keep. After his examination, he determined not long. The next day, he received orders to put the body in a coffin and to place it in his vault the next evening.[10]

Anxious to visit Belle and the new baby, her sisters, "who had not been notified of her illness," went to the home and "were horrified to learn that she was dead."[11] They demanded access to the body. Because a certificate of death from an attending physician was necessary to release Belle's body to them, a doctor furnished a blank certificate for them to fill out, and only then were they able to take Belle home.[12] As for the baby, the sisters resolved to send it to an orphan asylum until they could secure the means to raise it.[13]

Nine days later, their personal tragedy was made public when the *Sentinel* printed "Mysterious Doings: A Dark Transaction at the Home of the Friendless."[14] "Through some unknown means," hinted the paper, "news was brought to the Health officers that the DEAD BODY OF A YOUNG LADY had been shipped over the Indianapolis, Cincinnati and Lafayette railroad recently, in a manner having the semblance of mystery."[15] Over the next several days, the paper denounced the home and its administrators, accusing them of bringing about Belle's death by withholding medical care.[16] The *Sentinel* reconstructed Belle's lonely ordeal, asserting that

> the Matron provided no nurse or watchers for the woman in her distress; that she was allowed to occupy her bed unattended and alone; that in a Home for the friendless, this unfortunate lady died without a friend at her side to tell how she died. The death certificate notes the cause of death as puerperal convulsions, induced in part, it is claimed, from want of care and attention in the hour of peril. For this criminal negligence, if such it was, the matron of the house is alone responsible.[17]

The paper suspected the home of a raft of offenses, in addition to Belle's death. Some were financial in nature. The matron, the paper charged, "must . . . have been guilty of conniving at or countenancing crime, in undertaking this job for money" since the home was supported by public funds.[18] The paper wondered, might the home have maintained a lucrative blackmail business? Apparently, two "gentlemen," having read the *Sentinel*'s articles, paid a visit to the newspaper's editorial room to share letters they received from the matron asking them to cover the charges related to the confinement and labor of women they supposedly impregnated.[19]

When the matron publicly refuted all charges against her, the paper printed even more accusations against the home, including the treatment of Belle's body after her death. The paper imagined the matron thinking to herself coldly, "At all events the poor woman was dead . . . and the body must be gotten out of the way."[20] The doctor "neglected to report the death of his patient to the Board of Health, as required by law" because, the paper reasoned, "he was in league with the Matron in keeping the sad affair from the public."[21]

In the face of the *Sentinel*'s well-publicized indictments, the home's board of managers called an emergency meeting. The ladies of the board devised a plan to clear their names. They would ask the home's trustees to form an advisory committee to investigate the charges. A public hearing would be held for that purpose, at which they would testify, review all the facts, and set the matter right in public. The president called a full meeting of the board of managers for Friday, December 12, at nine in the morning.[22] The board guided the process toward their own exoneration by holding the hearing in one of the home's chambers, ensuring that they could exclude witnesses who might offer inconvenient testimony. A trustee of the institution presided, while another trustee "conducted the examinations" of witnesses.[23] No cross-examinations would be allowed. At least two of the five members of the advisory committee—trustee Charles Todd, husband of board treasurer Margaret M. Todd, and trustee Thos. H. Sharpe, husband of board member Elizabeth C. Sharpe—were married to members of the board they were supposed to be investigating.[24]

On the day of the hearing, the advisory committee of gentlemen convened, along with witnesses and reporters. Miss Brower was the lead witness.[25] She vigorously defended her actions and refuted all accusations. She testified that when Belle's sister Ettie first came to the home to inquire if Belle could be admitted, she had told Ettie that Belle not only was welcome to stay there but also would not be charged for her stay.[26] Ettie, however, insisted on paying. Moreover, it was Ettie who had inquired whether Belle could be there under an assumed name. The matron claimed that she had given her the alias "Smith" "for the sake of saving the sisters" from the shame of exposure to Belle's ill fame and that neither she nor anyone else personally received any money for Belle's care—all payments were placed into the board's fund.[27] As for the quality of care that she and the home provided overall, Brower insisted that people in the home attended to Belle during delivery and afterward and declared, "I could not have taken better care of my own sister than I did of her."[28] Brower also discussed the selection of shrouds and the health of the baby, noting there were no clothes for the child when it was born and that the women at the home were busy making them.[29]

Ettie Ward testified that she gave Miss Brower $10 for the care of her sister, and then, perhaps in fear of being blackballed and unable to earn a living, she echoed Miss Brower's claims by affirming, "My deceased sister told me that no one could have treated her better than did Miss Brauer [Brower] and the inmates of the institution."[30]

Dr. Bigelow, who had never seen Belle alive or dead, testified that he provided the undertaker with a certificate, stating that "a certain woman who died last week, had no contagious disease."[31] Dr. Jones, whose role in the saga was distinguished more by his absence than by his presence (he had seen Belle briefly, once before she gave birth and once after), noted that he had not been paid for his visits but had little else to say.[32] Not so the board's officers.

Reverend Mitchell traveled all the way from Lawrenceburgh to serve as a character witness for the Ward ladies. He "simply

reiterated what was published in the *Sentinel* as to the good standing of the sisters," explaining that changing Belle's name did not
suggest an attempt at secrecy "except insofar as the sisters would
naturally wish for, to keep the shame of their sister from the public."[33] Likewise, a parade of leading women in the city testified to
the virtue of the matron and the home.[34]

Mrs. Newcomer, incensed at the scandal, spun the hearing in an
"intensely interesting" direction. "With a good deal of spirit," she
pointed listeners toward the exonerating nature of all the previous
testimony, from which "she hoped the reporters would gather a lesson" that they "could find a good deal more wrong if they turned
their attention toward the men."[35] This category, as Mrs. Newcomer
articulated it, referred to the "seducers" who were charged with
the room and board of women kept in the home. The room full of
board members erupted in agreement, and "several voices insisted
that the reporters be investigated as to the source of the odious
charges."[36]

At the insistence of Mrs. Todd and on behalf of the board,
Mr. Fishback, editor of the *Sentinel*, was pressed to explain why he
circulated reports of scandalous dealings in the home and to retract
the stories.[37] He testified that

the whole matter had originated from the knowledge that there
had been a violation of the ordinance [regarding the disposal
of dead bodies]; and that a rumor had been afloat for some
years that there had been a blackmailing scheme played upon
the seducers, and this had a great deal to do in prompting the
publication of the details in the particular case in question.[38]

The last witness called was Dr. Wands of the Health Department,
who was critical of the handling of Belle's labor and subsequent
death. Moreover, he was defensive of the "gentlemen" who considered the extraction of payment to house the women they had

impregnated a form of blackmail. For this, "he was 'badgered' most unmercifully." The *Sentinel* reported that

> at this critical moment the ladies plied him with questions as to whether he had informed . . . [the] *Sentinel* that there was no physician in attendance at the time the woman was confined, and other information which tended to prove the alleged transactions at the Home. The doctor, however, maintained his equanimity through it all. . . .
>
> He inquired of them then in return whether it was not a fact that no physician was in attendance when Belle gave birth; but as there was no answer, it was of course taken for granted that there was no contradiction to the statement. Having settled that point the doctor propounded to them the question whether any of them would be willing to allow a member of their household, in puerperal convulsions, to go a whole night without the presence of a physician. They were at a loss what to reply, some of them said it was a very common thing, but did not say that they would be willing to be without one under such circumstances.
>
> At this point the assembly began to disperse, leaving Dr. Wands and the ladies of the Board in a confab of words, and the meeting in a commotion.[39]

After a "brief consultation," both the board of managers and the board of trustees' advisory committee nonetheless returned with a verdict to acquit Miss Brower (and by extension themselves) of all charges. The board of managers declared that the matron's conduct had been "noble and exemplary in the highest degree" and that the "evidence had fully and completely vindicated her character, and that a vindication could not be more triumphant and complete." The five trustees in attendance concurred: "We are satisfied that the affairs of the Institution, under the Board of Managers, has done and is doing a noble work: that it is entitled to and should receive the fullest confidence of our people."[40]

Two weeks later, the following was recorded in the board's monthly meeting minutes for the home:

> A girl, who had been brought there in the early part of [November] had been delivered of a child on the 24th and died on the 26th. The case was an interesting one and called for deep sympathy. The only known relatives were two orphan sisters, highly respectable who were intensely anxious to shield themselves from the disgrace, which they feared might attach to them if the name of the unfortunate girl were to become public property hence the adoption by the Matron of the name Smith by which she was known at the Home. The real name was however made known to the Board.[41]

The great dislocations occasioned by the Civil War left thousands of women—often young mothers with small children—widowed or abandoned and with few opportunities to earn a sufficient income. The economic crisis of 1873 exacerbated a situation that was already desperate for many. Working-class women and their children labored for starvation wages, often less than half of what men earned, and were denied the positions in factories they might have occupied, even at such diminished salaries. The few opportunities that did exist for women were in industries that did not rely on factory production, such as men's clothing, dressmaking, and millinery work.[42]

To survive, many struggling women turned to petty crimes, such as stealing food, jewelry, small sums of money, and even clothing and household goods. Some engaged in sex work, as it offered the highest economic return. Sex work operated under the cover of saloons, dance halls, and gambling houses and was attractive to a variety of women who were barred from other forms of employment.[43]

The criminalization of sex workers made them vulnerable to a growing network of institutions designed by reformers to contain the poor in the net of the law.

Criminal charges related to sexuality were not limited to the exchange of sex for money. Myriad criminal charges connected the law to sexuality, punishing adultery, fornication, and masturbation, alongside prostitution. In addition, a subcategory of public order offenses, sometimes called crimes against chastity or decency, applied almost exclusively to women and punished a wide range of behavior, including lewd and lascivious carriage, stubbornness, idle and disorderly conduct, drunkenness, and vagrancy.[44] Each charge carried penalties for women of all classes, but it was poor women—women without the means to pay the fines imposed on them or to hire an attorney—who were jailed, and it was their children who were sent away to poor farms, exacerbating the great divide between the upper and lower classes.[45]

The criminalization of sexuality, and in particular of women's sexuality, created a vast group of people subject to immiseration in prison and therefore in need of uplift by the benevolent elite. The reform movement blossomed with this grist for its mill. Reformers denounced the vice of a bad home and eulogized the virtue of a good home, contending that one was chaotic, promiscuous, unsettled, sensual, dirty, and unhealthy, while the other was orderly, modest, stable, rational, clean, and healthy. What was true of a woman was true of her children. The virtue of the children was dependent on the virtue of the mother. In the name of protecting the children from their idle and immoral mothers, reformers were willing to separate and condemn mother and child to their various and respective institutions of reform. By focusing on the moral regulation of poor women, reformers were able to effectively shift the blame for society's ills from the affluent and powerful to the poor and powerless: women who were widowed, divorced, separated, and unmarried with children. Poor single mothers—suspect since colonial times and ostracized from mainstream society—were prominent members of what was known as "the dangerous class." They were seen as a threat to American culture and to the very survival of the nation.[46]

Upper-class white women, who were themselves victims of sexism and gender bias, resisted and rallied against the dictates of conventional subordination by launching their careers as administrators of social reform. They set out on a mission to reclaim fallen women. As in all movements of major social change, almost by definition—whether because of a sense of possibility, the collapse of existing mechanisms of social control, or a religious or moral conviction—those previously subordinated often use such moments to take their place on the historical stage.

Religious reformers strategically used what they called "God's work" to divide people into "us" and "them" to maintain control over female behavior and to conserve the established order of society, traditional families, and social structures. The idea of a "calling," or the religious belief that one is divinely endowed with a life task or mission, provided reformers with a powerful moral justification for their worldly activities.[47] Capitalism fit neatly into this tradition, as reformers equated poverty and failure with sin, thus promoting a social and economic structure that elevated their own status and further devalued the status of others.[48] Thus, despite the religious frameworks in which they operated, well-connected reformers propagated the belief that the formerly powerful institutions of church and family could no longer adequately instill morality in society and that their newly established institutions could. In this context, the Homes for Friendless Women (HFFW) were born.

The Indianapolis HFFW was initially funded by the local Young Men's Christian Association (YMCA) under the auspices of Charles Coffin. As we have seen through Belle's story, the board of trustees read like a who's who of wealthy and politically connected men in Indianapolis—lawyers, bankers, doctors, and real estate moguls—while the board of managers consisted of their socialite wives, with the exemplary Sarah Smith initially in charge of operations. This arrangement solved knotty problems for the wives. As married women, it was socially unacceptable for them to be employed or to exercise power publicly, so they strategically positioned themselves in a way that gave them agency. By having their husbands serve on the board of trustees, the women were able to simultaneously maintain control of the institution and combat the stigma projected onto working women.[49]

The arrangement was not without its problems. Issues arose in the HFFW, including unwanted publicity when a member of the Indianapolis police force was caught cavorting with residents of the home. (He was charged with licentiousness and conduct unbecoming an officer.)[50] In addition to scandal, the everyday conditions of the home were troublesome. The premises were too small and the operational costs were too high. After an 1870 fire, a larger, more suitable location was secured in a better part of town. The new HFFW's construction was funded primarily by city and county funds, as well as by private donations.[51] As the home continued to expand, its well-connected founders convinced the Indiana legislature to enforce the collection of fines "for breach of the ordinance of said city for the suppression of vice or immorality, and for the suppression of houses of ill-fame, and for the punishment of the keepers, frequenters, and inmates thereof" to be paid to the city treasury and then released to the HFFW.[52] What was ostensibly a private philanthropy was now an institution financed by taxpayers and by fines levied primarily on the lower classes.

With the specific conditions in Indianapolis and with the general conditions in late nineteenth-century America spelled out, we can now understand Belle's predicament in fine-grained detail. Belle was subject to an overlapping set of economic and moral constrictions placed on working people, the poor, and women and on sexual and gender conventions. After her parents died, Belle was vulnerable, first to the predations of a manipulative fiancé and second to a punitive morality that forced her to hide her pregnancy from public view. Rather than labor with the assistance of her sisters in their boardinghouse room, or back home in their modest Lawrenceburgh house, perhaps with some expert midwives and the support of a loving community, Belle was forced to seek assistance from an institution set up to punish as much as to assist. The carceral nature of the HFFW is in full view in Belle's sad story, even though she was convicted of no crime. Belle may have gone to the home of her own accord, but it would be a great error of interpretation to ignore the brutally coercive nature of the ideologies of sex and gender that set her on a path to its door.

The coercive nature of assumption about "respectable" female sexuality highlights a fascinating aspect of this tragic tale. The constant emphasis on the Ward family's respectability, church attendance, and standing in the rural community serves to remind historical observers, and it would have affirmed to people at the time, that Belle was *not* from the lowest social strata. She and her sisters were not the poorest of the poor. They were middle-class people, insomuch as that category held in nineteenth-century rural Indiana, thrown into precarity by the early deaths of their parents and by the economic hardship of the Civil War, which was compounded by the fiscal crisis of 1873. What made the Ward sisters vulnerable to the home was precisely the toehold they hoped to maintain at this social level. Had they been solidly among the "thieves and prostitutes" who populated the elite's nightmares of the masses, they might not have cared about a pregnancy out of wedlock. They certainly would not have been vulnerable to exploitation by a man hoping to cheat them out of a house, since they would not have owned such a thing. Clearly, a crucial factor in this tragedy is the ideological predicament of a person only partially debased. Belle and her sisters had something to lose. Their embrace of the prevailing punitive, misogynist ideologies around class, gender, and sexuality ultimately led to the greatest loss of all: Belle's life.

With its first denunciation of the outrage at the home, the *Sentinel* made explicit the dual standards applied to poor versus respectable people. No supporter of the home, it charged, suspected the "wrong doings" it had uncovered, "other than such as must necessarily and naturally grow out of such a mixed community as existed within the lofty walls of the Home."[53] In other words, what happened to Belle may have happened regularly, but as long as it affected the appropriate segment of the home's "mixed community," it was fine. It was precisely the Wards' intermediate social position that made their story newsworthy.

Non-elites such as Belle and her sisters bought into such ideas at a great price, as Belle's story illustrates. While it would be wrong to blame them for embracing ideological conditions that both harmed them and, they correctly perceived, offered them some benefit, sometimes, in some situations, it would also be wrong to overlook their complicity and collaboration in what was ultimately their own oppression. Ideologies of "accountability" and "responsibility" function today in much the same way, coercing people who occupy social positions between the top and the bottom to support the toxic notions that most harm the poorest and that most cement the privileges of the elite.

When one class believes that another is better, they will allow themselves to be treated with disrespect and cruelty. Therefore, not all of the problems lie in the evil personalities or traitorous acts of those in power, but rather some lie in the socioeconomic and political orientation in which people believe that they get what they need by being careful not to offend the powerful. They desire to protect what little they have by not risking a fight for what they deserve, by believing that what they have is somehow a favor given to them by those in power. Reinforcing the constructs of all the isms, phobias, and other forms of discrimination enfolded in the negative impacts of identity politics amongst the bureaucrats who mask their Malthusian ideologies as benevolence are public policies on housing, health care, and education.

As for the elite in this case, the managers of the HFFW, their predicament was mild. Momentarily upset by a newspaper's sensationalist search for scandal, they quickly righted the ship. Calling in their powerful husbands, the managers created a scenario in which they could highlight their marital ties, rehearse their virtues, and even scold the wayward reporter for his inappropriate reach. The *Sentinel*'s change in tone by the third or fourth article confirms that its place in the social landscape was subordinate to that of the managers' husbands and therefore to the managers themselves when they positioned themselves deftly alongside their men. The welfare for those within their institution, respectable or criminal, barely mattered from the managers' lofty vantage point. No wonder they cared so little for the damage their decisions caused.

The Indianapolis HFFW, a "benevolent" institution, was part of a larger class struggle playing out in the postbellum era. Existing accounts—in their time and ours—border on the hagiographic, portraying charitable associations created by fine Christian ladies who established places of refuge for unfortunate and abandoned women making Indianapolis their home. In such accounts, the home's administrators were noble ladies, laboring without recompense for weeks and months for their community.[54] Yet for women like Belle Ward, refuge often came at a terrible price. Belle and the multitude of women she joined by getting pregnant were seen as sinful, willful vectors of contagion, loathed for being needy. To the affluent members of high society, the lowly were vulgar and criminal, their hopes and dreams easily dismissed, their names efficiently eliminated from history. Meanwhile the individuals responsible suffered no consequences for their acts and omissions, widening the disparity between the haves and the have-nots, buttressing the legacy that continues to structure criminal law and women's incarceration in the twenty-first century.

4

Sally and the Women and Girls at the Reformatory

Michelle Daniel Jones

The organizational hierarchy of the Indiana Reformatory Institution for Women and Girls, the first public prison for women in the United States, mirrored that of other prisons. James M. Ray, F.G. Armstrong, and Jos. I. Irwin, elite men of Indianapolis, constituted a board of managers. The reformatory itself was staffed by men and women: superintendent, Sarah Smith; steward, James Smith, Sarah's husband; matron, Elmira Johnson; teacher, Martha Pray; assistant teacher, Annie Mather; physician, Dr. Theophilus Parvin; engineers, Robert and William Gray; and watchman,

A portion of this chapter was presented via videoconferencing by Michelle Jones (Daniel), "Rhoda Coffin and the Fallout of the Cult of Domesticity in Indiana's Gilded Age," presented at the Indiana Women's Bicentennial History Conference, Hoosier Women at Work, Indianapolis, Indiana, March 26, 2016; Michelle Jones (Daniel), "Failing the Fallen: Sexual and Gendered Violence on Incarcerated Women in the Gilded Age," the American Historical Association Annual Conference, Atlanta, Georgia, January 7, 2016; Michelle Jones (Daniel), "Origins of the Indiana Women's Prison and the Criminalized Sexuality of Incarcerated Women," American Correctional Association Annual Conference, Indianapolis, Indiana, August 14, 2015; and "Sexual Violence Is an Old Hat: Criminalized Sexuality of Incarcerated Women in Indiana in the Gilded Age," presented via videoconferencing by Michelle Jones (Daniel) to Women and Gender Historians of the Midwest Annual Conference, June 12, 2015. I would like to thank everyone at those early conferences and institutions that gave us the opportunity to present our research via videoconferencing.

W.W. Moore.[1] One Quaker historical account of the reformatory described Sarah Smith's position as superintendent and her husband as "co-superintendent."

In addition to the reformatory's organization, a board of visitors was appointed, composed of the Honorable Conrad Baker, Indiana's fifteenth governor, Addison L. Roache, justice of the Indiana Supreme Court (1853–54), and Rhoda Coffin. Created by the 1873 legislative act that also created the reformatory, an appointed board of visitors received the power to "visit and inspect the Institution and examine as to its treatment, the employment and condition of its inmates and the management of its affairs."[2] The members of the board of visitors were charged with frequenting the institution at will and reporting on their findings.[3] This practice had already proven beneficial as a check on the operations at Jeffersonville Prison.

Sarah Smith desired two separate facilities, one for women and one for girls, but instead one large facility was built for both, with large sliding doors separating the prison side from the reformatory side. Each side had its own kitchen, washroom, laundry room, visiting room, etc.[4] A subterranean telegraphic alarm system connected to a nearby U.S. arsenal was sought to provide a level of security to keep the costs of guards at a minimum. It took four years to complete the facility.

Historians record that Rhoda Coffin and Sarah Smith's motivation for securing a separate prison for women was to provide a safe institution where women and girls could be reoriented to be useful to society, primarily as married women and/or domestic workers.[5] Smith shared that her methods included "special care in sickness, little acts of kindness," "commendation and encouragement," and "firmness and steadiness in the administration of discipline." The hoped-for results were "a well-regulated family; good religious influence; rules willingly obeyed; duties cheerfully performed;

Indiana Reformatory Institution for Women and Girls.

little punishment necessary; the use of tobacco dispensed with . . . [that along with] the religion of Jesus, [would] subdue the most hardened."[6]

The administrators sought to create a homelike environment of routine. The women and girls were dressed simply each day for work and education.

Sally Hubbard had been incarcerated for seventeen years at Jeffersonville Prison before the new women's prison opened in 1873. According to Rhoda Coffin, the Jeffersonville guards thought of Sally Hubbard as "a terror in the prison and exceedingly difficult to manage."[7] The guards' opinion of an incarcerated woman should be tempered with the prolific evidence of rape, sexual violence, physical abuse, and a culture of exploitation of the women, highlighted in chapter 1.[8] Incarcerated at Jeffersonville for all those years, Sally too may have been sexually violated at some point. Sally labored tirelessly at Jeffersonville while working directly for the warden in his mansion and being made to "do the work of all."[9] Rhoda Coffin recorded Sarah Smith and Sally Hubbard's first meeting:

Women cleaning the lawn.

The sheriff and two deputies brought her into the hall of the Administration building heavily manacled, and said, "Mrs. Smith, where shall we take her?" "Set her down," replied Mrs. Smith, "and take off her shackles." He replied, "We can't—show us the cell, she is an awful woman." "Take off her shackles," Mrs. Smith said, "she is my prisoner, not yours." They did so, and as the chains fell, she took the prisoner in her arms, kissed her on her forehead and said, "I receive thee as my child, and will be a mother, and I know thou wilt be a good daughter, let us pray, and ask Heaven to help us." They both knelt, Mrs. Smith's arms still around her. She plead for power to bring "the poor lost daughter home to God," and then rising with her prisoner, she said, "Come with me, dear, I have the loveliest little room for thee," and opening the door showed her her home for the remainder of her life.[10]

Sally Hubbard's infamous crime and her dubious reputation promoted by the Jeffersonville guards would soon give way to her image as the matronly "Old Aunt Sally," described as "very large, fleshy and in excellent health" in an 1875 profile of the new prison.[11]

Hubbard would become a stabilizing force at the reformatory, an enforcer of sorts in the prison, often quelling conflict and disruption on her own. Coffin reported that

> the prisoner became a new creature in Christ Jesus, old things passed away and a steady growth in grace was witnessed. She became quiet, gentle, unobtrusive, and faithful in service, always on the alert to see that there was no plot to do harm. *She was worth two guards*, and yet had the love and confidence of the fellow prisoners. For fourteen years she has led a meek and humble life.[12] (Emphasis added.)

Coffin depicted Smith as the benevolent mother and Sally as her lost child, despite the latter being in her seventies by 1875.[13] Smith's use of the word "family" is prevalent throughout the annual reports and can be arguably seen as a method to transfer power for social and sexual control inherent in families to a prison official.[14] It is not a far stretch to acknowledge that Sally believed she literally had been saved by Sarah Smith and the new reformatory.[15]

The board of managers, originally composed of all men, did not work well with Smith and the other women at the reformatory and often contradicted the women staff regarding financial decisions and the everyday operations of the institution.[16] As a member of the board of visitors, Coffin had little direct power or control of the reformatory. The board of visitors comprised herself and Emily A. Roache, until 1876 when they were joined by Lewis Jordan. Jordan told Coffin and Roache that the board of managers "to some extent has supplanted the Superintendent in supervising and directing the domestic affairs of the Institution." [17] Men were placed in charge of the board because many lawmakers didn't believe women capable of managing the finances of the first institution of its kind: a state-owned, separate prison for women.[18] Coffin stated that the new [male] board "had no conceptions of the real work intended.

We soon found that the machinery was cumbersome; the men had the money, the women had the internal management."[19] Finding the situation intolerable, Coffin and Smith authoritatively assembled all their political connections (current and former governors and senators) to seek a legal mandate.[20] Coffin said,

> We rallied all our forces to influence the Senators: ex-Governor Conrad Baker, . . . Thomas A. Hendricks, who was now the Governor, Senator Bell of Fort Wayne, and others of that body, Charles F. Coffin, Nathaniel Carpenter, Jacob S. Wiletts and wife, Sarah J. Smith, and many others whose names I cannot now recall, labored untiringly for placing the Reformatory wholly in the hands of a Women Board of Managers, who should control and manage the finances, see to the cultivation of the ground, and in every way conduct, govern, and manage for the best interest of the State, and the control of reformation of the women and girls committed by law to the Institution.[21]

The issue was of such importance that Coffin presented this argument before the fourth National Prison Congress in 1876:

> A woman's prison should be entirely under the control of women, from the board of managers to the lowest office. . . . But if a board of gentlemen for the financial management of a prison cannot be dispensed with, there should be a board of lady managers, to whom should be entrusted (in connection with the superintendent) the control and supervision of the convicts.[22]

Quite revolutionary at the time, no other state-owned carceral institution was managed entirely by women in Indiana or in the United States. Sharing power was out of the question at the reformatory, although Coffin didn't rule it out in other cases. The argument that convicted women should be under women's management was based on Coffin's observation that women held in men's prisons were provided no means for reformation and were made to labor for the incarcerated men, laundering clothes, mending, etc.[23] Coffin and her armada dismantled the current board and installed one composed entirely of women. She was elected board president in 1877.[24] Even though Coffin, Smith, and others asserted that the facility was run totally by women, notwithstanding the engineer and the watchman, it actually wasn't until 1884 that the core officers and employees were entirely women. This was accomplished when Dr. Parvin was replaced by Dr. Allison Maxwell in 1883, and James Smith, Sarah's husband, was replaced in 1884.[25]

After Coffin and Smith wrestled control of the reformatory's administration (finances, operations, etc.) from the elite men on the board of managers in 1877, the women became politically motivated to make the facility a success.[26] As Smith put it succinctly,

This being the only governmental prison known—either in the United States or Europe, under the entire management of women—we have felt the responsibility of our position and have sought to so discharge the trust assigned to us as to ensure success to the institution and to be an honor to our State, which has thus taken the advanced step of assigning to women the privilege of caring for, elevating and reforming her own sex.[27]

In other words, Sarah Smith and Rhoda Coffin had entered the national arena, and a successful demonstration of women reforming women was critical, which they endeavored wholeheartedly to achieve through securing speaking engagements and permitting visits to the reformatory. Accordingly, "only a constant defense of the new women's prisons . . . convinced the profession that women had both the right and the ability to control their own institutions."[28] Therefore, beyond their concern for the wayward girl or convicted woman, Coffin and Smith had staked their very identities and reputations and the state of Indiana's on the benefits of a separate female sphere, which they touted as the only means to reform "fallen" women.[29] This was the raison d'être of Quaker women reformers, and a failure would have great consequences. It could not be allowed to fail, even if that meant the women and girls lived meagerly. Smith admitted in 1881 that "all we have been able to do is just to live, but the institution has been managed too economically to be pleasant."[30] With the world watching, the pressure to be perfect cracked the benevolent veneer. As Ellen D. Swain, archivist and historian, articulates regarding late nineteenth-century reformers in general, "The boundaries between traditional benevolence and political activism were too blurred," and the stakes were high.[31] Coffin and Smith felt the pressure and prestige of being the first women to operate a prison of its kind and realized they would be harshly judged by male standards for any failures.

Very early on, newspapers, national journals, and books began to state that the Indiana Reformatory Institution for Women and Girls was a "model" facility led by a "model" superintendent, Sarah Smith.[32] But the reformatory managers were also met with opposition from men, who as members of the National Prison Congress thought it improper for women to run a facility devoid of men. One warden said, "Mrs. Coffin, I greatly admire you, your strength of character, and devotion to what you think is right, but you are not practical, you lack judgment, it can't be done, it is nonsense, I am an officer and I know it can't."[33] Another member argued, "I have seen women punishing women. They don't do it good." And another, "God has made man and women, and I believe the union of the two is better than a single individual, and special departments can be assigned to a husband and wife, so that they will perform each their distinct part, and do it in the best way."[34] These attitudes might explain why Sarah's husband, James, was recognized as the steward on the "Officers and Employees" pages of the annual reports to the board of managers, but he is wholly absent within the reports and everywhere else regarding the administration of the reformatory. Listing his name may have been a way to deflect criticism from those who continued to question Smith and Coffin's capabilities as administrators of a state institution.[35]

The reformatory also sought financial self-sufficiency. In addition to selling handwork (gardening and farming) and handicraft (caning chairs, knitting socks, etc.) and operating a laundry, the facility practiced a form of labor exploitation with a euphemistic name:

> The Board has adopted the Ticket of Leave system for the government of the Reformatory Department. When, in the opinion of the Superintendent, it becomes proper for a girl to be allowed an opportunity to again make her way in the world, the Board grants her a discharge conditional upon her good behavior. She, thus, remains a ward of the institution, without expense to it, and may be returned at any time upon her giving evidence of a want of reformation, or a lapse from good behavior, without a new commitment.[36]

Girls chosen for ticket-of-leave were the most trusted and indoctrinated. They would leave the reformatory on an early form of probation in a domestic service enterprise to labor in the homes of friends and associates of the reformatory staff.[37] Smith was quoted in testimony given in the 1881 investigation:

> We always aim to fit the girls for employment that they can get in the country, so that they shall not be compelled to stay in the city. The laundry business learns the prisoners to be practical laundresses, and I could always get employment for those who were experienced and could be recommended as reformed characters.[38]

Women feeding chickens.

Used to reduce the institution's population—and, therefore, the cost of operation—this convict lease ticket-of-leave system represented a way for the prison officials to profit from incarcerated labor. As Kim Baldwin will detail later, the state charged each county a fee for each woman and girl incarcerated in the reformatory.[39] To her fellow Quaker Friends, Smith shared in 1880,

> It really astonished ourselves to see the low, degraded women accepting Christ.... When they leave us and enter families who are willing to receive them, on our recommendation, so faithful and efficient have they proved that we cannot supply half the demands for the services of such.[40]

During Smith's and Coffin's reign as superintendent and president of the board of managers, respectively, the transactional aspects of ticket-of-leave were not recorded in the board's minutes. Fortunately, later administrators freely reported on a practice that was fundamental to the operations of the facility. On November 3, 1885, the board of managers reported that there would be a range of prices for the girls' labor: "In the matter of Girls on Ticket of Leave—On motion, it was ordered that the wages of girls sent out on tickets of leave be paid to the Superintendent. Also, that .75 cents, $1, and $1.30 per week be the price asked per week."[41] Interestingly enough, when Caroline Cleaver was released on ticket-of-leave to Mrs. Winsor of Illinois, $1.50 was paid by Mrs. Winsor "as compensation for the service of the said Caroline Cleaver."[42] A definite price increase. While it looked like a method to reintegrate women into the workforce, ticket of leave operated as a method to keep young girls tethered to the prison as "a ward of the institution without expense to it."[43] This means that young girls labored in these homes for their keep (i.e., food, meager clothing, and a bed), removing the cost of care from the prison. Yet as far as we can tell, the prison still charged the county of conviction for their incarceration.[44]

Labor in the prison also included working in the laundry. In addition to washing the linens and the simple uniforms they wore, the women and girls also labored in the laundry for profit. Smith and other administrators secured jobs from the local community, and in 1883 Smith reported that "the Laundry still stands at the head of our employments, and has yielded a better return this past year, in most cases giving satisfaction to our patrons, the demands upon us always exceeding our ability to fulfill."[45] The drive to extract labor from the women extended to manufacturing overalls and shirts with the Capital City Manufacturing Company. The desire to force incarcerated women to labor while captive under the regime of religious indoctrination away from the world can be summed up by Smith when she said, "Would that every State could separate its female prisoners and put them in care of Christian women, who will strive for their reformation as well as punishment,—out of sight and hearing of men—for as

Women laboring in the work room.

long as a degraded woman knows she can be heard by men there is no reformation probable."[46]

When Sarah Smith began the day-to-day management of the women and girls, she immediately met with difficulties. Forbidden to smoke tobacco, some of the women sent from Jeffersonville Prison rebuked Smith's "superior accommodations" and grand ideas of reformation. They smoked and chewed tobacco and/or ate opium and desired to return to the men's prison.[47] According to Smith, notwithstanding the implausibility of simply "working" off attachment and/or addiction to such substances, applying the women to labor would solve their substance use issues.

Smith, in one annual report from the reformatory, articulated that she felt "tasked" in reforming women and girls, who she thought were tainted with immorality:

Sarah J. Smith at the Indiana Women's
Prison.

So long as crime exists, punishment must be provided; and
punishment must be of such a nature that it will lift the criminal above the commission of crime; no easy task to perform,
when we understand the evil passions with which many of
them are sorely afflicted—revenge, jealousy, hatred, falsehood
and theft—sore evils that no power can eradicate but the power
of God in the heart.[48]

Smith felt the weight of her position and believed that failing to
"save" the women and girls in her charge would result in a world
infested with a contagious degeneracy:

Our position is felt to be one of no small responsibility, whether
in rescuing the little waif of misfortune, against whom all doors

seem to be closed, in striking contrast with the over-indulged and incorrigible, the orphan, or the one having a step-parent, which class, sad experience teaches us, is the ones most demanding our sympathy, as these are most frequently thrown upon the world, to be led captive by some designing man who robs her of her virtue ere she knows its value, and too soon she becomes the pest of society—betrayed herself, in pure revenge seeks to betray others, and at the same time spreading disease and immorality wherever she goes.[49]

According to Smith, the sex worker or ruined woman spread disease and immorality and did not belong in the community regardless of the circumstances that created her current condition. Here she disconnects criminal causality from life's precarity. Feminist criminologist Nicole Hahn Rafter asserted that the founders of separate prisons for women entered their work "believing that woman's mission included rescue of the unfortunate, . . . not serious felons or confirmed prostitutes, but wayward 'girls' who might be saved."[50] The argument is supported by the demographics. On average, the reformatory held one hundred girls, compared with the penal department, which held only twenty-seven.[51] Also, women convicted of sex work were not admitted to the reformatory during its first twenty-four years.[52] Smith acknowledged that men led women and girls to ruin, but she was very quick to condemn "tainted," gender-deviating sex workers and other ruined women, even though many were forced or coerced into sex work or sexual compliance.[53]

The priority was young girls, and apparently nothing was to be done about the designing men. Through indoctrinating religion and reifying a sex and gender system that privileged men over women, Smith and others sought a conversion and a refashioning. Sarah Smith reported that "daily religious exercises," Sabbath school, and services offered by the Young Men's Christian Association

The dining room.

(YMCA) were crucial to the effective operation of the reformatory.[54] In fact, at the third National Prison Reform Congress in 1874, Coffin explained to the attendees that "Mrs. Smith governed her prison by the power of the gospel; and no woman or girl had yet been brought to her who was impervious to the influence of that power." She continued, "Every woman in that prison . . . is now converted. In three weeks at the outside, the most hardened girls are brought under the influence of this extraordinary woman."[55] Those compelled to convert by force likely are included in that number. Smith provides one account of forced conversion:

A desperate character was getting tobacco surreptitiously from some workmen, and S. Smith knew it. One day she said to the woman, "Thee are very unhappy; what is the matter?" "Nothing" (in a loud angry voice).—"Yes, there is something, and I will tell thee what it is—tobacco."—"Tobacco! Who told you that? Oh! Every chew sends me nearer to hell!"—"Well,

thee must give it up."—"I can't!"—"Thee must."—"I won't. I am
going to hell."

The convicts' prayer meeting was going on, so S. S. told her
to come with her, and took her in. All the women were on their
knees; S. S. told them about her and asked their prayers. And then
she bid the poor trembling sinner kneel down.—"I can't."—So
S. S. took her by the shoulders and pressed her down, and *held*
her down, and prayed for her. Then she told her to pray for herself "God be merciful to me a sinner." S. S. says she repeated
this with a pause between, at least twenty times and told the
woman she *should* not rise till she had said it! At last she began,
"God be. . . ." no more—a great cry followed, loud and piercing
and the poor prodigal was rejoicing in the forgiving love of her
reconciled Father in Heaven.[56] (Emphasis added.)

Smith and Coffin attempted to mold women and girls in their own
image, albeit an inherently inferior version of themselves, and into
what they believed was their proper place, and they did it sometimes by force.

Finding a balance between kindness and firmness resulted in the
development of good conduct credits targeting women incarcerated with short sentences. The board and Smith agreed that "one-
year convicts receiving three or more bad conduct marks [will] be
deprived of any gain time from good conduct."[57] The rule was later
expanded to cover women in both the prison and the reformatory
and was made retroactive. It stated, "On motion it was ordered
that all convicts receiving three or more black marks during the
last year of their term shall lose all time gained by good conduct
rule and any rules upon the records conflicting with this shall be
null and void from this date."[58] Managing the diverse populations
of women and girls appears to have greatly challenged Smith and
others, requiring a check on good conduct credits.

Sarah Smith and the reformatory staff made great strides in

reforming fallen women according to Smith's own standards of morality. In 1873, Smith proudly acknowledged the fact that "woman is competent to govern the depraved and desperate of her own sex by womanly measures and appliances, without a resort to the rigorous means which are generally supposed to be necessary in prisons governed by men, and intended wholly or chiefly for male convicts."[59] She was likely alluding to the frequent use of corporal punishment and solitary confinement as standard disciplinary tools in men's prisons across the United States. In the 1878 annual report, Smith claimed an 82 percent success rate of women and girls reentering society.[60]

The facility was one large structure, and there was growing concern about protecting the girls from the bad influences of the "real" criminals—the women in the penal department.[61] The annual *Report of the Managers of Reformatory* for 1879 contains the following guidelines with respect to solitary confinement:

In the Reformatory Department a small room has been set apart for the most refractory. Confinement in this for a few days, on lessened diet (bread and water), is the extremity of punishment, and this has been rarely needed. In the Penal Department . . . separate confinement on bread and water, is the severest punishment that our Superintendent is allowed to inflict without an order from the Board. In but one instance has this order been called for.[62]

Yet all wasn't well. The small staff of eleven faced many challenges in supervising, twenty-four hours a day, an average of twenty-seven adults and one hundred girls, many of whom were undoubtedly uninterested in the reformatory's goals. Pockets of resistance amongst the women and girls emerged, particularly in matters of sexual agency.[63]

Efforts by the institution's leaders to violently wipe out these pockets of resistance resulted in an investigation by an Indiana state legislative committee initiated on January 13, 1881.[64] A reporter for the *Indianapolis Journal*, Gid Thompson, took note of the investigation, writing that there "had been more or less gossip for a long time, and I thought I would see what there was in it." He talked with four women and wrote their stories.[65] According to Thompson, some inmates and former staff alleged that the on-site physician, Dr. Theophilus Parvin, conducted operations on women and girls for reasons not given to them. As Anastazia Schmid explores in her chapter on the prison doctor, we now believe these operations included clitoridectomies and ovariectomies.[66] Others Thompson interviewed alleged that they found delivered babies in the cesspools near or on reformatory property. And some alleged that Sarah Smith had beaten women and girls, used the girls to hold down/tie down other girls, "ducked" them in cold water (a nineteenth-century version of waterboarding), hosed them down, denied them access to water closets, knocked their heads against walls, and placed them on bread and water diets as punishment, during which the women and girls were often stripped naked.[67] Punishment for what? Usually, for sassy, rude behavior but also for masturbation, then commonly called "self-abuse."

Sarah Smith and her employees were dedicated to reforming the women and girls at any cost, and as historian Estelle Freedman argues, "In the process of attempting to rescue and reform fallen women, . . . [reformers] established another mode of differential treatment, distinct from but no less oppressive than that of the custodial tradition."[68] When those who were already "out of place" as the result of a criminal conviction decided to indulge in masturbation or rude behavior, Smith and her staff responded swiftly.

Ida Harris (identified as "Ada" Harris in the reformatory's registry), an African American woman in the reformatory, appears to have been targeted particularly. She declared to Thompson that she was ducked, tied down, and struck on the head with a broom handle. Another African American woman/girl, Susie Sherman, saw her account of being ducked and punished appear as barely a blip at the bottom of the article that highlighted other women's testimonies.[69]

The legislative committee's investigation revealed that General Abel Streight, famed Civil War hero and state senator (1876, 1888), was apparently blackmailed by one of the reformatory's staff members for impregnating a young woman released on ticket-of-leave. The young woman worked in his home and appears to have testified in the investigation.[70] The Indianapolis newspaper *The People* reported that Sarah Smith had called on General Streight ten years ago and gave the reason why (regarding the young girl). Testimony was stopped, and Streight was taken into another room for "consultation" by the committee.[71] After nearly twenty minutes, he returned and was "not permitted to tell his story" on the record. He left shortly thereafter.[72] Counsel for the managers of the reformatory told the committee that it was improper to question a witness in private. A debate ensued, and the "Committee ruled that there would be no testimony given by [General] Mr. Streight and nothing was revealed by him which could be taken into account by the Committee."[73] Did the men of the committee protect a fellow man from incriminating himself on the record for the misuse of a young woman that worked in his home?

The chairman of the committee, Dr. Edwins, was a Democrat, and the reformatory was under Democratic management. Dr. Edwins initiated the investigation of the reformatory once the rumors surfaced of "acts of uncommon cruelty perpetrated upon the inmates there."[74] Did he assume that rumors of abuse and violence in the reformatory were false and that by taking the initiative he could control the investigation in the event of trouble? The committee was composed of Democrats and Republicans, but Dr. Edwins was the chair. When needed, he had the power to play a lead role as investigator and to not dig too deeply. One reporter stated, "It is possible that the investigation will not be as searching as it might be made if a lawyer of Mr. Duncan's capacity [the reformatory's attorney] was employed to question the witnesses and bring out the facts."[75] Perhaps Dr. Edwins thought it best to lead the reformatory investigation because Republicans throughout the state legislature had sought every opportunity to investigate institutions under Democratic control since 1875, starting with the investigation of Col. Shuler at Jeffersonville Prison.[76] Historians have attributed a series of legislative investigations, at the Knightstown Orphans' Home and State Prison South in 1885, and at the Insane Hospital in 1887, to political infighting, but they did not record the 1881 legislative investigation at the reformatory as being a part of the political fight.[77]

During the investigation, employees of the prison were split between defending the reformatory and corroborating the acts of violence. Dr. Parvin insisted that no harm had been done to anyone, while many other employees and former staff corroborated the allegations by the women and girls. Many women testified in the 1881 investigation. These are some of the reports.

Mrs. Nancy E. Clem testified that she was in punishment now because she refused to find out what Mrs. Talbott would swear to before the investigating committee.[78]

Francis A Talbott, the laundry teacher of five years at the institution, testified next. She said she witnessed Lizzie Smith, an inmate of the reformatory, who was thirteen years of age, "stripped, put in a bathtub and held by Aunty Smith while a large girl turned on the cold-water tap. The girl was ducked there for twenty minutes, then taken out, dried, spanked and sent to bed. This was for self-abuse [masturbation] and teaching the vice to the smaller girls." Talbott then went on to say that Smith "hit the girls on the head with her slipper, pulled their hair and pound their heads against the wall."[79]

Cynthia Beals was a nurse, who worked for two weeks at the Children's Hospital. She testified that "the children all had the itch (vaginosis) and syphilis. Beds were filthy, and the blankets, in which the children with running sores slept, were not changed during the time she was there." Beals claims she saw Sarah Smith, aka Aunty Smith, "jerk a little sick girl out of bed by the arms, and refuse her the medicine prescribed by Dr. Parvin."[80]

Mrs. Anna Buchanan, an ex-officer at the reformatory, testified to the committee that she had observed "Mrs. Smith take girls of twelve and fifteen years of age and strike their heads against the wall."[81]

Mrs. Charlotte Brown testified as well. Mrs. Brown received from the reformatory a young girl by the name of Jennie Solomon to work in her home. Jennie "became a little saucy," so Brown complained to Sarah Smith. Smith called for the girl, and when the girl returned, she had marks on her face and eyebrow. Brown added that Jennie said the punishment was inflicted by "Aunty Smith."[82]

Ida Harris remembered, "Mrs. Johnson and Mrs. Smith took me down stairs, made me take my clothes off, put my head under faucets and let the water run in my face till my breath was nearly gone. They did that several times, until the bath was nearly full. I was never ducked but once."[83]

Amanda Lampier, ex-prisoner, testified about the treatment of other women and girls and stated that one, Jane Johnson, was "severely beaten and choked" and that Susie Reynolds's mouth was "cut from the strap with which she was struck." She also saw others "when bathing, who had marks of straps upon their backs."[84]

Lizzie Cash, ex-prisoner, testified that she had been "whipped several times on her naked person" and that she'd seen Mrs. Smith "take a girl and pull her hair until some of it came out."[85]

Mary Jane Schweitzer, housed in the reformatory department, stated that "some of the prisoners told a falsehood about me and said I had stolen a whole loaf (of bread). Afterward they locked me up in my own cell, tore my clothes off of me, and turned the hose on me while I was standing in my cell. I had a chill afterwards, and never had any health since. Two men were sent that night to clean out the cell. I was thoroughly drenched, and the water was turned on for nearly half an hour. When I was shut up alone, after the ducking, they gave me no clean clothes, and I complained to Mrs. Coffin."[86]

Smith's bitter battle with Ida Haines seems particularly pronounced in this investigation. According to Haines, she met Smith at the Home for Friendless Women and that while at the reformatory she was ducked, held down for Smith, slapped in the face, hosed, denied medication, and had her head banged against the wall.[87] Haines also argued that when Smith slapped her in the face, she slapped Smith back. Smith argues that Haines was the worst woman incarcerated at the reformatory and that after Haines's sister died after leaving the reformatory, Haines visited Smith and said "that as a revenge, she would try and decoy to houses of prostitution every girl that left the Reformatory."[88]

For the good of the institution, Coffin and the board of managers closed ranks with Smith and the others to the point of outright contradiction with the staff, the girls, and, as Smith's testimony shows, the superintendent herself. The board reported the following regarding the investigative committee's conclusions based on the state's investigation:

> In the matter of Punishments: having investigated the punishments, the Board find that no "ducking" known as such in prison parlance, has ever been resorted to. That water punishment from the hose or by use of the bath tub was only resorted to in extreme or justifiable cases. And on motion, the action of the Superintendent in so punishing was approved.[89]

The board's minutes did not include how they investigated the punishments. But Coffin agreed punishment would be necessary, and as it was Coffin who decided the superintendent should have the responsibility of punishment, she trusted Smith to administer punishment within the boundaries agreed on.[90] As Coffin stated, "In order to effect this [reformation], punishment becomes more or less an adjunct, for the prisoner must be deprived of liberty and placed under subjection."[91] Herein, she admits violence was likely in the reformation of her own sex.

The testimonies of the women, girls, and staff suggest that when Coffin proclaimed before the National Prison Congress in 1876 that "flogging and shower baths should never be allowed in a female prison," she and the other staff did not view ducking, hosing, and beatings in the same light as those other types of violence, which were often found in men's facilities.[92] Further, Coffin insists that such "severe punishment, or fear, may deter a women from open violation of rules, and may produce an apparent, but never a real reformation; the debasing effects of such punishments, as a rule, only tend to sink her deeper, and complete destruction of her self-respect; and without self-respect she cannot be reformed."[93] Smith stated that she told the board every time the hose was applied.[94] How did Coffin reconcile her ideological beliefs with the shared experiences of the women and girls and the testimony of her own staff?

By the time it was Sarah Smith's turn to testify, the damning testimony must have weighed heavily on her. These allegations were shocking to the legislative committee, and Smith candidly testified why such devout Christians would resort to alarming physical abuse. Smith is representational of the white moral reformer, the "guardians" who focused on the sexual morality of the "abandoned"—women who were unmarried and without a protector. Devoted to the "cause of purity," white moral reformers "wrestled control of movement newspapers, petitioned to make seduction a crime, and built houses of refuge and industry. These moral guardians also continued to crusade against the solitary vice," masturbation.[95] By the 1850s, "fear of masturbation [became] a cultural phenomenon."[96] The pervasive sentiment was that the "aroused female cannot be trusted" and the "sexually awakened girl is for the brothel."[97] In other words, Smith's position on masturbation and unruly behavior was informed by widely held social and religious beliefs that pathologized and demonized women's sexuality. It is within this context that the following excerpts from three hours of testimony can be viewed:

We had hoped that we would be able to do without whipping. . . . Mrs. Smith then described the consequences of self-abuse [masturbation] on the part of the children, and to cure this, she said, we adopted the bathing which has been called ducking. I could not stop it by any other mode of punishment than by using cold water. . . . I do not deny that we have punished severely in some cases, but I could show fifty letters from prisoners thanking me for the treatment given. . . . I never used anything but the hose, the slipper, and the strap, to punish any of the inmates. . . . I never knocked a girl's head against the wall *except on slapping their faces. . . . I have never whipped any woman with the strap,* except up on the shoulders and arms—not any other part of their persons. . . .

I positively deny that I ever deliberately knocked any girl's head against the wall. *I have slapped their face, when they were impudence to officers. I have often pulled their hair when they have done the same to other girls, to let them see how they liked it.* I have done that also, when the prisoners have threatened to assault me, to subdue them. . . .

I thought that the whipping was the best means of teaching them that they had to work. . . .

The bath was used as a punishment fourteen times, and in every case it was beneficial, and there were no evil results. The girls were always rubbed dry, dressed and put to bed. Mrs. Johnson and myself were the only persons who used the hose. No girls ever fell enough to knock anyone down. I have never whipped any woman with the strap, except upon their shoulders and arms—not any other part of their persons. The girls I used to strike on their naked persons. . . .

A baby was found in the cesspool, and Dr. Parvin said it was not possible for any woman to have been deliverer of that baby. He told the coroner that no woman in the institution could have been its mother.

At one point, it appeared that Smith grew confused with her statements, stating one thing at one point and then the reverse at another.

We never turned the fire-hose on anyone but Mollie Scott. . . . *I never used the fire-hose on any inmate in the Reformatory.*

The handcuffs have never been used in the Reformatory. . . . *When we put handcuffs on Lizzie Cash she kicked me in the bowels.*

When I used the bath, I did it entirely for the purpose of frightening them and as a deterrent. . . . *I have no recollection that cold water was used in the bath when they were first put in. The water from the faucet was cold.*[98] (Emphasis added.)

Smith confessed that she beat women and girls in the face and body "severely" with "slippers," if they were found masturbating or committing acts of violence. Smith described an environment wherein she felt threatened and unsafe to go among the women and girls, especially without the threat of or actual use of punishment. She was embroiled in various assaults, arsons, and attempted murders, and yet former governor James William and other visitors were thoroughly impressed with Smith and the facility. At the same time it is important to see that from Smith's point of view, life at the reformatory was equally a fearsome hell and a pleasant oasis.

The picture is strained. Smith believed that kindness, Christianity, and a firm hand could reform any woman or girl. When defending herself against testimony that she couldn't fully discredit, she relied on the criminal history of the women to make her case, as occurred with Jennie Switzer:[99]

The woman, Jennie Switzer, came here a very bad woman; it took nine men to arrest her; she was reported to be the worst woman in Laporte County; she was the most profane woman that was ever here.[100]

Smith, however, didn't respond to the allegations that Switzer was operated on by the prison doctor. Smith did object to the fact that Switzer apparently remained in bed for two days after being hosed.

Near the end of her testimony, Smith argued that it was the board's failure to create laws regulating punishment that caused her to take matters into her own hands and to violate the women in her charge.

> The board makes the rules to govern the institution, but there is no law regulating punishment. I believe the Lord called me to take charge of this institution. I suppose also that the Lord directs my methods of management.[101]

Further, Smith's open retelling of the violence she inflicted reveals she felt culturally, religiously, and morally justified in her actions. Smith's actions were supported by the philosophy of the white moral reformer movement entrenched in the culture by the 1880s.[102] Christian doctrine instantiated sexuality as "born in sin" and "notions of the flesh" as sinful.[103] This doctrine was the ethos through which people were thought naturally deviant. In 1874, just five months after the reformatory opened, Smith shared with a reporter that "there is but one dark cell, with an iron door in the prison. The Superintendent told us they had never had the occasion to use it, for generally ordering them to their rooms proved sufficient punishment."[104] Smith rationalized that in circumstances where one was in "sin," physical violence was a necessary evil. In fact, when Smith told the board on April 7, 1879, that she had confined Nellie Shea in the "dark cell in manacles" for insubordination, the board sanctioned confining Nellie "until thoroughly subdued."[105] It seems that Smith defined "insubordination" as sin as well.

Illustration of a woman being forced into a dark cell.

Reporting to the board on May 5, 1879, Smith said that she "had changes made in the Dark Cell, as ordered at last meeting, but that she had delayed having [an] iron door placed in [the] Engine house and would suggest that it be bricked up leaving only small door, which should be and [sic] made fire proof," which was ordered by the board.[106] Was the dark cell next to or within the engine house? Were these changes made to improve safety or to make a better dark cell? No report on Nellie Shea was given at that time. It was not until June 2, 1879, that Smith reported to the board that she had "released Nellie Shea from the Dark Cell on promise of good conduct, she having surrendered completely" after nearly eight weeks of confinement.[107] With Smith's ready admissions of the violence she enacted on others and with that method's apparent success, it is a wonder that Nellie Shea's experience in the dark cell is the only report of its kind in the board's records through 1887.

Smith recognized that direct physical punishment of the women and girls in her charge was unsustainable. She testified that "I think that the cells will deter them from violating the rules better than any other punishment," even though she thought solitary confinement severe.[108] She also admitted that housing the women and the girls together was a mistake. Smith and Coffin thought that they would be able to keep the women and girls separate, but Smith felt that the girls could hear the "demoralizing language" of women on the penal side, and she blamed the insubordination at the facility on the fact that women and girls were incarcerated together.[109] When questioned about forms of water punishment and the use of cold water, Smith remarked that the boilers were old and in need of repair and that as a whole everyone in the facility was doing all they could to "just live."[110]

Smith's assistant superintendent, Elmira Johnson, testified and admitted that water closets were often locked to prevent congregating and talking and that warm water was placed in the tubs before the cold water was turned on.[111] She described Mary Jane Switzer (Schweitzer) as mentally unstable and Jennie Williams as simply "crazy." Johnson was the only one to address allegations of race discrimination by refuting its existence at the reformatory.[112] Anna Dunlop (bookkeeper), Martha Pray (teacher), and other staff, along with members of the board of managers, Mrs. Thomas A. Hendricks and Rhoda Coffin, testified before the committee as well. All testimony glowingly affirmed Smith. Coffin said, "I do not think Mrs. Smith has an equal in the world." They all supported her manner of punishment and refuted any suggestions that Smith had become too old to effectively manage the institution.[113] The investment in the woman-run institution echoed again when Coffin said, "We have tried to show to the world that institutions of this kind under the management of ladies could reform women and make them new again, and I think we have succeeded admirably."[114] Reiterating the stakes involved in managing the reformatory, Coffin reminded the committee that Dr. Wines, the distinguished prison reformer, called the reformatory a "model" institution. Coffin claimed that the form of punishment advocated by the board was designed to resemble that which a mother would give to her child. It is unlikely that nineteenth-century middle-class mothers performed the type of violence on their children that women and girls experienced at the reformatory.

During the legislative investigation, testimony was also given by several formerly incarcerated women and girls, who argued that they received the best care and treatment from Smith and Johnson, the assistant superintendent. Sally Hubbard, the "Wabash Murderess," testified on Smith's behalf:

> Have been in prison twenty-two years; was at Jeffersonville before I was brought here; I am a life prisoner; was one of the first prisoners that went to the Reformatory; the treatment of the prisoners is good; when any of the prisoners get sick they are treated very well; they are generally fed from the officers' table when sick; I do not think some of them are half-punished in accordance with the treatment they give the officers; I have often told them that I wished they were down in Jeffersonville where they could get the cat.[115]

Sally clearly speaks disdainfully of the women and girls who she thought were tarnishing the great reputation of her savior, Sarah Smith. Sally wanted to impress on the legislative committee and the women with whom she shared such information that conditions at the reformatory were superior to those at Jeffersonville. Further, she wanted to demonstrate her elevation in class status and to mark the difference between her and the other young women and girls.

Smith strategically used Sally's testimony to demonstrate the reformatory's ability to reform, while the news media divulged Sally's crime of conviction but counted her as belonging to a "better class of prisoner." [116] When women like Sally demonstrated their ascription to the middle class, women prison reformers "won an ideological victory. Its values had been affirmed; its symbols of status had been accorded validity by women of the working class." [117]

The committee thoroughly examined seventy witnesses and concluded that the discipline at the reformatory was "maintained, as far as practicable, by kindness and appeals to the moral sense of the inmates and resorts to hard punishment only when other methods have failed." [118] One of the strangest turns of events following this investigation was the resurgence of solitary confinement as one of the primary modes to discipline and control the behavior of young girls and its sanctioning by the state legislature. Results of the investigation brought the following changes: "punishment by the bath and water, we find, has been abolished. We would earnestly recommend the abolishment of corporal punishment on the naked persons of young females and recommend instead confinement in the lone cell." [119]

The Indiana state legislature set up solitary confinement and physical violence in an "either/or" formulation. Prison discipline, which originally was based on corporal punishment and little to no solitary confinement, now swung in the opposite direction. Curtailing corporal punishment apparently could not happen without allowing solitary confinement. The committee also questioned incarcerating older, "hardened" girls together with children under the age of fourteen years, expressing concern that said children would be contaminated by association.[120] But the younger girls would not be removed to their own facility until after March 9, 1907, when the act that created the Indiana Industrial School for Girls passed the legislature.[121]

Smith was cleared of any wrongdoing and was exonerated. She

continued to serve as superintendent for two more years. The incredulity of the testimony provided by the many women, girls, and staff against Smith and other staff may have been motivated by the fact that the reformatory was the pride of Indiana and was an internationally known "model."

> Your committee are fully aware of the fact that Indiana is entitled to the proud position that she contains within her borders the only female prison in the world governed, guarded and financed by females, and when we see its condition from a sanitary and moral standpoint, its freedom from political convulsions, its surroundings so wholly consonance with female instincts and character of what is and should be womanly, we cannot but express our admiration of the pioneers of such a movement.[122]

Should the ready admission that the Indiana Reformatory Institution for Women and Girls was the first of its kind in the country and that Indiana held a "proud position" because of it, along with Dr. Edwins's investigation of his own politically affiliated institution, plus the notion of "vigorous examination" being wholly speculative, add up to a complete disregard of the testimonies from the women, girls, and staff of the reformatory? Does reporter Gid Thompson's claim that the investigation was part of a conspiracy led by Republicans to discredit Democrats and Democratic-affiliated benevolent institutions fully discount and discredit what some of the women and girls experienced?[123] Only two years after the investigation ended, Sarah Smith and Dr. Parvin both resigned. Dr. Parvin accepted a new job as chair of Obstetrics and Disease of Women at Jefferson College in Philadelphia.[124] In the *Tenth Report of the Managers of the Indiana Reformatory*, Smith cautioned succeeding superintendents about disgruntled officers and ungrateful incarcerated women who would make false claims against the facility.[125]

The two leading histories of the reformatory, Rafter's *Partial Justice* and Freedman's *Their Sisters' Keepers*, make note of Smith's accomplishments but ignore the extent to which her actions diverged from her stated principles. Consider the timeline. The reformatory opened in 1873, and Smith published her principles on reformation and punishment in 1874, which limited punishment to "confinement in cell, with privation of social privileges, and a diet of bread and water, till subdued."[126] In 1875, she discovered women and girls were masturbating, and she immediately instigated a regime of harsh punishment.[127] By 1881, Sarah Smith and the reformatory staff were under investigation for allegations of sexualized abuse against imprisoned women and girls.[128] Most historians of Sarah Smith see her moral character as mostly benevolent; however, scholars like Freedman and Rafter fleshed out the limitations of Smith's and other women reformers' approaches to incarcerating women and girls.[129] Analysis of the gulf between principles and performance can give a clearer picture of Sarah Smith, can demonstrate the complexities of human experience, and can reveal the subversion of Smith's best intentions.

Sarah Smith resigned from the position of superintendent in 1883, after reports of failing health.[130] As the annual reports show, she remained active in the institution for a time as a member of the board of managers.[131] Smith's resignation from the board occurred in March 1885, when Martha M. James took her place. According to Rhoda Coffin, who wrote and published a memorial for Sarah Smith, Smith left the public sphere to care for her husband, James, who died in January 1885. It is reported that Smith died suddenly of heart disease in December that same year.[132] Accounts of Sarah Smith's work lived well beyond her death, as Coffin's memorial of Smith's life was published widely.[133]

After Smith's death, the reformatory appears to have undergone a great deal of adjustment. Throughout 1885 and 1886, there were constant shifts in the superintendent, assistant superintendent, matron, teacher, and laundress positions. Concepts like vacation days, sick days, job descriptions, roles of subordinate officers, and the overall organizational power structure appear for the first time, with extreme detail, in the board's minutes. Smith's absence in the facility is clearly legible in the record. Changes came quickly.

In 1884, as a part of regular business of the reformatory, the board of managers instructed the superintendent to have an existing "retiring room" converted into a room for the "confinement of refractory prisoners." This is the point when solitary confinement was relocated from the "Dark Cell" to "over [the] prison ironing room, which took a month to complete."[134] It is here that the parameters of physical punishment were spelled out definitively and recorded in the minutes. The assistant superintendent was explicitly limited to "slippering," and all "heavier punishment" required the consent of the superintendent.[135] Further, it was decreed "that inmates be locked up on bread and water when it became necessary to punish whenever possible as the Board is opposed to indiscriminate whipping."[136] Here, the new management is deciding all over again what punishment should accompany the incarceration of women and girls.

No longer would staff be paid a salary, "all officers of this Institution will hereafter be employed for one month at a time."[137] The board also ordered that "all officers dispense with the service of the girls as attendants in their, the officer's rooms, except at the time of cleaning and putting the room in order in the mornings."[138] This suggests that some of the girls had served the staff as personal servants. In March 1886, the board also fired the long-serving Mr. Petrie, who was the day watchman, stableman, and driver of the wagon, because they wanted a woman in that position, likely to ensure that all positions at the reformatory were held by women.[139] All these efforts reflect an effort to right the reformatory's ship. The reformatory remained a wonder, and people continued to visit and study the facility.[140]

Ultimately, the 1881 investigation changed the trajectory of Coffin's life and likely damaged her reputation. Quite publicly, after the investigation, she fought against Mrs. E.C. Hendricks and Mrs. E.J. Dodd, the other two members of the board. Mrs. Dodd nominated Mrs. Hendricks for the presidency, as she felt a "rotation in such offices and under such circumstances is eminently right and proper." Hendricks declined a previous nomination, but when Coffin would not step down of her own accord and when Hendricks was nominated a second time, she "declined to waive what she regarded as her rights."[141] In actuality, a Democratic legislature in 1877 had placed the administration of the reformatory's financial affairs into the women's hands, and Hendricks was awarded a term of six years; Coffin, four years; and Roach, two years. Hendricks was a governor's wife and felt she should have been named president, but Coffin was chosen.[142] Hendricks and Dodd disagreed with Coffin on money. Specifically, "Mrs. Hendricks was unwilling that the expenditures in any contingency should exceed the appropriation. She opposed the making of debts on any pretext. She insisted that the Institution should live within its means." Coffin's position related that she had plans for the reformatory that were not yet actualized, which required she retain the presidency.[143] Coffin attempted once again to rally "friends" to her cause, each friend arguing that Coffin was best suited for the position. While others responded that "no one imagined that Mrs. Coffin would hold on to the office so tenaciously or accept the nomination of any other member as a personal affront."[144]

When Coffin submitted her resignation, Governor Porter said

Rhoda M. Coffin, from a 1910 publication,
reproduced from a photograph.

that "nobody could regret more deeply than he did the resignation
of Mrs. Coffin, for she had worked so long and earnestly for the
institution and her experience in such matters had been so great." [145]

Is it possible that more was at stake? The reformatory came
through the 1881 investigation successfully but with scars. The *Indiana State Sentinel* reported, "The Female Reformatory of Indiana,
though no longer an experiment as a successful institution, is the
first in the world. Though early thought idle and visionary, time
has abundantly tested its sterling qualities." [146] Hendricks made
a point to emphasize that "in the united struggle for success, if
anything hitherto unpleasant has occurred, it was not noticed." [147]
Here Hendricks is distancing herself from the investigation, and

by doing so implying that others did know something "unpleasant" had occurred and did nothing about it, as "things were developed in regard to the punishment of the inmates that were not
altogether countenanced by the public." [148] Nevertheless, Coffin was
credited with bringing the reformatory through the 1881 investigation with "one of the highest Christian sentiments." Yet when
she tried to hold on to the position of president, her detractors
claimed that making the board presidency "a place for political reward would not have conduced to its health and growth; it would
have also been in poor taste." [149] It is interesting that Coffin became
so completely a political figure in this reading, while Hendricks,
wife of former governor Thomas A. Hendricks, did not.[150] The situation highlights the blurred lines between traditional benevolence
and political patronage. As Lori Ginzberg notes about similar well-
connected and powerful women organizing in New York, "No one
involved in these early successes remarked on the inconsistency of
the women's proximity to politics, including the men who sometimes spoke to city governments 'to support [the women's] claims
for patronage.' " [151] Coffin ultimately resigned "rather than serve in
any other capacity than president." [152] Did the reformatory, originally thought to be a potential failure and "now a legitimate matter
of State pride," require a clean slate and distance from its scandalous past?

In 1884, Charles Coffin's involvement in a bank scandal at the
Richmond National Bank, of which he was president, coincided
with the end of Rhoda Coffin's presidency. He loaned thousands
of dollars to his sons, to himself, and to others for several failed
ventures and embezzled well beyond the bank's capital, and the
bank collapsed.[153] The turn of events contains not a small amount
of irony. Rhoda and Charles Coffin spent the whole of their adult
lives teaching and preaching their religious and moral beliefs to
convicted men and women and "deviants" in *their* institutions, and

one privileged, respected, powerful man embezzled hundreds of thousands of dollars *from their own community of believers* and from others, ruining family farms and businesses, and never spent a day in prison.[154] Embroiled in scandal, the Coffins moved to Chicago.

Later denounced from the Quaker faith in 1886, Charles and Rhoda led far quieter lives in Illinois. Rhoda Coffin died in 1909, and in her obituary that ran shortly thereafter, she could not shake the specter of her husband's behavior. Charles Coffin's actions were recounted right after Rhoda Coffin was heralded as "one of the leading charitable workers in England."[155]

Criminality intersects race, gender, sexuality, and class in those colonial origins of natural deviancy and deviancy through affiliation. Criminality profoundly disadvantages women by limiting or removing access to resources and opportunities for success through the ascription of a stigma, a taint.[156] When criminality intersects race, sexuality, and gender, the marginalizing effects of these interwoven constructs exacerbate the oppression women experience. From their culturally ascribed place above men on the social morality scale, women criminals suffered greatly in their "fall," because as the "guardians of morality, when a woman transgressed she seemed to threaten the very foundation of society."[157]

Historically, social reformers and prison officials have been known to use violence to reinforce universal norms and values, and in institutions of power, like prisons, violence has consistently been legitimated.[158] Evidence of violations was seen by men and women outside the prison system. But no one arrested the prison officials or reformers for committing violent acts against incarcerated women. Assault, sexual assault, rape, and battery are all criminal offenses, so why weren't the offenders prosecuted? Michel Foucault suggests the reason lies in the fundamental makeup of prisons as moral institutions of power:

Prison is the only place where power is manifest in its naked state, in its most excessive form, and where it is justified as moral force. . . . It reveals itself as tyranny pursed into the tiniest details; it is cynical and at the same time pure and entirely "justified," because its practice can be totally formulated within the framework of morality. Its brutal tyranny consequently appears as the serene domination of Good over Evil, of order over disorder.[159]

What makes prisons ideal spaces in which to commit atrocious acts on its inhabitants? Foucault's concept of heterotopias describes spaces, real or imagined, existing everywhere in which undesirable, disposable, deviant, and criminalized persons are tucked away, out of sight from normative spaces and "respectable" people.[160] This concept is helpful here. There are two kinds of heterotopias. One is the "space of crisis," for individuals who find themselves in temporary spaces of exclusions, like prisons or mental hospitals.[161] This may be one of the reasons prisons are often located great distances from major metropolitan areas and tucked away in rural communities.[162] The other is the "space of deviance," for those who operate outside accepted social norms.[163] Prisons are both kinds of heterotopias. Further, heterotopias are spaces against which white, patriarchal "noncriminals" establish and measure themselves, and they are spaces where people labeled deviant are divorced from society.[164]

Secrecy is foundational to heterotopic spaces like prisons. Hidden from the public eye, as in the case of Jeffersonville Prison, the reformatory, and other institutions, "outrages" against women went unchecked for extended periods of time. One late nineteenth-century newsman suggested that abuses in a heterotopic space can be prevented only when prison officials accept that "a certain amount of arbitrary authority is essential to a prison system, and with such authority, and the secrecy which prison walls obscure, only high personal character in the warden and his assistants can prevent iniquities." [165] When Rhoda Coffin pressed the chaplain to confirm what the incarcerated men told her, "he was loath to say anything for fear he would lose his position, but finally admitted that it was all true and much more." [166] In a heterotopia, keeping a job can equate to keeping secrets, secrets that supersede a moral and religious directive to help those subjected to immoral and egregious violations.

Yet high personal character in a warden alone is not sufficient to prevent violence in prisons because violence is constitutive of prisons. This fact by no means lets Smith and company off the hook. The goal of Smith and others was to remake these women, thought deviant but redeemable, into their own image and to teach them to imitate and live by middle-class social and religious norms. However, efforts to control sexuality and subdue gender nonconformity through the use of violence were ripe for the victimization of those same people the prison officials were charged to help. For confined women and girls at the reformatory, masturbation was not a private act. They had lost their right to privacy. The policing of their sexual agency and the egregious victimization of those who expressed themselves thusly demonstrate that the reformatory staff were also perpetrators of sexual violence. Culturally instantiated in religious and social norms, sexual violence was used to deter "self-abuse" because masturbation was a "sin." [167] Women and girls caught masturbating represented too great a "sinful" practice for the "benevolent" reformers to reconcile easily, and various violent strategies were used to reorient them. As shown earlier, the reformatory was interested in compliance and obedience to the institution's ideals and requests, whatever that entailed, and violence was justified in the resolution, which is inherent and constitutive of all prisons.

Let's close with Sally Hubbard. In the *Fourteenth Report of the Managers of the Indiana Reformatory*, the superintendent emphasized that women with life sentences or long sentences proved the reformatory's ability to reform. By all accounts, Sally was a model prisoner. She settled conflicts between women and helped Mrs. Smith to maintain order.[168] Sally died on January 13, 1887, after serving thirty-one years. In the remarks column of the reformatory registry, it stated she was "a great novel reader; now quite changed."[169]

Women playing in the yard.

5

Jennie and the Economics
of the Reformatory

Kim Baldwin, Molly Whitted, and Michelle Williams

We know little about Jennie Solomon, other than that her name appeared in *The People*, an Indianapolis paper that covered the 1881
investigation of abuse at the Indiana Reformatory Institution for
Women and Girls. We think Jennie was reformatory inmate #123,
listed in the official prison registry simply as "Jennie."[1] If so, Jennie Solomon was thirteen, orphaned, poor, and illiterate when she
arrived at the reformatory, sometime between May and November
1875. She had not been convicted of any crime and on her arrival
was deemed by officials to be in good health with "good capacity."

Jennie's early childhood was likely wrought with trauma. Born
in the midst of the U.S. Civil War, perhaps fathered by a soldier,
she was almost surely impoverished even before the Panic of 1873,
which led to the country's first great depression and lasted the rest

This chapter is based on Kim Baldwin, "Counterfeit Decency: Charity as Exploitation in Creation of Women's Reformatories," presented at the Annual Conference of
the American Historical Association, Atlanta, GA, January 6, 2016; and Molly Whitted and Michelle Williams, " 'But I Only Wanted Them to Conform': A Detailed Look
into the Initial Cohort of Girls at the Indiana Reformatory Institution for Women
and Girls between 1873 and 1884," *Midwest Social Sciences Journal* 22 (2019): 180–202.
Video of Kim Baldwin's presentation to the AHA can be viewed at www.youtube.com
/watch?v=DHnKfRGI9h8&t=9s.

PERSONAL.

—Hon Will Cumback, who wasn't elected U. S. Senator, but who will be permitted to keep his Internal Revenue collectorship, was in the city last week. We reckon he was at Harrison's blow out.

—Dr. C··lbertson, the skillful and experienced oculist and aurist, can be consulted relative to all diseases of the eye and ear, between the hours of 9 a. m. and 12 m., and 2 and 4 p. m., at his office, 26 West Washington street.

—Lawyer Josh. Flores, wife and baby, have returned from the Paris of America, where they have been spending time leisurely and happily and taking in the hill tops, smoke, fog and other beauties of art and nature in the Queen City.

—Herman Schierling, who formerly stood at the general delivery window of the post-office, died on last Tuesday morning, of lung fever. He had been connected with the post-office for twelve years, and was highly esteemed and respected by all.

—Val Meier, lately deceased, did not forget his poor creditors when he made his will, in which he requests that they should be treated forbearingly. This is creditable to his head and heart, and yet he made no loud professions of Christianity.

—A delightful surprise party took possession of the residence of John A. McGaw and his estimable lady, on last Wednerday night. They made things lively about that portion of North Mississippi street, and the last we heard was the familiar refrain:

"We won't go home 'till morning."

—Col. Edward H. Wolfe, the new State Auditor, has made a clean sweep in his office Piercy, Messick and Baker all having to go to make room for John W. Coons, J. Wright Wharton and Isaiah Piatt. It is stated that this is the first instance in which a clean sweep was ever made by an incoming State Auditor.

—Judge Newcomb says "we will be laughed at for giving our dollars and taking no security for their return"—if we subscribe $100,000 to the proposed Southern Coal road. Now no one likes to be laughed at. Let's keep our dollars and not run the risk of getting laughed it.

—Among the candidates named as successor to Gen. John Love on the State House Board, are Col. B. C. Shaw, Thomas Cottrell, J. P. Dunn, Gen. M. D. Manson, Austin H. Brown, Hughes East, John H. Piercy and John A. Reaume. A Democrat must be appointed according to law. The Governor, Auditor and Treasurer of State make the appointment. They will endeavor, of course, to select the best Democrat.

—If you want to be taxed $300,000 for coal roads, vote for the subsidy to the Coal and Southern road, on Monday. Two other roads are waiting anxiously the result, and if it is favorable to the road they will each demand $100,000, and you know it won't do to make fish of one and flesh of another. With three additional coal roads, God only knows where the price of coal will get to. Way out of sight, we reckon.

—John C. Shoemaker, of the Sentinel, who is one of the incorporators of the proposed Coal and Southern road, which the citizens of Center townshep propose to snow under on next Monday, in an editorial endorsing the project, on last Wednesday, observed; "Let us, therefore, take a broad and enlightened view of this question and avail ourselves of the opportunity presented to procure cheap coal by voting for the donation to the coal road." "The opportunity presented," is the donating of $100,000 to the Coal and Southern road projected by John C. Shoemaker. You may rest assured, John, that the citizens of Center township will "take a broad and enlightened view of this question" and vote against it. They will, John, they will.

Vote against the Coal Road Subsidy of $100,000.

Better than Government Bonds.

The Franklin Life Insurance Company of this city, on the 8th of January, paid to the widow of Wm. B. Gentry, of Arcadia, five thousand dollars insurance on the life of her husband. The insured had paid only $496 90 in premiums.

Superintendent of Printing.

No appointment yet. The Governor, Auditor and Secretary seem to have an unusually hard time of it in deciding upon their printer. There were about fifteen candidates, but it is said they are now narrowed down to four. It is probable no choice will be made until next week.

Miss E. Webber, manufacturer and dealer in human hair, No. 10 East Washington street, is offering some very fine masquerade wigs, natural water waves; also sole agent for Fetherly's Parision Complexion Compound.

CHRISTIAN PUNISHMENT

At Indiana's Female Reformatory.

HAIR PULLED OUT BY THE ROOTS

And Girls Beaten Over the Head Until They Become Deaf for Life.

The Legislative Committee renewed the examination of witnesses in reference to the alleged cruelties practiced upon the inmates at the Female Reformatory and prison, at the office of Messrs. Duncan, Smith & Duncan, on last Monday night. Only two or three witnesses were examined, and their evidence was simply corroborative.

Mrs. Charlotte S. Brown, who lives near the Reformatory, had seen marks of punishment upon some of the inmates; these marks were on Jennie Solomon, who lived with her. The girl became a little saucy while working for me. I complained to Mrs. Smith, and she sent for her. It was when she returned to me that I saw the marks on her face and eyebrow. She was only gone a few minutes. She said that the punishment was inflicted by Aunty Smith.

The following was developed on Wednesday night. We take the News' condensation of the evidence:

Mrs. Amanda Lampier, an ex-prisoner, discharged October 26, testified as to the punishment of Jane Williams, a crazy woman, by Mrs. Smith and Mrs. Johnson. The woman was severely beaten and choked. Mrs. Lampier had seen a mark on Susie Reynolds' mouth, which she said was a cut from the strap with which she was struck. The food was good enough generally. Several times the meat was bad. A serious cause of complaint among the convicts was that the water-closets were kept locked two or three hours at a time. Mrs Lampier had seen prisoners, when bathing, who had marks of straps upon their backs. Mrs. Gwyn, the matron, was kind to the prisoners.

Mrs. Anna Buchanan, an ex-officer at the Reformatory, testified that she had seen Mrs. Smith take girls of twelve or fifteen years of age and strike their heads against the wall. Mrs. Buchanan did not think herself competent to say whether Mrs. Smith was a humane superintendent.

Emma Thomas, who served three years for larceny, couldn't say any thing against her treatment. Had never been ducked, but had seen others punished that way.

Lizzie Cash testified that she had been whipped several times on her naked person. She had seen Mrs. Smith take a girl and pull her hair until some of it came out.

Mary Ellen MacIntyre said she had been strapped and dragged all over the floor by Mrs Smith. The prisoners have been denied access to the water closets. She had seen three or four persons around Jane Williams, the crazy woman, pulling her hair and whipping her.

The committee, after hearing the above testimony, adjourned until Friday afternoon at 2 o'clock.

The Coal Road Again.

To the Editor of the Indianapolis Journal:

Allow me space in your paper to notice the address of the corporators of the "Coal and Southern railroad" in this morning's Journal, and your editorial comments thereon.

Although the address does not purport to be an answer to my article you published on Tuesday last, I am authorized from its tenor to assume that its appearance is due to that article.

The adddress charges that opposition to the donation asked for by this company, and criticism on the sufficiency of the present statutes to secure to the public the benefits promised as a return for the donation, comes from paid attorneys of other roads. If this remark was intended for me, the worthy gentlemen who signed the address have shot wide of the mark. I am not the attorney of any railroad company. What I wrote was in the interest of the people who are asked to vote and pay the $100,000.

The address virtually concedes that I was correct in the legal proposition advanced, that should the road at any time be sold on a foreclosure decree and a new company should become the owner, then the contract the present company is to execute for cheap freight on coal cannot be enforced against the new corporation. This proposition has to be admitted, for it is too plain for argument.

But in the address the corporators propose to obviate the necessity of additional legislation by a promise which will be noticed presently.

In your editorial comments on the address, you say:

"It is true there is no provision in the act o 1879 that such a contract as that which the incorporators of the coal road propose to make shall be a lien on the road, but there is no necessity for any such provision in the act.. It can be made a lien without any such provision by the terms of the contract, and by a mortgage contemporaneously executed, and this is precisely what the incorporators propose to do."

We do not read the proposition of the incorporators alike. I find no promise in it to execute a mortgage contemporaneous with the contract to secure the performance of the latter. What they do say is this:

"We hereby pledge ourselves that no contract, bond or mortgage shall be executed upon the property that does not acknowledge this obligation as a first lien upon the road within the township."

This is the individual promise of the present stockholders that in any mortgage they may place upon the road they will reserve a lien in favor of the township, on so much of the road as lies therein. This is good so far as it goes, and if we could know that the road would forever be in the hands of as public-spirited and substantial residents of this city as now compose the company, the public might feel safe without any further guarantee; but suppose that in a few years Jay Gould, Vanderbilt, the Panhandle combination, or some other railroad anaconda should conclude that this coal road was a needed link in some great consolidation, and should purchase a controlling amount of stock, would there be anything in the promise of the present incorporators to prevent other mortgages from being placed on the road, ignoring the contract with our county commissioners? Such veteran railroad absorbers would smile at the suggestion that the promise made in to-day's Journal was binding on them.

As a continuing security, the promise made in the address is valueless. A few years hence none of the stock may be owned by the present incorporators, and their promises as to what they will or will not do can have no binding force to prevent future owners from indulging in those common schemes by which undesirable obligations of railroad corporations are sponged out. Your suggestion of a contemporaneous mortgage, to secure the performance of contract, is quite another thing.

H. C. Newcomb.

February 2.

A Bill of Particulars.

Ferdinand Schellschmidt who, with others, was thrown down an embankment by the upsetting of Charles E. Shover's wagon while returning from Crown Hill in October last, sues Shover for damages, and files the following bill of particulars:

Loss of musical instrument	$ 75
Physician's bill	50
Loss in business	500
Pain and suffering	1,000
Permanent disability	1,200

altogether a fair shake.

POLITICAL NOTES.

From the number of looming, if not "boom"-ing, candidates for the mayoralty, who are mentioned and announced, it is suggested that Uncle John Caven's mortgage to the office is to be hotly contested. It is understood that Horace McKay is quietly marshaling his friends, and that he will be found a formidable competitor for the nomination. Mr. McKay has had experience in the practical administration of city affairs, and the Republicans might go further and fare worse than the election of McKay to the mayoralty. To some part of the conduct of the Board of Public Improvements, with McKay at its head, The People objected, but he would no doubt make a live, popular Mayor. His energy about the State Republican Committee rooms in the late campaign proved him to be a man of prodigious capacity and sagacity.

Should the Police Judge bill pass and become a law, and Calvin Rooker fail to receive the nomination for Mayor—then it is pretty thoroughly understood that C. F. Rooker will be the best man for this new office. For our part we think C. F. would also make an excellent Mayor, but the will of the people must be obeyed.

Death of Tyler Mason.

The well known temperance worker, Tyler Mason, died suddenly at Champaign, Ill., on last Thursday, as is supposed of heart disease. Most everybody throughout the State knew Tyler Mason. He kept hotel with his father in this city for many years, and at one time he was quite dissipated, but some four years ago he straightened up and became a temperance lecturer, taking care of his father in his old age, who is now in this city in very feeble health. Tyler Mason had some very fine points about him, which developed of late years and gained him many friends. He was one of the largest men in the State, weighing 446 pounds.

Vote against the Coal Road Subsidy of $100,000.

BREVITIES.

Florida Crook cigars at the Circle House.

Cadwallader's photos are the finest made.

Uncut papers at 40 cents a hundred, for sale at The People office.

Ten Pin Alley and pool room at No. 91 East Washington street. Lunch daily.

Go to Huegele's Oyster House, 60 E. Washington street, for the best 25 cent dinner.

The boss, Max Herrlich's saloon, No. 143 East Washinton street. Lunch at 10 a. m.

Call and see the $3 photographs for $1, at the New York Galery, next to the New York Store.

Huegele's fried oysters are delicious. They can't be beat. Try them at 60 East Washington street

Dr. Rogers' vegetable worm syrup instantly destroys worms and removes the secretions which cause them.

Treasurer of State-elect Hill has purchased the residence of M. L. Cox, on Park avenue, and will remove to the city at an early day.

Persons in search of masquerade costumes for the approaching carnival should call at Mrs. Grauman's, Nos. 108 South Illinois street.

The report of H. Clay, State Inspector of Mineral Oils, to the Governor, has just been issued in neat style by Carlon & Hollenbeck. It is down on "Hyperion."

Dr. Jordan, the celebrated throat and lung physician, of Terre Haute, Ind., can yet be consulted at his rooms, Spencer House, southwest corner Union Depot.

The magistrates complain that 'Squire Schmidt is cutting rates. He married a couple the other day for a keg of beer, but the worst of it is he didn't get the beer.

Hunt & McCurdy will close out the stock of boots and shoes at No. 40 West Washington street, at retail auction, beginning on Monday next. See advertisement in another column.

Joseph Lewis, an employe of Fahnley & McCrea, was seriously burned one day this week by the explosion of gasses in a base burner, the ashes of which he was shaking down. It is feared that he will lose one of his eyes.

Isaac Haworth and John F. Holloway, who hail from Hamilton county, were arrested on Monday night last, charged with passing and possessing counterfeit money. They were committed for future examination.

James Kelly, proprietor of the Marble Works, No. 60 West Maryland street, is receiving a choice invoice of marble, suitable for monuments etc. Mr. Kelley has been turning out some of the finest specimens of monuments and tombstones found west of the Alleghanies.

We understand from undoubted authority that the postmen regulate their own clothing —so far as whether they shall wear overcoats or not—and they concluded this season they would not wear them, the cape being so much in the way in carrying their bundles. So, if they freeze it is their own fault, and not that of the P. O. authorities, who do not control the overcoat business.

Minnie Von Specklen was taken into custody one day this week, at Brightwood, charged with stealing articles from the residence of Heddrich, corner of East and Washington streets, in whose employ she was formerly. A portion of the missing things were found in her possession, which she claimed were presented to her by a beau—but the worst of it was Miss Von Specklen could not procure the beau or tell where to find him.

STEALING

THE SUCCESSOR (TRIES HIS HA

And Gets Away Wi $500 W

When Ed Stewart, th at the postoffice, about a went to the penitentiary of the registered letter another saddle-colored place. You would have sugar would have melte so truly good did he app upon as one of the colo studying for the minist cense to preach, althoug a very presentable "man est and unassuming, an ment. Col. Holloway h and he had the general r

A week or so ago Wil from Cathcart & Cleland to the clerk at the stan the money. It was subs that the bill, when it left was for only 50 cents. B of this at the time—ev utmost confidence in the of the Methodist persuas

When Superintendent make up his stamp acc January, he discovered short some $350, and was discovered that wh pally 15 cent stamps ha Edgerton, a special P. C be in the city, and afte little he came to the conc could be no other than son, and the Rev. John into custody.

He at first denied stre the thief. He wouldn't But on the way up to hi and confessed all. He s up to it by the man who bish or waste paper al pulled out of his over sheets of two and five boy who applied at the stamps was made to disg He said that a man had to sell them. Wilson al ing burned a lot of fift he couldn't get rid of, keep, and when, with th at his home, he pulled other lot of stamps. burned about $300 in fift this can be conclusivel will not be called upon

How long the Rev. J carrying on this stamp t to tell—but as stamps h before, probably he tells says it has only been since he fell from grace. prosperity, and went wr he fell. The Rev. John month or two ago to o an amiable and excelle He has no excuse for h he pleads what many a before him, financial em

Wilson was taken bef ers, but, waiving examin ted to jail in default of but very little doubt th his predecessor, Ed Stew some service.

Wilson took the stamp Holloway's room, to wh cess—frequently being se cials for stamps for imm the easiest matter in th smuggle entire sheets at

Col. Holloway remark tried both a good and ba loss to know whom next senger. Why not try once?

Footpads

On last Monday night Robert W. Heidlinger, of the Merchants' Excha home, he was set upon after he had passed th knocked down and rob book containing $72, an been playing pool with the Grand hotel bar roo thinks the parties who hangers-on about the have the money.

Sudden

John Harris, an Englis 53 years, in the employ freight depot as night dead at his residence sho duty on last Tuesday mo

He had been conversin he fell, but had complain time of not feeling well, urer of the St. Paul's and a very honest, deser a wife and numerous fri sudden departure from t of the decade. After being orphaned—or possibly abandoned—Jennie was sent to the reformatory.

To get to her destination, Jennie might have traveled, perhaps by buckboard, from as far south as the Ohio River or from as far north as the border of Lake Michigan. She might have seen the Coffins' horse-drawn carriage resting in front of the two-year-old brick building that would become her home for the rest of her adolescence. Jennie was assigned to the reformatory wing of the institution, with the other children. The statute that authorized the institution mandated that only those under the age of fifteen could be committed to the reformatory and that they must be released by the age of eighteen. The penal department housed girls aged sixteen and older and women convicted of crimes.

Using data from the prison registries from 1873 to 1876 and from 1881 to 1884 (the eight years when the registries are most complete), we determined that the typical girl at the reformatory was fourteen years old when she was first admitted, was white, had at least one living parent, and was judged on intake to be of average to above-average intellect with good health. Though some girls were there for crimes such as larceny, others had been deemed to have incorrigible conduct, and some, at least in the early years, were simply orphans. Those who were not orphans often arrived there because their parents had been persuaded by Superintendent Sarah Smith that they were unable to care for their daughters and that they should abandon them to the institution.

The cost of running such a large establishment was high, especially if it wasn't fully occupied. During the fiscal years of 1873/84, the annual cost of feeding, clothing, and housing each girl fluctuated between $136 and $200. These estimates were calculated each year by the institution's steward (Sarah Smith's husband) and reported to the state. Counties were responsible for exactly half of the expense per girl that they had committed for every year of her stay, and the state paid the rest.[2] But if there were few girls there, the cost per child increased, which possibly discouraged counties from sending more, with the resulting deficit falling on the state and the inevitable opprobrium falling on the reformatory's founders.

Thus, within a year of the prison's opening, Indiana's former governor Conrad Baker, who was a member of the institution's board of visitors, wrote to his successor, Governor Thomas Hendricks:

> As long as there are so few inmates the expense of the institution must unavoidably be comparatively high, and it is to be hoped that the different counties will, in view of this, avail themselves of the advantages of the Institution by committing to its guardianship some at least, of the girls which are to be found in every community who need and are entitled to such guardianship.
>
> It is believed that the people as yet, do not generally understand that *a girl need not be an offender against the penal laws of the State to justify her committal* to the guardianship of the Reformatory Department of this Institution.[3] (Emphasis added.)

To increase the number of girls in the reformatory, the board also sought to raise the upper limit of the age that girls could be initially committed to the reformatory from fifteen to eighteen and to lengthen the duration of stay for the girls in the reformatory by raising the mandatory discharge age from eighteen to twenty-one.[4] When young women were convicted and sent to "prison," the financial burden was all on the state. For girls in the reformatory, however, half the bill was footed by the county. As a result, the number of girls in the reformatory increased, and girls were sent there from counties across Indiana.[5]

A few years later, however, the board again requested a change in admission policy, this time limiting admission to girls between ages twelve and sixteen. "There are, at present in the Reformatory quite a number of small children. It surely cannot have been the

intention of the Legislature to make this a State Orphan Asylum,"
opined the board.[6] Sarah Smith affirmed, "The age of ten is quite
too young, unless guilty of crime. A necessity is felt, with increase
of numbers, for some better means of giving them regular, useful and profitable employment than our present arrangement will
admit of."[7]

From the outset, economic exploitation was set into the laws governing the institution. "The Superintendent of said Institution shall
have power to place any girl committed to the reformatory department thereof at any employment for account of the Institution."[8] Indeed, the goal of the managers was always to have every girl at the
reformatory profitably employed. An axiom of prison government,
they proclaimed, is that "the best prisons are self-supporting."[9]
To minimize the costs of running their institution, the managers
sought to exploit the human capital of displaced children.

The goal of being self-supporting took on new urgency when
Rhoda Coffin successfully deposed the all-male board of managers,
replacing it with an all-female board, of which she was president.
The new managers quickly increased revenue. Local news sources
reported that "the current expenses per year had been $21,500 since
the ladies had charge of the Institution," while when "the gentlemen had the management [the expenses] were $28,000."[10] Indeed,
the cost per prisoner per year had plummeted from an estimated
$200 per annum in 1874 to $146 in 1878,[11] a 25 percent drop. How did
the new board of managers achieve such remarkable savings? By
selecting profitable enterprises and by forcing all the women and
girls to work longer hours under harsher conditions.

The first annual report of the board of managers declared, "Plans
of labor, in addition to systematic education will be adopted, with
the purchase of suitable materials for work, so that the industry of
the inmates may produce the best results practicable, in aid of the
funds of the institution."[12] From the start, the principal remunerative work of the institution was washing. So as not to compete with

Laundry work room—washing.

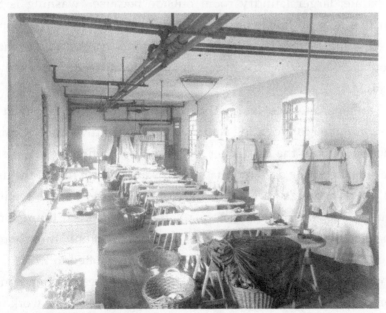

Laundry work room—ironing.

the poor women of Indianapolis who were economically dependent on laundering work, a glove-making business was introduced,[13] plus caning chairs, knitting, and sewing. When these businesses did not turn a profit, the reformatory adopted a new method of laundering, used first in the penal department and then in the entire reformatory. Before a girl could be discharged from the reformatory, "she must . . . be able to do laundry work in the new style."[14]

Laundry work was not only the most practical and lucrative business for the reformatory but also the most effective way to control the girls. As Rhoda Coffin so coldly observed, "It subdues the excitability of the system, and makes submission easier."[15] It also imperiled the children's health. The laundry rooms, originally located in the reformatory basement, were small and "kept damp" by the miasmic "steam from the boiling soap-suds," posing a serious health hazard to the girls. Yet the board's main concern was expanding the size of the operation and putting more girls to work. They asked the state for appropriations to build a separate, larger laundry room outside because "washing is by far the most profitable business."[16] Once the new laundry rooms were built in 1880, the number of girls working there more than doubled.[17] More than likely, this is where Jennie spent most of her days.

The superintendent and the board of managers always claimed to be committed to providing a mix of education and vocational training throughout the day. Thus, in Sarah Smith's first report as superintendent, she declared that the girls are "taught half of the day in a well organized school, the other half devoted to cane-seating chairs and household duties in rotation."[18] However, the reports that actually break down the girls' day show that only three hours were allotted to school, while six hours were allotted to work, five hours for meals, recreation, and religious exercises, and ten hours for sleep.[19] This remained the schedule until 1884, when work increased from six hours to seven hours a day, cutting back an hour from meals, recreation, and religious exercises.[20] A journalist who visited the prison in 1890 observed that all the girls were taught to work in a style termed *rotation of the crops*. A certain detail would wash for half the day, then iron clothes, then sew, then scrub, then cook, in addition to weaving cane-coated chair bottoms.[21] Girls turned out 4,500 "cane-seating chairs" in 1884 alone. Some girls were "profitably employed" sewing and repairing all the clothes for the institution, as well as the clothes of other facilities.[22] To get an idea of what was expected of them per day, consider that the girls put out 3,384 tailored pieces in 1876, 2,808 pieces in 1878, and 3,122 pieces in 1884.[23] All the while, scripture was read aloud to the children when they worked. Sarah Smith was fond of quoting 2 Thessalonians 3:10: "Our motto has been if you don't work, you shall not eat."[24] Religion was at the root of Smith and Coffin's ideology for reformation. Smith wrote in her first report, "We willingly admit that it is no light task to take the ungovernable and vicious from a life of idleness and crime, and by firmness and Christian kindness, make them obedient and industrious, restoring the victims of neglect to virtue and usefulness."[25]

In 1874, the board adopted the ticket-of-leave system, an early form of parole/work release.[26] This novel program provided underage girls as domestic servants to affluent homes in the neighboring community and eventually in other parts of the state. To be granted this "privilege," girls were required to cook well, bake the best sort of bread, make a dress, and do laundry in the new style.[27] The ticket-of-leave program proved "invaluable" to Smith, giving her "greater power over the girls,"[28] for if they failed to perform their duties they were subject to recall,[29] even for minor offenses. Thus, when orphaned Jennie Solomon got a bit "saucy" while working for Mrs. Charlotte S. Brown and living in her home, she was almost surely on ticket-of-leave. That is why Mrs. Brown reported Jennie's impertinence directly to Sarah Smith and why Smith felt empowered to put "marks on her face and eyebrow" as punishment.

The *Thirteenth Report of the Managers of the Indiana Reformatory* noted that sixty-three girls had been out on ticket-of-leave "in various parts of the state" and declared that "this system . . . we consider one of the largest factors in working out reformation."[30] Perhaps. But it also proved quite lucrative. We were unable to find in any of our sources whether the homes hosting the girls paid them for their services. However, the institution financially profited from this collaboration. Jennie Solomon was still considered a ward of the reformatory while living in Charlotte Brown's house on ticket-of-leave, and as such, the county from whence she came was still required to pay its yearly portion of her housing costs.[31] With her bed at the reformatory now empty, a new commitment could take her place, paid for by another county, thus doubling the income stream.[32] Perhaps Jennie's bed at the reformatory was full at the time of Mrs. Brown's complaint and that was a contributing factor to Smith striking Jennie rather than recalling her.

According to the board, "Idleness is one of the most fruitful sources of crime, and laziness its twin sister. These are two mighty evils with which we have to contend. Constant employment is therefore an absolute necessity, that they may be taught the means of earning an honest livelihood." The board went on to note with pride that "a number of those who have left are making good and reliable house servants."[33] Unfortunately, Smith and Coffin appear never to have considered whether their charges were capable of being more than servants. Whether engaged in forced labor at the reformatory or while on ticket-of-leave,

> it can hardly be expected that the majority will ever reach very high positions in social life, but all can be taught to make themselves useful in some appropriate sphere. We regard knowledge of cooking, house-keeping, sewing, washing, ironing, mending, etc., as indispensable for all.[34]

In selecting remunerative work for the girls, the board made a list of requirements:

work must be such that she may continue at it when discharged
work that must not degrade the woman
work that will not interfere with the honest working women
of Indianapolis
work must be profitable to the institution.[35]

Some of the girls—including perhaps our Jennie—did realize they were considered servants and felt that the work they were forced to perform was degrading. Their feelings found expression in the following passages from the annual reports: "We find . . . no work more beneficial than that which qualifies them for household duties. Many of them have the false idea that it is 'degrading,' that by following some trade they can dress better, and have more leisure, which too often proves their downfall."[36] And "great care is taken to infuse into them a pride in, and a love for, labor, instead of the feeling that labor is derogatory to a woman."[37] Clearly, these girls had more faith in their abilities and held higher aspirations for themselves and their future than those responsible for their care.

Ironically, the girls' staunchest advocate for a more beneficial future came not from the women sworn specifically to uphold their interests but from a man. As Anastazia Schmid describes elsewhere in this book, Dr. Theophilus Parvin, the prison's physician, found many ways to exploit the captive population there. Yet as early as 1874, he advocated for more education and for more creative and satisfying work:

Among the children in the reform department there will be found some possessing a natural talent, a special fitness or

aptitude for modes of industry that are more productive, receiving higher remuneration than sewing, knitting, washing,
ironing, and chair work. Might not the state . . . go a step far-
ther by giving those who manifest undoubted talent . . . at least
a commencement in education for such work? Bookkeeping,
music teaching, telegraphing, drawing and painting, picture
coloring, and engraving. . . . There are children here whose tal-
ents if properly cultivated . . . could be rendered independent
of all aid here-after, and capable of lucrative work.[38]

Stonewalled, Parvin went a step further in his 1876 report to
the governor by offering himself as the instructor.[39] To no avail.
The board declared in 1878, "We do not aim to give the pupils
in the Reform School a finished education."[40] And again in 1882,
"A common, plain education only is given. No attempt is made in
higher branches."[41] Their unwillingness to educate these children
in anything but domesticity reveals their true intention of making
servants, versus reforming young women who might have a pros-
perous future.

Through founding and governing the literal "civilizing institutions" of the era, upper-middle-class reformers like the Smiths and
the Coffins imposed their moral agendas, perpetuating a belief that
certain classes of people could not be trusted to make decisions
regarding their own values. The new elites believed that the formerly powerful institutions of church and family could no longer
adequately instill morality in society and that newly established
outside institutions, such as prisons, orphan asylums, poor farms,
and reformatories, could. Their institutions were underpinned by
economic and cultural injustices, which linked and reinforced each
other. The result was a vicious cycle of cultural and economic subordination and social injustice, which became the cultural norm
(and still is).

Rhoda Coffin and her husband, Charles, exemplify the cruel

The visiting room.

hypocrisy of this system. A genuine power couple of the Gilded Age, the Coffins were movers and shakers in Indiana, where they maintained a surprisingly lavish lifestyle, especially for Quakers, complete with a ballroom in their mansion. They were sought-after speakers, both nationally and internationally, on many topics, especially prisons. As Michelle Daniel Jones describes, they were also frauds, using their bank customers' hard-earned savings to pay not only for their own glamorous lifestyles but also for their four sons'.

Theft without culpability shaped the fate of the Coffins. True, they had to flee to Chicago to avoid arrest and were disowned by their Quaker Monthly Meeting.[42] And two of their sons later went to prison for other financial scandals, while a third—a disgraced stockbroker in New York—eventually committed suicide.[43] Yet most historians treat these matters as mere footnotes to the Coffins'

storied careers as social reformers. Rhoda is celebrated to this day
as one of Indiana's greatest women. Yet it is worth noting that the
sum total of financial loss resulting from the Coffins' misdeeds
was exponentially greater than *the combined total of all the economic
crimes committed by the women imprisoned by Rhoda and Sarah* in the
nineteenth century. Which leads to the inescapable conclusion that
when theft is small and when it is committed by marginalized people it is a crime, but when theft is large and when it is committed by
elites it is merely an unfortunate business outcome.[44]

Jennie found herself in a system of justice where it's better to
be rich and guilty than to be poor and innocent. She had committed no crime, yet she found herself committed to the guardianship of an organization that prioritized imprisoning her over
protecting her. She was poor. Quite often the poorest people are
the best versed in what it takes to survive simply because their
focus is not on lining the pockets of the rich. Jennie's focus was on
what would allow her a few small pleasures through the ticket-
of-leave program. But there came a point in time when she had
suffered enough. Since she had nothing to begin with, she had
nothing to lose when she stepped out of line and got "saucy" with
Mrs. Brown. In fact, some would say that Jennie gained a lot more
than she lost that day. She gained a sense of who she really was.
As far as Smith was concerned, though, when Jennie was no longer obedient, she was no longer special, she was unworthy and
easily disposed of.

But politeness filtered through fragility and supremacy is not
about manners. It's about a methodology of control. Sarah Smith
knew this when, under the facade of civility, she struck Jennie.
Smith felt no remorse. Jennie gained no value or insight from the
physical punishment, other than the notion that people like Sarah
Smith and Rhoda Coffin are there to get what they can and to block
the way so others cannot pass without meeting whatever arbitrary
standards they create. And if they are not appeased, to prevent

any real progress from taking place while they reap the benefits of counterfeit decency.

Jennie Solomon and those like her were not weak; they were perpetual towers of strength who lived in situations where it wasn't okay to identify or talk about problems. Denial became a way of life—a way of dealing with hardship. We all have days when we cannot push any harder, cannot stop focusing on fear, cannot be strong, when we expose our tiredness, irritability, or anger. Jennie allowed herself to be human when she asserted herself. Her inner strength and determination provided her the energy to move forward. She was a true champion of fortitude.

PART II

Sex, Sexuality, and Control over Women's Bodies

6

Mary Jane and Dr. Parvin
at the Reformatory

Anastazia Schmid

Mary Jane Schweitzer was sent to the Indiana Reformatory Institution for Women and Girls in 1877. She was not convicted of a crime but was placed there merely "on suspicion of committing arson." Mary Jane told the *Indianapolis Journal* that during her two years there she was "punished very frequently. For most of one year [she] was not allowed to speak with any other person. Was kept in solitary confinement for one month, fed on bread and water, ducked, and had no clean clothing."[1] Starving and ill, Mary Jane took bread from the prison kitchen. Finding her eating, Superintendent Sarah Smith attacked her, beating her with a pair of shoes. She was taken to her cell, stripped naked, and drenched with a hose by two men "for nearly half an hour." After describing repeated altercations with prison officials and an unsuccessful appeal to the assistant superintendent, Rhoda Coffin, Mary Jane recalled,

This chapter is dedicated to the loving memory of every historical woman identified here within and to every incarcerated woman I have known and to those who remain unknown and unnamed who have lost their lives in prison, and to other incarcerated women who are survivors of prison rape and sexual abuse or medical experimentation or who have lost their lives in indefinite sentences, lost their body parts, or lost their children while serving state-sanctioned prison sentences.

I was visited by Dr. Parvin. I was very sick, and he was to examine me with instruments. Mrs. Smith on that occasion dragged me out of my bed and into another room. I told her what I thought of being treated that way. Dr. Parvin said I was to lie in bed for several days after the operation.[2]

The historically obscure Mary Jane Schweitzer was one of several prisoners Dr. Theophilus Parvin (1829–98) forced to be a surgical and experimental subject while incarcerated in the Indiana Women's Prison. There are few surviving testimonies from women such as Mary Jane, but those that remain speak volumes, revealing subjugated knowledge gleaned from lived experience that challenges the dominant historical narratives of medical advancement and scientific progress, as well as of prison history, and illuminating the difference between popular and scholarly narrative.

If his victims are little known, Parvin is the opposite—he remains a prominent and lauded figure for his work in the then-budding fields of gynecology and obstetrics. His colleagues held him in high esteem. According to one historian of surgery, Parvin "should be designated a catalyst in his branch of medicine."[3] Deemed an expert in matters of female reproductive anatomy, Parvin held chairs at the most prestigious societies and medical colleges and served as the founder and president of the American Gynecology Society, president of the State Medical Society in Indiana, and eventually as president of the American Medical Association (AMA). His most celebrated work, *The Science and Art of Obstetrics*, was issued in several editions in the late nineteenth century.[4] His name was noted and his works cited in prestigious medical journals, both nationally and abroad. In a memorial tribute, Dr. William Parish wrote,

Dr. Parvin can be rightly classed among the great men who have illumined the medical profession with their intellectual attainments. . . . Dr. Parvin was a thoroughly religious man and a thoroughly good one. Of an intense nature, his dislikes and his friendships were intense. He did many acts of friendship, and I believe that he never deliberately did any man a wrong.[5]

Likewise, G.W.H. Kemper, a fellow member of the State Medical Society, credited Parvin with being "instrumental in elevating the standard of medicine, as well as laying the foundation of our present State Medical Association." Another colleague said of Parvin: "He was the purest man I ever knew, and apparently wholly without faults or vices."[6] Yet Parvin's fame relied on the hidden spaces in which he perfected his craft and on the invisible, discredited, vulnerable bodies he used to gain knowledge there. Although his magnum opus *The Science and Art of Obstetrics* appeared in 1886, after he had moved to Philadelphia to take up the chair of obstetrics at the Jefferson Medical College, an Indiana colleague noted that "the book was written while Dr. Parvin was a resident of Indianapolis. On the eve of his departure for Philadelphia he told the author of this paper that he must 'dress the work up a little.' "[7]

Parvin's contributions to medical science must be reconsidered in the context of the work he performed while employed as the sole physician of the Indiana Reformatory Institution for Women and Girls, using the captive bodies of women, including Mary Jane Schweitzer. This context calls into question Parvin's benevolence and demands a redistribution of the credit for the "catalyst" of his discoveries. Parvin founded this field of knowledge, and found great fame in it, from brutally experimenting on the bodies of incarcerated women for a decade.

This chapter reveals the stories not told about Dr. Theophilus Parvin. It relies on under-consulted documents, including newspaper reports, Parvin's numerous medical publications, clinical lectures, and medical collaborations, and the annual reports of the prison where I spent the better part of nearly two decades of incarceration. These sources tell of sex, gender, class, race, science and medicine, and human captivity along the continuum of social control from internalized hegemony to the most abusive forms of forced surgical experimentation. This chapter challenges popular narratives of medical progress through a critical inquiry into Dr. Parvin's relationships with his captive patients. The story of Dr. Parvin's interconnections with scientific, social, religious, and political elites, critical to his work using captive patients inside institutions of social control, illustrates the ways elite men relied on and buttressed their power over the female body through the practice of medicine and actual physical captivity. This story also reveals the overlap between slavery and incarceration, often wrongly considered autonomous institutions with separate histories.

The first part of this chapter tracks the relationship of science and medicine to institutions of social control during the nineteenth century. It focuses on physicians' use of the bodies of vulnerable populations, from people subject to chattel slavery to those in penal reformatory institutions and asylums. It begins with a better-known gynecologist, Dr. J. Marion Sims (1813–83), whose use of enslaved women for his medical experiments foreshadowed Dr. Parvin's use of imprisoned women. The "advancements" these men and their cohorts made in female medical science highlight expansive practices of bodily control via the medicalization of the female body and human reproduction. The history recounted in this section places the joined institutions of social control—slavery and prisons—in relation to race, sex, and class, noting the specific bodies used to spark medical advancements. In scientific and medical advancement, who counts as human? Whose bodies can be used as a means to an end?

The second part of the chapter details Parvin's work at the reformatory. Despite the gaps Parvin left in prison records, his published work allows a detailed picture to emerge. Parvin experimented on incarcerated women with both drugs and surgeries, often with disastrous results. Parvin, Sarah Smith, and their cohort shared a certainty of moral rectitude that permitted them to attempt to control women's sexuality and to limit female sexual pleasure, leading to torturous punishments for masturbation, which Parvin denied, and bloody messes of abortions. As I narrate, I identify the women and girls used as Parvin's medical experimental subjects, naming them whenever possible and believing their stories.

Medicine and Institutions of Social Control

A critical chapter in the history of the use of human medical test subjects takes place in pre–Civil War Alabama. Dr. J. Marion Sims, Theophilus Parvin's predecessor and later colleague, used enslaved women he leased or purchased for the purpose of perfecting gynecological surgeries. Gynecology would grow through Sims's surgical experimentation on enslaved women, feeding not only the medical field but also the linked institutions of slavery and capitalism. Indeed, just as Sims's experimentation on enslaved women not only "provided for the maintenance of sound black female reproductive bodies" but "also served to perpetuate the institution of slavery," as Deirdre Cooper Owens has shown, so too did Parvin's experimentation on incarcerated women help perpetuate and deepen what I call the prison-industrial-medical complex.[8]

Sims's provision of medical "treatment" to enslaved women must be understood not as altruism or even benign condescension but as a component of slavery's political economy. Enslavers held a profound interest in keeping their workers healthy to sustain their productive and reproductive value. In Sims's case, the experimental use of enslaved women's bodies produced medical practices that could restore reproductive capacity not only to women whom enslavers wanted as "breeders" but also to affluent white women with similar ailments. I begin with the story of Dr. Sims because it clearly links medical science and institutions of human captivity and also

Dr. Theophilus Parvin.

neatly foreshadows the story of Dr. Parvin and his captive patients at the Indiana Reformatory Institution for Women and Girls.

Sims began his medical practice in Alabama and haphazardly fell into the treatment of women's diseases. He was called to attend to a woman who sustained a pelvic injury from a horseback riding accident and subsequently devised the speculum by using two spoons to facilitate an internal examination:[9] "I saw everything as no man had ever seen before. . . . I felt like an explorer in medicine who first views a new and important territory."[10]

Sims found his experimental medical subjects in enslaved Black women suffering from then-incurable vesicovaginal fistulas.[11] Over a four-year period (1845–49), Dr. Sims leased approximately fourteen enslaved women and performed surgical experiments on them, without anesthesia, in a makeshift hospital he built in his yard. One of his slaves, Lucy, nearly died in the process. Another,

Anarcha, would go under his knife thirty times before Sims found surgical success.[12] In 1855, Sims moved from rural Alabama to New York, where he continued his exploitative work by providing free surgical "treatment" to the indigent, poor, primarily Irish, immigrant women.[13]

Sims's success in using humans for medical experimentation secured him entrance into elite circles of power and wealth. The backers of Sims's New York hospital included a Civil War general, New York's lieutenant governor, and the founder of the *New York Times*, among other political and economic elites.[14] Sims's fame grew, and practitioners flocked to the field he anchored. Between 1876 and 1881, the number of American periodicals devoted to gynecology doubled, and the number of American gynecological societies increased from six to eleven.[15] The fraternity of gynecology was thus born.

In 1894, a statue of the late "father of gynecology" was erected in Philadelphia to commemorate Sims's life work and his contribution to medical science. Many influential gynecologists and obstetricians participated in bestowing this honor on Dr. Sims. Among the attendees were several faculty members from the Jefferson Medical College, Sims's alma mater, including Theophilus Parvin.[16]

The fall of slavery bled into the rise of criminal confinement. Emancipation created a great need for cheap labor. Convict leasing, a system historian David Oshinsky proclaimed as "worse than slavery," was one of the initial answers.[17] With convict leasing, the "criminal," unlike the enslaved person, was expendable—if a person died in servitude while incarcerated, they were easily replaced by simply leasing another imprisoned person from the state.[18] Because incarcerated people were blamed for their condition, in some ways they were better choices for medical research subjects than enslaved people.[19]

Deviance, as historians of medicine have pointed out, structures the concept of disease. Disease can function "as a conceptual form organizing phenomena in a fashion deemed useful for certain goals. The goals, though, involve choice by man and are not objective facts."[20] Medical treatments provided by a physician, a person assumed to be morally sound by virtue of their position, were assumed to provide a "corrective" therapeutic boon to people of questionable morality or of "immoral" or "filthy" habits. In this regard, Parvin's use of imprisoned people's bodies to advance medical science fed a vicious cycle of oppressive control. His captive patients already were deemed deviant and hence were disregarded and discredited by society, which in turn made them prime candidates for "reformation" and experimental "treatments" as forms of bodily control. In addition to all this, their institutional locations hid them from the outside world, keeping them far from any public sphere in which they might protest. As we'll see in subsequent sections of this chapter, Parvin's partnership with Sarah Smith and the Indiana Reformatory for Women and Girls would provide the ideal laboratory for human control via medical power over the body.

The continuum of slavery and incarceration is starkly backlit by Sims's and Parvin's choices of experimental subjects. Sims laid the foundation for gynecological research on powerless women. Parvin seems to have been among the first to build on this foundation with women in prison. In this sense, incarcerated women such as Mary Jane Schweitzer stand in direct line of descent from enslaved women such as Lucy and Anarcha. The medical conquest of these vulnerable women's bodies provided a means for gynecology and obstetrics to extend their authority, reaching for control of *all* women's bodies—and the communities of men and children organized around them—by elite white men.

The reverberations of this patriarchal affront to women's health echo across time, continuing to affect women and children today. Rooms full of white male politicians still feel perfectly justified in deciding questions of women's health.[21] The connections between gynecology and obstetrics and eugenics are also ongoing. Up until 2013, for example, California routinely subjected incarcerated women who gave birth in custody to tubal ligations, in violation of state and federal policies. Dr. James Heinrich, who performed the operation at least 148 times at the Valley State Prison for Women in California, defended the surgery on a brutal cost-benefit basis: "Over a ten-year period, that isn't a huge amount of money . . . compared to what you save in welfare paying for these unwanted children as they procreate more."[22] Vulnerable populations remain the target for sterilization tactics. Poor women and women of color— particularly Native American women in egregious disproportion— are sterilized with woefully inadequate processes of informed consent. As Andrea Smith compellingly argues, the "conquest" of targeted populations via sterilization is a form of genocide.[23]

It is crucial to place Sims and Parvin in their rightful positions of notoriety, to recognize them as key figures in the history of using captive women's bodies for experimental surgery. Sims's legacy fueled Parvin's work, which then paved the way for further medical experimentation on imprisoned women. The use of captive people for experimental surgery is the legacy (to this day) of the agricultural-labor institution of slavery that permanently branded (and continues to brand) a person as less than human. Understanding of the historical continuum of medical experimentation, which relies on the continual stigmatization of vulnerable bodies, even as the specific contexts of those bodies change, provides deeper insights into medical modes of social control that continue to affect the lives of women today. The use of incarcerated women, and others described as "unfortunates," "degenerates," "deviants," and "criminals," as experimental subjects rests on a warped sense of experimental treatment as a "therapeutic" benefit to the recipient and as a necessary step toward medical advancements for the benefit of all.

Controversies abound among both doctors and historians as to whether the benefits of experimental surgeries justify the harms done to those on whom they are developed. It is critical to consider the perspectives offered in historical accounts, or perhaps the lack thereof. More recent accounts of Sims's career and his contributions to the medical field include and even highlight his use of enslaved females and/or Irish immigrants, but that was not always the case. In 1952, chronicling "The Rise of Professional Surgery in the United States," Courtney Hall lauded Sims's "greatest achievement, the conquest of the vesico-vaginal fistula." She explained that "publications of these cases [fistulas] in 1852 made Sims famous," and she admired "his great idea for a special hospital and clinic for women, a plan pursued against great odds but with a final success in the organization of the New York State Women's Hospital in 1855," all of which made his reputation "world-wide."[24] While Hall noted Sims's path to greatness disrupted by "misfortune," she fails to mention that he strode to success on the aching backs of enslaved women and poor immigrant women.[25]

Historians are beginning to delve deeper into the workings of power and control within medical procedures and to consider the experiences and contributions of the subjects of these experimental procedures. Perhaps no better example is the work of the brilliant historian Deirdre Cooper Owens, whose scholarship is coupled with public advocacy and fueled by her own experience of abuse at the hands of racist gynecologists.[26] Cooper Owens's timely work coincided with the controversy over, and eventually the removal of, the commemorative statue in Central Park that honored Sims as the father of American gynecology.[27]

Contemporary historians' and activists' reassessment of Sims's medical legacy is beginning to challenge the dominant historical omission of the role of white male privilege in the creation and sanctification of elite banks of knowledge. More and more, observers are calling attention to the ethical implications of celebrating elites without considering how their contributions were achieved. Cooper Owens's research demonstrates that "slavery and Irish immigration were intrinsically linked with the growth of modern gynecology."[28] My research adds the bodies of incarcerated women to the tally of casualties intrinsic to the expansion of these fields after the Civil War. This work points to the ways that even today, ideologies that reinforce and expand racism and sexism make institutionalized people easy targets for medical experimentation based on their supposed "deviance" and need for (medical) "reformation." Just as Cooper Owens presents the enslaved women and Irish women immigrants used by Sims as "complicated, whole, and fully human" individuals,[29] we must also give voice and validity to the testimonies of incarcerated women and acknowledge the women as credible sources of knowledge whose subjugation was (is) imperative to medical advancement and social control and whose lived experience constitute a key link in the interconnected histories of power and social control. The next section takes further steps in this direction.

Parvin at the Reformatory

Even though Parvin was the head physician at the Indiana Reformatory for Women and Girls for the first decade of its existence, there is little in his writing that gives insight into his work there, and he himself left few clues about his patients or their lives. In the prison's annual physician's reports, Parvin made no mention of having operated or performed surgical procedures on women or girls at the reformatory.[30] His annual reports fail to record instances of venereal disease or other gynecological problems or treatments. He provided no details of pregnancies or births. These are peculiar omissions for a man striving, in print and lecture form, to represent himself as an expert on such diseases and medical practices.[31]

Parvin's prison reports instead reflect the best intentions of a classic "good doctor" trope. In these yearly memoranda, Parvin professed his belief that the imprisoned women needed fresh air,

Dr. Theophilus Parvin.

exercise, and milk. He advocated for a new drainage system. He mentioned his treatments for malaria and dysentery and the vaccinations for smallpox, tuberculosis, measles, mumps, and typhoid.[32] For details on his medical work, we must turn to sources other than these rose-colored reports, principally, the fourteen articles Parvin published during his years at the reformatory, several of which were clearly based on clinical research on women and girls confined there, as well as his celebrated 1886 textbook *The Science and Art of Obstetrics*.

Parvin's published articles make clear that he considered the people incarcerated at the reformatory fair game for experimentation. He wrote in the *American Practitioner*, for example, of his use of sulphate of cinchonidia to treat fever. He explained that he had tried a smaller dose, then created pills with tartaric acid and water, then raised the dose. He began by treating twenty-four women, and then a few weeks later, "many more." Parvin conducted medical trials at the prison and then proudly reported his results to colleagues.[33]

Parvin also imperiled his charges by forcing even young girls to care for the sickest among them and to dispose of hazardous medical waste. In 1879, the girls' reformatory had an outbreak of typhoid fever that sickened thirty-nine girls between the ages of seven and eighteen, two of whom died. These numbers were unremarkable. What was remarkable was who died and why. The first was "S.W.," just thirteen years old, who "acted as nurse for the first typhoid-fever patient, being with her almost constantly for nearly four weeks."[34] The second was identified only as fifteen years old and "colored," whose "duty it was to disinfect and bury the evacuations from this [first] patient." Parvin notes that "it would seem as though, being constantly with a person ill of typhoid fever on the one hand, and on the other having to dispose of the typhoid excreta, gave them the typhoid poison in larger quantity. Each of these girls—one white, the other colored—was, prior to being taken sick, an excellent representative of good physical development and of robust health."[35] I claim that Parvin was responsible for their deaths.

Another telling example of Parvin's attitudes toward his patients appeared in his article "An Illustration of Xenomenia," published in *Transactions of the American Gynecological Society* in 1877. Parvin chronicled the case of a sixteen-year-old girl at the reformatory whom he referred to as "A.P." The girl had stopped menstruating "for six months when it then reappeared," though decidedly "abnormal." The abnormality was that the lips (of her mouth) were engorged with menstrual blood. Parvin seems to have been thrilled to have this unusual case in his sights. As this young woman "hemorrhaged" from the mouth, Parvin studied her, reporting that the abnormal condition repeated itself for several months after his initial exam. Alas, "soon after the third recurrence of this abnormal menstruation," Parvin lost his golden opportunity: A.P. "made her escape from the Institution." Parvin lamented A.P.'s departure, calling it "an unfortunate escape both for her own good, and for the interests of professional study." [36]

Parvin neglected to disclose in institutional reports the surgeries he performed on women inside the prison, while documenting the surgeries as case studies for publication. These acts of omission are recurrent in doctors' descriptions of medical treatments given to incarcerated people. It is precisely in such *lack* of detail that the hidden abuses and mistreatments lie. Facts surrounding medicine practiced in institutions of social control are chronically overlooked by those who lack the firsthand experience of incarceration. Those with firsthand experience are aware the abuses they have suffered are purposely omitted from records, to protect the system and the powerful within it.

Parvin's publications and notes regarding institutional deaths provide further discrepancies. The prison's annual reports from the Parvin years include demographic numbers recording deaths. Most of the deaths go unexplained in his physician's reports. Where deaths are mentioned, Parvin largely fails to provide names or details. One illustrative exception is Parvin's note in the 1879 annual report that on "June 1, Margaret Conrads, a prisoner, committed suicide." He provided no further details, but Sarah Smith's report from that year included more information: "one poor woman hung herself after being with us but three days, an opium-eater for many years." [37] Left to contend with withdrawal alone, Margaret was found hanging. She was buried in the Green Lawn Cemetery. [38] He also subjected Fannie Morris, "a convict, forty-one years of age, but apparently fifty-five or sixty," to the same drastic strategy, for he believed that "the way to quit opium-eating is to quit, to quit at once and forever, not to gradually unloose the coils of this serpent-habit, but to slay it outright." [39]

Within the prison's annual reports, Parvin's one mention of a gynecological issue was the note that a woman named Kate Lindsey died from uterine cancer. No details are given regarding her condition or any treatments Parvin might have administered to her. Kate is one of the few deceased women he mentions by name, and she was African American. Race plays an important factor in considering patient privacy and confidentiality. In all of Parvin's publications, the *only* time names are provided in any context is when the person is African American and/or a prisoner. More information about Kate emerged in 1881 during an investigative inquiry on abuses inside the reformatory. When Sarah Smith was questioned about Kate, about forcing Kate to work while she was sick, Smith admitted that she had told the patient, "Now, Katie, let's run up and down the floor." She justified forcing Kate to exert herself with the odd claim that Kate "was in a condition that exercise was necessary." Why a woman dying of uterine cancer should be forced to do pointless, strenuous exercise was not explained. Shortly after this episode, Smith acknowledged, "she took to her bed [and] never left it again until she died." [40]

Parvin's medical experimentation at the Indiana Reformatory for Women and Girls was made possible by the larger ideological context in which he lived and worked, a culture organized around Victorian ideas of sexuality and female sexuality. [41] Perhaps nothing reveals this context and the abuse it made possible more than Parvin's (and his contemporaries') terror over female sexual pleasure. Parvin, Smith, and their fellow administrators feared the female orgasm even when it resulted from reproductive sex conducted within the institution of heterosexual marriage, but they feared it with a frantic terror when it came from female masturbation. Reformatory officials sought to control this frightful scourge through medical intervention and punishment.

The rhetoric of godly morality framed the work that reformers, including Smith and Parvin, understood themselves to be performing. During the 1881 investigation for abuses committed inside her prison, Sarah Smith claimed that her methods of punishment came not from herself but from God. "I believe the Lord called me to take charge of this institution," she proclaimed; "I suppose also that the Lord directs my methods of management."[42] Smith insisted that her methods were not meant to inflict suffering but to inspire change, for there could be "no faith in the permanency of a reformation which is not founded on a Christian basis—A THOROUGH change of heart."[43] This did not mean she would shrink from punishment. On the contrary, she expounded,

> So long as crime exists, punishment must be provided; and punishment must be of such a nature that it will lift the criminal above the commission of crime; no easy task to perform, when we understand the evil passions with which many of them are sorely afflicted—revenge, jealousy, hatred, falsehood and theft—sore evils that no power can eradicate but the power of God in the heart.[44]

Such a change of heart, inspired at the reformatory, would "fit them for the responsible positions of wife and mother," Smith contended.[45] Nowhere else does Smith better reveal her hopes of moving women from one institution of sexual subservience into another, her intentions of removing women's autonomous ambitions and keeping them under elite and patriarchal control. An interesting concept for a Quaker woman who herself enjoyed the fruits of an egalitarian marriage.

Moral deviance and righteousness were easily translated into expressions of sickness and health. Nineteenth-century elites easily conflated medical and moral deviance. Illness and vice could be one and the same. Historian of medicine H. Tristram Engelhardt Jr. commented on the relationship between ideas about morality and notions about sickness and health: "Although vice and virtue are not equivalent to disease and health, they bear a direct relation to these concepts. Insofar as a vice is taken to be a deviation from an ideal of human perfection, or 'well-being,' it can be translated into disease language."[46] Parvin clearly subscribed to this notion, using the unequivocal term "evil" to explain the great need to regulate masturbation and other sexual practices he deemed excessive. "Countless evils come upon individuals and upon society for their unregulated sexual passion," he explained in 1894.[47]

The nineteenth-century desire to control female sexuality guided Smith and Parvin. A striking illustration of this is seen in Parvin's 1886 article "Nymphomania and Masturbation," which, he lamented, was a "combination well calculated to wreck a woman's life."[48] In the article, Parvin discusses a forty-two-year-old widow who, he claimed, complained of "excessive desire for sexual intercourse"; there is no proof the woman herself made this claim, and Parvin is the only one to claim that she had. Parvin raped his female patients by digitally "examining" them. When he induced orgasm, he then declared their bodily response was "proof" of a woman's sexual deviance and disease:

When I subjected this woman to examination . . . I found some peculiar phenomenon. When the finger was introduced into the vagina, as soon as the clitoris was barely touched, there were produced irregular movements of the hips and pelvis. As the finger was advanced the muscles about the vagina were thrown into a state of contraction, which it closed tight on the finger, and this caused a sense of gratification to the woman.[49]

Women who masturbated challenged elite mores directly—and were punished accordingly. Sarah Smith was dismayed to learn of masturbation among her wards. "In 1875 I discovered that a general practice of self-abuse was going on among the girls," she explained in the context of the 1881 investigation.[50] Parvin also noted the epidemic within the institution, in which one incarcerated woman was taught another "by example, or at least had it suggested and explained by a worse, if not older companion."[51] The consequence for such behavior was dire: a nineteenth-century form of water-boarding. Smith explained, "We have adopted the bathing which has been called ducking,"[52] which consisted of repeatedly forcing a person's head under cold water, holding it under water for several seconds, then pulling it back up just long enough for the victim to gasp for air before being forced back under the water.

Smith lamented that for those "inmates of the Reformatory who have committed no crime, but . . . are addicted to filthy habits"[53] (in other words, nonconvicted orphaned girls who had been abandoned to or rounded up by the institution and were brazen enough to masturbate while confined to the reformatory), there seemed to be no remedy other than the brutal application of cold water:

> The punishment was effectual. I never allowed them to remain in the tubs more than three or four minutes. . . . The inmates would often use the most abusive language that could be thought of; some of them were the most filthy and degraded girls that could possibly be found in the State. . . . I simply wanted to have them know that they must be governed and conform to the rules of the Institution.[54]

During the 1881 investigation, one of the prison's employees, Francis A. Talbott, testified about one such case. According to a Cincinnati paper, "The severest case of punishing [Talbott] has ever seen was the ducking of Lizzie Smith, age thirteen. . . . This was for self-abuse and teaching the vice to smaller girls."[55] Smith stripped a thirteen-year-old girl naked and held her in a tub while another prisoner turned on the cold water tap. The young girl was ducked for twenty minutes, spanked, and sent to bed—nearly drowned for the crime of masturbation.

Parvin clearly approved of similar methods. In an 1875 paper,

Lawn photo of the Indiana Women's Prison, 1914.

Parvin detailed how he prescribed cold shower baths for urinary in-continence.[56] The "shower bath" was a device resembling a shower stall with a chair inside in which its occupant was strapped in place by means of wrist and lap restraints. A large spout positioned above forcefully releases mass quantities of water over the occupant's head to create a sense of drowning. Like ducking, the process is repeated multiple times, often to the point of unconsciousness. Nevertheless, Parvin's sworn testimony to the 1881 investigatory committee affirmed that in his six years of employment at the institution, "no punishment that was cruel had ever come under his notice," asserting further that "he did not believe that treatment in the reformatory was hurtful to the health of inmates."[57] Parvin's ideology gave him this tremendous certainty in his self-righteousness; historical retrospect can see a bit more clearly.

In addition to the evidence of abuse inflicted on women and girls via medical experimentation or "treatment," there is compelling testimony of more conventional forms of sexual abuse at the reformatory. The notorious Nancy Clem, the purported mastermind of fraud and murder in the 1868 Cold Springs tragedy, reported on sexual misconduct between the night watchman and several women inside the prison. Clem also reported on abortions being performed on the women and girls and claimed dead babies had been found inside the prison.[58] During the 1881 investigation, Sarah Smith dismissed these and all other claims of illegitimate pregnancies and abortions. There was "not a word of truth in Mrs. Clem's story," she insisted. Nor was there "a thread of foundation for any stories of abortion in the institution." As for pregnancies, Smith contended there were none for which the institution was responsible: "Seven children have been born in the Reformatory, and three in prison. In all cases the women were pregnant when they came to the institution."[59]

The institution's annual reports do not name the ten children Smith acknowledged here, nor do they document which women were pregnant and whether they arrived at the reformatory in that condition. This distinction was only recorded in a few cases of recidivism, with women returning to the reformatory pregnant after a violation on a ticket-of-leave (essentially a parole violation). To be raped while in forced domestic servitude (a condition of confinement) is to experience compounded (sexual) punishment. The annual reports do provide numeric data recording births and deaths within the institution but do not give names. No name is ever listed in the births and deaths of infants, children, or mothers.

Against Smith's insistence that there were zero miscarriages and abortions at the prison, Parvin mentioned in a scientific publication that a woman called "P" "was delivered of a fully developed fetus that had been dead some days."[60] While it is not clear whether Parvin performed the procedure on any of the imprisoned women in his care, he details how to empty the uterus of its contents in cases of miscarriage in an 1880 article in the *Obstetric Gazette*.[61] He described the technique in gruesome detail:

Let the patient lie on her back, upon a hard bed, her hips brought to its edge, lower limbs strongly flexed; then introduce Neugebauer's speculum, and bring the os [vaginal canal] fairly in view; now catch the anterior lip with a simple tenaculum, or better, with Nott's tenaculum forceps, and then, if there be any flexion—and it is not uncommon in cases of spontaneous abortion to observe this—use gentle traction to straighten the bent canal; at any rate fix the uterus by the instrument. Now take a pair of curved polypus forceps of suitable size, or, better still, Emmet's curette forceps, and gently introduce the closed blades into the uterine cavity, open them slightly, then close them and withdraw, when the fragments of membranes can be removed, and the instrument re-introduced. Repeat this three or four times, if necessary, until all membranes or placental fragments are extracted.[62]

This description amply confirms Parvin's wide experience performing the procedure. Particularly telling is his recommendation of specific tools to achieve an "even better" result, implying a process of experimentation with multiple tools.

In 1881, Smith's own testimony admitted a dead baby on the grounds, with a strained attempt to deny the most likely scenario:

A baby was found in the cesspool, and Dr. Parvin said it was not possible for any woman to have been delivered of that baby. He told the coroner that no woman in the institution could have been its mother. It was a very fine nine-pound baby, and it did not belong to any one in the institution.[63]

If women were suffering male sexual abuse at the reformatory, there were only two likely candidates, because only two men worked at the prison at the time of the allegations: the night watchman and Parvin. In 1883, after the reformatory was threatened once again with investigation for prisoner abuses, both Smith and Parvin resigned from the institution. Three years later, Parvin created a lifelike OB-GYN manikin. Was this innovation to compensate for the loss of the large pool of experimental subjects the prison had provided?

A colleague of Parvin's praised the quality of the model, describing "a life-sized figure, possessing a form proportioned with the nearest approach to nature possible."

> The joints are mobile, so as to permit of all the various movements and to allow of the figure being placed in any desired posture. . . . The pelvis is an exact reproduction in brass of the most perfect bony pelvis obtainable, and is completely and smoothly covered with soft leather. . . .
>
> Further, a soft leather pelvic floor is added, which readily allows the exit of the foetus, or the use of instruments, palpation, or manual extraction, as desired. . . .
>
> The entire external surface of the manikin, with the exception of the head, is covered with soft leather; and the figure itself is light enough to be freely movable upon the operating table, or carried from place to place.[64]

This colleague, Dr. J. Clifton Edgar (also a member of the American Gynecological Society and the AMA), embraced the figure, which he explained "more fully fulfills the requirements for obstetric teaching and demonstration than any other now in use."[65]

The breadth of the procedures this teaching tool made possible was impressive. Edgar went on to claim that with the manikin and "accessories together with an abundant supply of foetal cadavers of various sizes—there is scarcely an obstetric operation or procedure that may not be performed or demonstrated."[66] The operations and demonstrations that could be accomplished with the manikin, he enumerated, were not limited to but included accidental hemorrhages; embryotomy; induction of abortion, forcible delivery, and perforation; craniotomy; decapitation; evisceration; and amputation of the extremities.[67] There is no mention of where an aspiring doctor might obtain an "abundant supply of foetal cadavers in various sizes" or of the number of times these procedures were performed on women to create the perfect obstetrics model on which to practice the procedures.

A life-size, moveable, bendable female doll covered inside and out with "soft leather" was possibly intended for other uses as well. In one illustration, Parvin's manikin is posed in the knee-chest posture with buttocks in the air and wearing a pair of thigh-high striped stockings.[68] The misogynistic sexualization of the practice of medicine is an ethical breach with deep links to the history of women's incarceration.

Evidence of sexual abuse at the reformatory is ironic given that the reformatory opened *because* of the outrage over sexual violence,

Dr. Parvin's manikin.

rape, and the birth of children at the Jeffersonville State Prison. A former prisoner, Harrie J. Banka, had written of imprisoned women impregnated by prison officials and bearing their babies at "Old Jeff." [69] Clearly, the practice did not end with the reformatory's "reform," just as it has not ended in our day.

Only after examining Dr. Parvin's work and words in careful historical context do the implications of Mary Jane Schweitzer's 1881 testimony, which opened this chapter, become clear. Mary Jane experienced severe medical and institutional abuse at the hands of Sarah Smith and Dr. Parvin. Solitary confinement, a starvation diet of bread and water, hosing, waterboarding, an examination with instruments, and a mysterious, nonconsensual surgery were the reality for a woman sent to prison for two years on "suspicion of committing arson." Unfortunately, the 1881 investigation closed without indicting Dr. Parvin (or Sarah Smith) for their nefarious deeds against their captive women and girls. But this is not surprising considering the entire investigative board was made up of their peers.

Parvin's eventual resignation (which failed to come under public scrutiny) from the reformatory left no stain on his name, allowing him to move to Philadelphia to occupy the chair of obstetrics at the Jefferson Medical College, to build an obstetrical clinic in conversation with international colleagues, and to work overseas, garnering him national and international acclaim during his life and posthumously. Meanwhile, his captive "patients," Mary Jane, Jennie, Molly, "P," Lizzie, Fannie, Stella, Mary M., Margaret, Anna, Mary Ann, Nancy, and countless, unfortunately nameless others, went uncelebrated, barely even seen as human while alive and all but forgotten in the end.

Conclusion: Ethics, Consent, and Knowledge

The women who suffered under Parvin's "treatments" and knife were treated unethically and were subject to gross violations of their civil and human rights. Historians of medicine (while often lauding medical advances made by these physicians) have chronicled the widespread abuses and have rejected the noxious notion that people in the past should be held to lower standards.[70] Still, many people often fail to critique medical abuses—then and now—thanks to a warped cost-benefit analysis, what L. Song Richardson refers to as a "social benefit bias": the notion that some people's suffering is justified if it produces a "therapeutic" benefit to *all* of society.[71] The math in this cruel equation, however, only works if the suffering is on the part of devalued people such as the enslaved, "unfortunates," "deviants," "degenerates," and "criminals."

The Indiana Reformatory Institution for Women and Girls housed only 17 women when it opened in 1873. Today, over 115,000 women are incarcerated nationwide. Of the number of women incarcerated in the world, 1 out of every 3 is incarcerated in the United States. Numbers fail to illustrate the sobering reality of incarcerated women's lived experience. That is why we turn to history, for the full and human narration of the shape of life. We must not assume, however, that history is past. As William Faulkner said, "The past is never dead. It's not even past." Every nineteenth-century woman's story highlighted in this book has a modern version. My fellow incarcerated and formerly incarcerated sisters and I are living embodiments of nearly two centuries' worth of captive American women denied the rights to our own bodies and progenies. Our losses reflect corporeal captivity for women far and wide. Abuses in the realm of medical care continue to be particularly egregious.

Critical historical analysis giving credibility to the voiceless creates space to bring awareness to their lived experience and to implement change. In *Possessing the Secret of Joy*, Alice Walker imploringly declares, "Human compassion is equal to human cruelty and it is up to each of us to tip the balance."[72] Historians, scholars, activists, critics, and reformers, and, perhaps even more so, the common public, need to heed the echoes of these abusive practices performed on people in prison, for these practices continue to shape both medicine and incarceration and the way we live our lives. The day is yet to come when the "advancement" of some is achieved independently of the debasement and dehumanization of others.

7

Johanna Kitchen—
The Grand Lady of Stringtown

Anastazia Schmid

Stringtown was a site of vice and a central target for reform in late nineteenth-century Indiana. Now called Haughville, it was a suburb of Indianapolis, situated west of the White River, along the National Road.[1] Stringtown was occupied mainly by coal miners and industrial workers and was generously populated with saloons, taverns, and houses of ill fame. Local newspapers constantly reported on the town's most notorious characters, scandals, and sensational occurrences: "Those Dead Babies,"[2] "Pitiful (Drunken Teen),"[3] and "How Subjects Are Procured for the Dissecting Table:

Parade in Haughville, formerly Stringtown, circa 1920.

Negroes Murdered. Horrible Revelations."[4] On occasion, they also showcased the "do-gooding" efforts of the town's religious elite. Composed of the Temperance Union, the Indianola Mission, and the Third Presbyterian Church, the "Christian fellowship with a vengeance" existed amidst the seedy tumult of Stringtown and were united in their various political agendas to wage war against vice and to annex the area into greater Indianapolis.[5]

Most notable among Stringtown's houses of ill fame was the notorious Duchess of Stringtown's brothel. The Duchess of Stringtown was a woman of mystery, allure, and prominence. She was the illustrious madam of Indianapolis's most notorious house of ill fame. Though she played a central role in Indianapolis history, few written documents exist about her, most of which amount to news sources that sensationalize her through scandal and ill repute. Women like the Duchess often are discredited through notoriety or historically erased by those in power. The Duchess's life is a soap opera, an open-ended mystery, and a story in need of critical (historical) inquiry. An analysis of scandalous press items of the time, with careful handling of their validity and credibility, reveals much about women's labor and the political reconstruction of greater Indianapolis. The Duchess is a missing link in the evolutionary story of power and control in the rise of American carceral institutionalization of women. She also provides a lens for critical analysis of media representation and how it shapes social and political ideologies.

The epitaph on the Duchess of Stringtown's grave immortalizes her as "Joanna Kitchen," yet she was a woman of many names: Ann, Anna, Johanna, Joanna, JoAnna, and a cadre of surnames. Perhaps an anomaly for a woman of her time, the Duchess, as she was commonly referred to, was married six times during her short, forty-year life, to men of prominence and infamy.[6] A woman of wealth, she owned her own hotel and brothel, where "more than fifteen hundred women and girls" worked over the course of her

Grave of Joanna Kitchen *"The Duchess of Stringtown," d. 1872). Crown Hill Cemetery, Indianapolis.

life.[7] She had power, wealth, and fame, albeit a celebrity based mostly on outrage and sensation, in a time when, in retrospect, most women were blurred into nameless, faceless supporting entities in a landscape of industrious white men and a few "virtuous" white women. For this reason, we need to read beyond the sensationalism of her life as represented in the contemporary media.

For the journalists of her day, the suburban Stringtown provided the perfect backdrop for her seemingly wanton, delinquent lifestyle. Bootleggers, drunks, thieves, murderers, adulterers, whores, swindlers, dirty cops, and gangs ran the neighborhood.[8] At the same time, church groups infiltrated the debased borough through proselytizing, picketing, and religious and political conversion.[9] Throughout the early 1870s, news articles highlighted the efforts of the Stringtown Protestant clergy to transform the area into a respectable place. The Indianola Mission would cordially invite all to attend its holiday festival in December 1870.[10] Stringtown was a space for conquest within the greater Indianapolis region in view of political annexing and industrial expansion. The ongoing push and pull of crime and corruption, along with the "rage for real estate," provided the catalyst for Stringtown's reformation.[11] In 1872, the *Cincinnati Enquirer* speculated that Indianapolis's population would double within the "next five years." As signs pointed to the inevitable annexing of the suburbs, purportedly all of them, "save that of Stringtown," showed "substantial improvement."[12] The Duchess was a key figure in this political intrigue.

The story of the Duchess was most often told through her many marriages and divorces. Of her six husbands, four appear, in some fashion, in newsprint alongside her.[13] Shortly after her final marriage, to John Kitchen, a news editor claimed to have witnessed the Duchess assist "a couple of huge Bucktown darkies" to hurl a *Sentinel* newspaper Ku Klux Klansman into a coal cart and then quickly drive away, heading toward "Pogue's Run."[14] It's debatable whether this would have been considered an act of altruism or defiance on the part of the Duchess, though given the Klan's racist infiltration throughout Indiana's political and media institutions (and given the *Sentinel's* white supremacist Democratic Party affiliation), such reports were likely intended to provoke further disdain for the woman.

Between scandalous talk about her many husbands and her associations with Black enemies of the Klan, we find a charitable side of Johanna Kitchen. In March 1871, the Ladies of the Third Presbyterian Church canvassed the Duchess's establishment. They proudly announced that the Duchess "intended to reform her manner of life as much as was possible and close up her establishment."[15] The Duchess's supposed declaration came with a sizable donation to the Indianola Mission and Sabbath School, which opened a "public school building in Stringtown for $2000" by April 1872.[16] That June, the *Indianapolis News* printed a lengthy report on the "Sunday School Work" of the Indianola Mission, mentioning its purportedly "large numbers of teachers and pupils" and including Reverend David Stevenson's commentary acknowledging the work of the school's matrons and the success of the school.[17] By June 1874, the man who started the Indianola Mission was reported to have substantially decreased the number of saloons and houses of ill fame in Stringtown and to have built up a "flourishing church," making "a decent settlement of the burg."[18] By midyear, attempts were made to change the name of Stringtown (so named on account of houses strung along the Vanderburgh County road) to Pleasantville, as the face of the burg was shifting toward annexation into Indianapolis and a new dawn of reformation.[19]

The "very sudden" death of the Duchess of Stringtown may have spurred on this transformation. In February 1872, the Duchess's name appeared nearly daily across news publications announcing her demise, scarcely over the age of forty, speculating about the particulars of her impressive estate.[20] An inquest was held at the request of her brothers, who believed "her death hastened by poison." Questions arose as to whether the poisoning was by her own hand or by the hand of "some of her vile companions." Perhaps the long-standing battle to clean up Stringtown was the catalyst for removing one of the town's most powerful and influential inhabitants. Nonetheless, Coroner Hedges pronounced her death to be the result of "natural causes."[21]

The papers reported that Johanna Kitchen had amassed considerable wealth, having a "considerable sum of money on deposit in one of our banks." Another news article reported the sum to be $5,000, deposited in the Fletcher's bank. Perhaps because of such reporting, she was known as "the most noted Cyprian of Stringtown" and a "remarkable woman."[22]

Her funeral was held at the Crown Hill Cemetery, "ordered

upon the expensive scale, and the finest burial caskets in the city [to] encase the remains."[23] At least two of her six husbands made an appearance, though the papers fail to say which ones. Reverend David Stevenson, of the Indianola Presbyterian Church, officiated the service, which was open to the public.

A scene unfolded at the Duchess's funeral that was reported to have been "one of the most remarkable and impressive ever witnessed in this vicinity." Mrs. Sarah Smith, then the matron of the Home for Friendless Women, attended the funeral. The *Indianapolis News* reported that Smith "rose and addressed the audience" from the same text the reverend had preached from. Mrs. Smith claimed that despite the Duchess's many good qualities, her "great sin" amounted her goodness to "nothing."[24] She went on to admonish select members of the audience, warning them to take advantage of the time they had left to change their ways. Her graphic depictions of the wages of sin were delivered with "the highest pitch of feeling and leaving scarcely a dry eye in the house," which wrought the audience to a "fever point."[25] One can only assume Smith feared the dire consequences of the Duchess's influence over "hundreds of human souls."[26] These were, we can assume, the souls of the claimed "fifteen hundred women and girls" who had worked for the Duchess and whom Mrs. Smith desperately sought to save, most likely in one of her institutions that targeted just such women and girls.[27]

Stringtown would be "taken into the city limits, and the name changed to 'Pleasant Valley.' "[28] Upon her death, "one half the odium was removed from the locality, and with the completion of the new bridge, a new era will be commenced in its history." A new era indeed, in which Indianapolis expanded its network of institutions of state-sanctioned social control, including, among others, the House of the Good Shepherd and the Indiana Reformatory Institution for Women and Girls.

8

The Duchess of Stringtown Play

Michelle Daniel Jones and Anastazia Schmid

In researching Sarah Smith, one of the founders of the Indiana Reformatory Institution for Women and Girls, we discovered an article in which Mrs. Smith took over a funeral service and preached her own sermon. The deceased woman was brothel owner and businesswoman Johanna Kitchen, called the Duchess of Stringtown. Sarah Smith condemned Johanna to hell, along with the 1,500 women Sarah estimated the Duchess had led into vice.[1]

The Duchess died, of suspected poisoning, the first week of February 1872 at the age of forty.[2] Five days later, Stringtown was annexed into Indianapolis. The discovery that the Duchess's death coincided with the annexation of Stringtown was suspicious to us.[3] As Anastazia Schmid explores in the previous chapter, a range of parties stood to benefit from the Duchess's death, including city officials desiring to absorb Stringtown into greater Indianapolis, men of industry who wanted to expand commerce in the area, and Sarah Smith herself, who had made it her mission to save "fallen" women. Our play takes place in January and February of 1872 and posits that the Duchess was murdered via arsenic-laced cosmetics to facilitate the annexation and sanitation of the vice district.

Scene 2—Predicament in Benevolence

SARAH SMITH at Indianapolis, at the Home for Friendless Women (HFFW). Sarah Smith is at a writing desk going over papers. MABLE enters, frantic and scared.

MABLE

(knocking loudly)
Uh, excuse me, where is my baby?!

SARAH SMITH

Oh, Mable. Please come in. Have a seat.

MABLE

No, not until you tell me where my baby is! Where is my baby?

SARAH SMITH

Your baby is fine. She is in the nursery. My name is Sarah Smith and I run this home. Dr. Parvin gave you something to help you sleep. We thought it best that you get some rest. You were exhausted and in tears when you got here last night and in no state to care for yourself, let alone your baby. Both you and your child are perfectly safe and cared for. Please, have a seat.

MABLE

Can I see her?

SARAH SMITH

Sure, of course, don't worry at all. But first, can you tell me how you happened to come by us? *(pause, leaning in)* You mentioned you came from the Perdue farm. You were working for a very prestigious family.

MABLE

Yes . . . I . . . I worked for Mister Perdue and the family for the last six months. My aunt got me a job working in the fields. I worked really hard and everything was good for a while.

SARAH SMITH

So what happened, why did you leave?

MABLE

(*stammers*) Uh, um . . . do I really need to say? When I helped bring in the harvest last year, Mister Perdue saw me, and he asked me to help him in the barn. (*beat*) I did and he . . . he . . . uh . . . he took me. (*breaks down sobbing*) Then he started sending for me to help him in the barn over and over again. It wasn't long before I was with child.

SARAH SMITH

Good heavens, child! How old are you?

MABLE

I just turned fourteen. When Mister Perdue noticed my belly and that I couldn't work in the fields as long, he hid me in the barn and locked me in. I was so scared, so scared.

SARAH SMITH

Oh, dear girl. He held you prisoner? Good heavens! How long did you stay in there?

MABLE

I bore my babe in that barn. My aunt helped me, but something went wrong. Mister Perdue sent for Doc Peters, and when he arrived, he went to the big house and asked who was having distress in childbirth. Mrs. Perdue came with Doc Peters to the barn, and when she saw me and Mister Perdue in there, together, she was mad as all hell fire. She started rantin' and ravin' and talkin' about killin' us all. She knew.

SARAH SMITH
What did Mister Perdue do?

MABLE
He told her the baby's father was the stable master. But she looked at me, and she knew he was lying. As soon as I could stand, I took my baby and ran.

SARAH SMITH
My child, you've walked a great many miles, and with a newborn babe! You brave, brave child. The Lord surely has guided you here. It is by the grace of the God you and your babe have survived.

MABLE
You don't know how grateful I am to be away from there. Can I see my baby now?

SARAH SMITH
Yes, and we will find you decent work. I know of a few good families through the church needing help. We will also help with proper care for the child.
(*Knock on the door. SARAH SMITH stands quickly.*)
Oh, that must be Dr. Parvin. Head on up to the nursery, it is right up the stairs, on the left.

MABLE
Thank you, Mrs. Smith.
(*SARAH SMITH opens the door and ushers MABLE past DR. THEOPHILUS PARVIN as he enters.*)

DR. THEOPHILUS PARVIN

Are you feeling better, my dear?

MABLE

Yes, sir. Thank you so much. Excuse me.
   (*MABLE exits.*)

SARAH SMITH

I'd nearly forgotten you were here. Have a seat.

DR. THEOPHILUS PARVIN

What are you going to do with that girl's baby?

SARAH SMITH

No worries. I've got it covered. Do tell me how Belle is faring.

DR. THEOPHILUS PARVIN

I fear I bring sad tidings. She was showing signs of premature labor that was advancing far too quickly, which poses a grave risk to the mother. I was left without choice but to perform an embryotomy and extract the fetus to save her life.
   (*SARAH quietly mutters a prayer.*)

SARAH SMITH

I receive your news with a heavy heart but am gracious for your steadfast service. I do not profess to understand your science, but I do believe the good Lord works miracles through your hands, doctor.

DR. THEOPHILUS PARVIN

Thank God and science that my hands were of assistance in saving the mother's life.

SARAH SMITH

I am grateful too. There are so many of these unwed women with children with no place to go. I shudder to think of the absence of their medical care. What is to become of a society overrun with these sad cases?

DR. THEOPHILUS PARVIN

The miracles of modern surgical medicine are indeed providing us answers, Mrs. Smith. Rest assured, my work will prevent further unwanted pregnancies. These women won't have to endure such misfortunes again.

SARAH SMITH

We are indebted to you, doctor—and working at no expense.

DR. THEOPHILUS PARVIN

I wouldn't be a proper Christian physician without charitable service. This has been worthwhile, which is why I shall be the head physician at the reformatory. Wouldn't you agree that as president of the American Medical Association I am the most qualified and the best choice?

SARAH SMITH

Certainly, doctor. Being a man of God, you've proven your worth here at the home, and your principles are in line with our mission.

DR. THEOPHILUS PARVIN

Indeed. I am at your service. I've made arrangements for the baby's remains with the medical college. Now, if you'll excuse me, I need to return to my office for another appointment.

SARAH SMITH

Have a blessed day, doctor.

(*fade out*)

Scene 3—The New Arrival

The following week at the DUCHESS's brothel hotel. An expansive, opulent brothel in the heart of Stringtown. Women are draped on the laps of men at gambling tables, drinks are flowing, smoke is wafting, and there is uproarious laughter. We see women ascending the stairs with clients.
BELLE enters, disheveled and weary in the midst of all the activity, walking in front of it. SALLIE leads her into another room of the hotel.

SALLIE

Come this way. We heard you were comin'. The Duchess has a room for you. Everything's gonna be alright.

BELLE

Thank, thank you. I—I didn't know where else to go . . . I didn't know what else to do . . . (*beat*) I—I don't have anyone. I don't have any money and they—

SALLIE

Did they really take your dead baby?

BELLE

(*hesitates*) Yes, they did.

SALLIE

No burial, no prayers, no nothin'?

BELLE

No. Nothing. My baby was just gone. (*pauses, SALLIE urges her to go on.*) I went to Mrs. Smith trying to find my baby, she told me Dr. Parvin took it. I said to her, "What do you mean he took it? Took it where?" She said Dr. Parvin didn't know why it died and so he took my baby to the medical college.

SALLIE

The medical college? I can't believe it. It's one thing for a prison to do that but the Home for Friendless Women?

BELLE

Yea, she agreed with him. She thought it was a perfectly acceptable thing to do. She did not fight for me or my right to bury my own baby. Can you imagine!?

SALLIE

Naw, and you a fully white woman too. Lawd have mercy! Christ help us.

BELLE

(*crying*) Sure, I'm white, but not white enough in Mrs. Smith's eyes. In her eye—having a baby out of wedlock, I am as soiled as anyone else.

SALLIE

Hush now. Don't you worry 'bout a thing. You just rest in here. The Duchess'll be right up.

    (*SALLIE exits.*)

    (*BELLE is nervous. She warms her hands.*)

    (*DUCHESS enters.*)

    (*BELLE is awestruck by the DUCHESS. BELLE relaxes.*)

DUCHESS OF STRINGTOWN

It's alright my dear, you may sit down. Your name is Belle, is that right?

BELLE

Yes, ma'am, that's right.

DUCHESS OF STRINGTOWN

My servant, Mary, will be up shortly with a tray. You must be starving.

BELLE

It is kind of you to offer, but I have no money.

DUCHESS OF STRINGTOWN

I know why you're here. I am not concerned with money. I will send in some clothes after you've eaten, and Mary will draw a bath for you. We have what you need. No one will harm you here. You can stay as long as you like.

BELLE

(*tearful*) It has been so hard. I can't believe my life has come to this.

DUCHESS OF STRINGTOWN

I am well acquainted with pain. You can talk to me.

BELLE

I come from a good home. You know, my family is highly respected in the community, but my fiancé left me—you have no idea.

DUCHESS OF STRINGTOWN
Try me. I understand better than you think. A well-to-do woman such as yourself taken advantage of? You'd be surprised how often that occurs. It's almost cliché.

BELLE
(*takes a deep breath, the DUCHESS listens with genuine concern*)
It all started when I was introduced to the son of my father's friend. He was my parents' choice for my husband but not mine. He spent every minute talking about himself and I was bored to tears. I couldn't take it.

DUCHESS OF STRINGTOWN
Understandably. Then what happened?

BELLE
I ran into the most handsome man I'd ever seen. It turned out he was the younger cousin of my betrothed. I know I should not have entertained his advances, but he courted me relentlessly. When he asked for my hand, how could I refuse?

DUCHESS OF STRINGTOWN
As has been the case for many of us, my dear.

BELLE
I'm so ashamed that I fell for his lies! He didn't marry me, and he left me with child! I had nowhere to go but to the Home for Friend-less Women. Despite my delicate state, those wretched women nearly worked me to death. And when I collapsed from exhaustion, they handed me over to that—that butcher! He, he took my baby! (*breaks down sobbing*)

DUCHESS OF STRINGTOWN

There, there. I most certainly understand. (*handing a handkerchief to BELLE*) You know, I have a less than savory story of my own. (*beat*) My fourth husband threatened to kill my daughter if I didn't lie about a murder for him. He nearly left us in ruins because of his greed and hunger for power. I worried about my daughter every day, because he was connected to many powerful men. Oh yes, I understand far too well.

BELLE

(*recovering*) Really? I would never have thought you'd gone through any of that. You seem like you are doing so well now, for . . . for a . . . for a—

DUCHESS OF STRINGTOWN

A brothel owner? Oh, yes, I am doing quite well.

BELLE

I didn't mean to offend. I just, I just never expected a life like this would be, well, so . . . extravagant.

DUCHESS OF STRINGTOWN

It's okay, dear. We women find the best way to play the hand we have been dealt. There are ways for women to attain money and power. Even after brutish betrayals and tragedies. We have a valuable asset in our very flesh, and those who claim it, can never be trampled on again.

BELLE

I really loved him.

DUCHESS OF STRINGTOWN

Love is a gamble. My current husband, Mr. Kitchen, leaves much to be desired as well. But as we know, love is often blind, and we roll the dice and try again.

(*transition*)

Ah, but I digress. We have everything you need right here. You have complete freedom to rebuild your life as you see fit. I'll send Mary up with the tray and to see how you're faring.

BELLE

Oh, thank you for your kindness and generosity.

(*DUCHESS exits and scene fades out.*)

Scene 8—Men of Science and Medicine

It's the next day. DR. PARVIN's office. A meeting with DR. THEOPH-ILUS PARVIN, DR. CALVIN FLETCHER, DR. STAUGHTON MOR-RIS, and DR. AMOS SIMS. Put emphasis on them referring to one another as "doctor."

DR. THEOPHILUS PARVIN

Gentlemen, I've called us together to discuss women that are categorically criminal. Fallen women need to be controlled by any means necessary. It is imperative that I continue to study female anatomy. Which is why I told Sarah Smith that only I should run the infirmary at the new reformatory.

DR. AMOS SIMS

Right you are, doctor. The problem is inherent in these women and must be mastered by the physician's craft.

DR. CALVIN FLETCHER
Before their craft masters us.

DR. STAUGHTON MORRIS
I've heard, Dr. Parvin, that you are on the cutting edge in female deviance and degeneracy.

DR. THEOPHILUS PARVIN
A quick study you are, Dr. Morris. Female deviancy goes against the nature of both God and man. Doctors, as my work in the *Ohio Medical Journal* states, it is not natural for a woman to have desire for sexual intercourse—it is submitted to as a duty, and those that willingly do it for money and enjoyment are not women, they are rutting animals.

DR. CALVIN FLETCHER
Certainly, doctor, but is such a state biological or social? I have encountered women who are as sexually ravenous as wild beasts! Does your research apply only to whores?

DR. AMOS SIMS
It is a good question. All women may be suspect. Every medical journal there is professes that the origin of female hysteria resides in the uterus.

DR. STAUGHTON MORRIS
AND the clitoris if I'm not mistaken.

DR. AMOS SIMS
Absolutely, doctor. That organ is inferior in design to that of the penis. It is useless beyond being an attributing factor behind female deviancy.

DR. STAUGHTON MORRIS

Dr. Parvin, you've written articles on nymphomania and masturbation . . . tell us, doctor, of your methods of detection. I'm most interested to learn your methodology.

DR. THEOPHILUS PARVIN

It's true, Dr. Morris, I have examined a great many women in my years, but in those so afflicted I found some peculiar phenomenon that I believe are the telltale signs of such deviance.

DR. CALVIN FLETCHER

Do tell.

DR. THEOPHILUS PARVIN

I had a widow in my care at the home. She said she was unable to stop abusing herself. The mere mention of her ailments caused her to begin disrobing in front of me.

DR. STAUGHTON MORRIS

You mean she stripped right there, right in front of your eyes, no curtain?

DR. THEOPHILUS PARVIN

Yes. I tell you, doctors, she was all but hysterical and insisted that I examine her right then and there.

DR. CALVIN FLETCHER

Sounds like a few women I know.

(*some of the men laugh and nod their heads, others look horrified*)

DR. THEOPHILUS PARVIN

Doctors, this is the ungodly study I have lectured on at the medical college. I confess this to you in the name of science.

DR. AMOS SIMS

No righteous physician could fault you for speaking the gospel of medicine! Do go on, doctor.

DR. THEOPHILUS PARVIN

Well, I scarcely had trouble getting her to place her legs into the stirrups on my table and to open up so I could have a look.

DR. STAUGHTON MORRIS

A look? You looked right at it?

DR. AMOS SIMS

Of course he looked at it. Why, the speculum serves that very purpose. This is part of the work of being a gynecologist, Dr. Morris.

DR. THEOPHILUS PARVIN

In this case, the speculum was unnecessary. As I was saying doctors, she did insist that I physically examine her, so I introduced my finger into her vagina.

(Dr. MORRIS *gasps, appalled by what he's hearing. DR. CALVIN FLETCHER leans back.*)

DR. AMOS SIMS

(*to MORRIS and FLETCHER*) Doctors, there is no need to be flabbergasted. This is purely scientific business. Do go on, Dr. Parvin.

DR. THEOPHILUS PARVIN

I continued her internal examination, and as soon as her clitoris was barely touched, she produced irregular movements with her hips and pelvis.

DR. CALVIN FLETCHER

Wild beast indeed!

DR. STAUGHTON MORRIS

Good God, man! Surely you didn't say such things in a clinical lecture?

DR. THEOPHILUS PARVIN

Of course I did, Dr. Morris. We have a moral duty to publish our medical findings so we can advance science. (*DR. PARVIN hands a medical journal to DR. MORRIS.*) Read it for yourself.

DR. STAUGHTON MORRIS

(reading aloud from the journal)
"I further advanced my finger deeper inside her, which then caused the muscles about the vagina to be thrown into a state of contraction! She then closed tight on my finger and fell into exhaustion, seeming to be thoroughly gratified." If I hadn't just read it in the medical journal, I would scarcely believe it!

DR. THEOPHILUS PARVIN

Believe me, doctor, AND her behavior proved to me that she is indeed inflicted with these dually horrific diseases.

DR. CALVIN FLETCHER

Well, you did what any good doctor would do. You helped that poor woman.

DR. STAUGHTON MORRIS

Good gracious, doctor, but were you not horrified?

DR. CALVIN FLETCHER

I've heard tell that this sort of woman's vagina is more powerful than the jaws of an animal.

DR. AMOS SIMS

Why, you're lucky to have retrieved your finger, doctor! I myself can confirm the vagina's viselike capacity. (*grabs and squeezes DR. MORRIS's finger*)

DR. STAUGHTON MORRIS

I fear what would become of other . . . appendages should they be inserted inside such a woman.

DR. CALVIN FLETCHER

I shudder to think . . .

DR. THEOPHILUS PARVIN

My case study *penis captivus,* published in the Jefferson Medical College's journal, proves that a woman's vagina is capable of holding a man's penis captive.

DR. STAUGHTON MORRIS

Heavens have mercy! Did this happen to your finger when you examined the widow, doctor?

DR. THEOPHILUS PARVIN

Fortunately, no.

DR. STAUGHTON MORRIS
What did you do to alleviate that woman's future bouts of hysteria, doctor?

DR. THEOPHILUS PARVIN
Well, I've experimented with cocaine treatment. As you can read in my research (*Parvin takes the book and finds the page*), I applied a muriate of cocaine to her clitoris and then prescribed her vaginal cocaine suppositories. Doctors, I can assure you the effect was wonderful! The vagina at once behaved as the most virtuous vagina in the United States!

DR. CALVIN FLETCHER
Excellent, doctor! We should all be using cocaine. (*MORRIS laughs, PARVIN and SIMS glower.*)

DR. STAUGHTON MORRIS
But Dr. Parvin, you also wrote that clitoridectomy and ovariectomy might do good in some cases. When do you suggest such surgical treatment?

DR. THEOPHILUS PARVIN
That question actually brings me back to the business at hand. Surgeries of the sort would permanently solve many of our problems. My work in the reformatory will allow me to collect data and conduct such experimental surgeries. I hope I have your support in my research. In the event ethics come into question.

DR. AMOS SIMS
Absolutely, doctor. You do have a private practice, so I see no reason why we'd ever need to reveal that your research is being conducted in a prison.

DR. CALVIN FLETCHER

I can only hope to be as fearless in medicine one day as you are, Dr. Parvin. I'll do whatever I can to assist you.

(*fade out*)

Act 2: The Death of the Duchess and Stringtown

Scene 2—The Duchess's Funeral

The funeral hall is extravagantly and opulently decorated, fit for a memorial service for true royalty. No expense has been spared. The seating is in two sections, separated by the podium, platform, and casket in the middle. The DUCHESS's GHOST is perched on top of the casket, observing the proceedings. She periodically powders her nose throughout the scene. Friends and associates of the DUCHESS are gathered together in the back of funeral hall, near the food table. JOHN KITCHEN is drinking heavily and carrying on with SALLIE. As the scene begins, DOUGLAS and DANIEL are watching JOHN KITCHEN's display.

DANIEL

Look at the way that John Kitchen is acting. I bet he's had a nip or two.

DOUGLAS

Good way to hide the guilt.

DANIEL

Good God, man, it's her funeral! It's unseemly! Uncivilized.

DOUGLAS

Her body's not even cold yet. (*DOUGLAS approaches JOHN KITCHEN.*) Carrying on in public with these trollops.
How dare you!

DANIEL
(*following DOUGLAS*) Damn you! You should be locked up. You have no right to be here.

JOHN KITCHEN
I have the right to anything that has to do with my wife!

DOUGLAS
(*grabs KITCHEN by the neck*) Wife? Barely. In what sense, as an up-start pimp? After what you've done? My sister's body isn't even in the ground yet!

JOHN KITCHEN
What I've done? You know nothing of it. You fool!

(*JOHN KITCHEN stalks off. DOUGLAS and DANIEL make their way to seats as JAMES SMITH is entering near the casket. DR. THEOPHILUS PARVIN and DR. CALVIN FLETCHER approach JAMES.*)

DR. THEOPHILUS PARVIN
James, good to see you.

DR. CALVIN FLETCHER
Have you heard the news?

JAMES SMITH
News? What news?

DR. CALVIN FLETCHER
Stringtown has been absorbed into Indianapolis.

DR. THEOPHILUS PARVIN

And most prosperously for our reformatory project.

DR. CALVIN FLETCHER

The Duchess's death has been officially ruled a natural one.

DR. THEOPHILUS PARVIN

Naturally.

JAMES SMITH

(*growing in agitation*) Natural? Really? You'd call death of a forty-year-old woman in perfect health natural?

DR. THEOPHILUS PARVIN

Perfect health? Come on, James. Every learned man knows women of this sort are vectors of disease. (*to FLETCHER*) To be quite honest, she would be a perfect specimen for study.

JAMES SMITH

She's a human being, not an animal.

DR. CALVIN FLETCHER

How would you know?

JAMES SMITH

I ministered the gospel to her just days ago. Give the deceased the proper respect she deserves.

DR. CALVIN FLETCHER

Ministering the gospel to a fallen woman is a waste of air.

DR. THEOPHILUS PARVIN

But she might BE closer to an animal. My colleagues assure me such a woman would even entertain wild beasts. Her death is a blessing.

JAMES SMITH

Don't be so crass, Theo! We're talking about a life here! Didn't you take an oath to uphold life?

DR. CALVIN FLETCHER

What does it matter how or why she died? The fact that she did is good news for us all.

JAMES SMITH

This is a travesty! This is unbecoming of men who call themselves good Christians.

(*JAMES SMITH storms off and sits down. FLETCHER and PARVIN move to their seats. REVEREND DAVID STEVENSON enters, ushering in remaining guests.*)

DOUGLAS

What's taking so long? It's like a circus in here! Who else are we waiting for?

DANIEL

Everyone is here. Let's get on with it already.

REVEREND DAVID STEVENSON

My apologies, we've never had such a crowd for a funeral.
(*DOUGLAS and DANIEL takes seats again. REVEREND DAVID STEVENSON crosses to the podium.*)

Please be seated. (*all begin taking their seats*) Shall we begin? Today we are gathered to acknowledge the passing of one Johanna Kitchen, otherwise known as the Duchess of Stringtown. In her we find a . . . uh—gracious, uh—decent, uh—tenacious, yes, a tenacious woman. It is sad that she has gone before she repented of her ways, because God loved her, and he loves you and me. But he hates sin. Oh yes, yes he does. And to sin before God and not to repent is to be condemned to the fiery pits of hell.

The Duchess was a generous sort. Always helped out with the local charities. But I tell you, the Lord knows those of us who have repented and chosen Him and only those, I say, only those who have repented of their sins will be saved. Every good deed, donation, or help you've given another soul will matter for naught until you have repented and turned away from your wickedness. Turn away before it's too late. The Judgment comes, and when it does, it just might be too late. Why just the other day—

(*REVEREND is cut off by music—maybe "Kashmir" by Led Zeppelin. SARAH SMITH, RHODA COFFIN, and the ladies of the TEMPERANCE UNION and THIRD PRESBYTERIAN CHURCH enter. SARAH SMITH crosses toward the podium. The ladies line up to the left and to the right of the podium.*)

SARAH SMITH

To hell! Sinners unrepentant of the Lord, go to hell! When we, the weaker sex, fail to uphold what is right and just. How much more does the fabric of our society need to unravel? With cunning and the illusion of family, she created that den of hell, roiling with cavorting fornicators and girls so broken in iniquity and shame that only the Lord can save them! We are called to hold our fair sex, our communities, and our nation itself together! (*ladies vocally affirm SARAH's statements*) By these very hands I have toiled in the service of the Lord, never considering myself while women like the

Duchess besmirch the very name of woman to satisfy her greed and ambition.

(*she moves from behind the podium and the ladies echo, "Hell"*)
You, each of you, destroy woman's respectability and taint the sacred holiness of the womb. You are all sinners, vile, vengeful, vectors of disease, infecting the very fabric of our moral society. You are placing this nation in great danger! Those of you, who by some miracle weren't arrested and taken to Ol' Jeff, change your ways and come to the Home for Friendless Women. You will be saved. Stay in this life and you will go to hell! You need to fall down on your knees right now and repent, repent or go to hell. Repent or go to hell!

(*rumbling amongst the prostitutes*)
The Duchess gave you nothing but an express ticket to hell. You're sitting here supporting her, but don't you know, she's in hell? You want to be like her? In hell? If you don't stand up, stand up with me now, you too will go to hell!

SALLIE

(*as some of the prostitutes begin to respond*) Sit down!! Why, I can't believe y'all! You fallin' for this nonsense? This woman has no right comin' in here, railin' at us and the Duchess. The Duchess looked out for us when the church wouldn't give us a crust of bread. She took care of us.
(*to SARAH*) Infected? Diseased? If we so diseased, so too is half the men over there! (*points to the elites*) Who you think buys our wares? Ain't that right, Doc Calvin?
(*DR. CALVIN FLETCHER nearly faints from being called out.*)

SARAH SMITH

You blasphemous harlot!
(*SARAH SMITH jumps SALLIE. Fight ensues as others join in. Music under. The DUCHESS's GHOST rises in smoke and low thunder.*)

DUCHESS's GHOST

Stop!!!

(Everyone freezes except SARAH SMITH, who rises out of the scuffle in great fear. All hear the ensuing. SARAH alone can see the DUCHESS.)

You know nothing! The truth is far more shocking. Things are not always as they seem . . . you must listen to the truth.

(DUCHESS's GHOST glides into the circle of prostitutes and reaches for MINNIE, which animates MINNIE.)

MINNIE

I will never forget the creepy feeling I had when that door to the convent was opened by these unseen hands. I could never have known the dreadful journey I was about to take. They stole my name and hid my identity, forcing me to work as a slave in their laundry. I never thought I'd nearly be killed by people of God! I was forced to run away to save my life. The Duchess saw this lost and vacant child and helped me. She gave me a safe place to stay, fed me, clothed me. And never once judged me. I slept in a clean bed. A real bed. I didn't mind helping out in her house. The Duchess was good to me. This was a better family than any I had known. God works in ways maybe you don't understand, but these are my sisters.

(The DUCHESS's GHOST reaches for BELLE and BELLE rises.)

BELLE

I gave my "respectable" fiancé everything, even my virtue. When my parents passed away, I inherited their house. Suddenly everything became about the property and how much it was worth. He took everything I had, then broke off the engagement and deserted me, leaving me . . . pregnant. I went to Mrs. Smith's home, and she worked me to near death! When I collapsed, she handed me over to that villainous doctor. He cut my baby out of me! It felt like I was in unending torture and when I could, I ran. That was when I met the Duchess. She was the first woman who didn't look down on me. She understood and answered with opportunity. I learned that there is still worth left in this body.

(The DUCHESS's GHOST reaches for SALLIE and SALLIE rises.)

SALLIE

(to ELITES) Our "worth" ain't our own in your eyes. I've sought help from Christians in the past and was refused food and clothes. Then the very Christian men who refused me work quickly give me money for immoral purposes—arrest me, po' weak girl, and throw me in prison because they say I have sinned! Is surviving a sin? When we women fall so low that none will traffic with us, we are arrested. Tried by the very law that aided in our ruin. Sent to prison by the law. And then outraged by them enforcers of the law. Humph! Those guards fought each other like devils to see who would insult me first! Did I ever commit a crime so bad as what they did to me in that filthy cell house from the very beginning?

(to SARAH SMITH directly) You know very well, Mrs. Smith, that there was not a day that passed in Ol' Jeff that I or some other girl wasn't insulted by Colonel Merriweather. Next came the guards, which Merriweather shamelessly charged $10 a month to use us. We poor girls—instead of being mistress to one or two men were forced to act as mistress to twenty. Now you're building a prison of your own. You're no better than the rest of 'em. Your vile reform makes a brothel a haven!

DUCHESS's GHOST

Now they know the truth of about almost everything, Mrs. Smith.

(She returns silently to the casket; the crowd is reanimated.)

SARAH SMITH

(*to the casket, a crazed woman*) You can't speak through them, and no one believes your vicious lies, Johanna! You're dead and they are all whores! You can't justify the evil you do or they do. Get behind me, Satan!

SALLIE

Who the hell are you talkin' to? You crazy ol' biddy. Have you lost your mind?

(*JAMES SMITH runs up to comfort and quiet SARAH.*)

SARAH SMITH

(*to SALLIE*) And you. A brothel a haven? Brothels are the dens of iniquity, where Satan devours the ignorant and lost! Your sanctuary? Is that your haven? Jesus is the only sanctuary!!!

SALLIE

When my time was done at Ol' Jeff, I was thrown out like some trash with nothin'! No one provided me work or a roof over my head. Where was your sanctuary then? Only the Duchess, helped. She treated me nice and taught me I was worth somethin'!!!

SARAH SMITH

Worth something!? Laid out on your back?

SALLIE

I am worth somethin'! The Duchess taught me that! I'd do anything to help her with the hotel and the girls.

SARAH SMITH

Apparently, that wasn't all you helped with! I suppose caring for Mr. Kitchen came with the house!?

SALLIE

You bitch!

(SALLIE storms off to her seat. JOHN KITCHEN runs to the casket and speaks to the casket.)

JOHN KITCHEN

Did you even love me? Didn't I give you *everything*? Wasn't I worth some of what you had? You never did nothing but take what you could get and look down on me, while you courted highfalutin men.

(to JAMES SMITH and SARAH SMITH)
And you! You and all your righteousness! What sort of reformation did you have for my wife? With your frequent visits. Is that what you call preaching the Gospel? Or were you worried that her influence over you and Stringtown would prove dire for your plans?

(SARAH SMITH tries to go at him. DR. CALVIN FLETCHER jumps up to rein in JOHN KITCHEN.)
(to the casket) Did you ever love me?! Was I only a pretty face?!

DR. CALVIN FLETCHER

Of course she loved you. *(whispering)* Pull yourself together, John. You need to be of sound mind. We can't afford you to be ruled incompetent over the estate.

(Church ladies start thumping their Bibles and singing a hymn. Once again, the whole congregation is in an uproar. REVEREND DAVID STEVENSON charges to the podium, attempting to regain control.)

REVEREND DAVID STEVENSON

Enough! What's this? What impropriety has sullied this solemn occasion? Why this is—

JAMES SMITH
(cutting off the REVEREND STEVENSON at the podium)

Listen! Listen everyone. We have indeed come to pay our respects to a woman who . . . yes, I visited her home to minister the Gospel to her in her final days, because of her influence on the young women and girls in Stringtown. (*gazes at SARAH SMITH imploringly*) It was always my hope the Duchess could use her influence in a different way and become more like my beloved wife, Sarah.

(accusing everyone else)

Many had something to gain from her demise. Dr. Calvin Fletcher! You of all people have waited for her to go down. Miffed by her rejection, I'm sure you would seize any opportunity to get revenge. And Dr. Theophilus Parvin! How dare you call yourself a Christian? You scrape and scourge at any opportunity to examine a dead woman's body. And John Kitchen! Isn't it you who has the greatest interest in her untimely death? We all know she owned the hotel, and you have nothing. She told me how she took pains to hide the vile ways you assaulted her, while you gallivanted with girls in her employ. For a man like you, murder wouldn't be a stretch, would it?

JOHN KITCHEN

How dare you! Are you trying to pin my wife's death on me? It's a sham, these murderous accusations! It's a sham, I'm no murderer. In fact, I wasn't even around on Tuesday.

SALLIE

John!

JOHN KITCHEN

(*to JAMES*) Where were you?

JAMES SMITH

Don't be absurd. (*beat*) Wait, Sarah, weren't you there on Tuesday?
(*attendees all look to SARAH SMITH*)

SARAH SMITH

The Duchess confided in me that her life wasn't what she desired. We all know that women living the life she lived would be burdened with self-loathing for the iniquity and sin upon her soul. Her vanity has done her in. Trying to be a fair lady requires more than paint. You can't cover up lifelong transgression—even with arsenic-laced cosmetics. Surely, as evil and as steeped in sin as the Duchess was, her demise was inevitable.
(*DOUGLAS and DANIEL jump up and confront SARAH.*)

DOUGLAS

How did you know that our Johanna was poisoned by arsenic?

DANIEL

(*overlapping*) How did you know it was her cosmetics?
(*Attendees appalled, whispering*)

SARAH SMITH

Well, I, uh . . .

JAMES SMITH

(*rushes up to embrace his wife*) Sarah, it's all right dear. (*to everyone*) Leave her alone!

DR. THEOPHILUS PARVIN

Gentlemen, gentlemen! Calm down! Who could possibly think such nefariousness from this virtuous woman? Who does so much in this community to *help* fallen women? How could such a godly woman as she possibly be involved in any foul play? Why, it is beyond comprehension!

(*whispering subsides*)

I remind you that the coroner's report affirmed that Mrs. Kitchen did indeed die of natural causes. The inquest concluded that this is NOT a matter of foul play. Let us not be blighted by our emotions. Both God and science have ruled in this matter. Only those without religion or intelligence would think otherwise.

(*lights flash and thunder rolls*)

DUCHESS's GHOST

(*DUCHESS's GHOST rises from the casket.*)

Silence!

(*All freeze except SARAH SMITH. Again, she alone sees the apparition, and she begins muttering fearful prayers. DUCHESS's GHOST points in accusation at SARAH.*)

YOU! (*mockingly*) "Mistress of Benevolence."

(*coming face to face with SARAH SMITH*)

You know you're responsible for what's happened to me! You and your group of self-righteous elites—out to control everything and everyone! You may have these people fooled, but someday the truth will be known. *Your* immoral deed will be revealed. As you say, what is done in darkness shall *always* come to light. Isn't that right, Mrs. (*draws out "Mrs."*) Smith?

SARAH SMITH

You are a blight upon womanhood and Stringtown! You've never been a *true* woman, no matter how much money or how many marriages you've had, or how many husbands you've tried to steal! No one will ever question the death of a common whore.

DUCHESS's GHOST

Oh, but that's what *you* think. Someday my voice will sound from the grave. The truth of all of this will indeed surface. This isn't over yet!

(*DUCHESS's GHOST maniacally laughs. She disappears. Fade to black.*)

THE END

9

Hazel at the Indiana Girls' School

Nicole Hayes

Hazel France was tried before the U.S. District Court of Eastern Illinois on March 7, 1912. She was charged with "unlawfully and feloniously" causing two teen girls "to be transported in interstate commerce from Indianapolis, Indiana to Danville, Illinois for the purpose of prostitution and debauchery."[1] The prosecution claimed that twenty-two-year-old Hazel had brought the girls from Indiana to Illinois to pursue sex work at the Danville Hotel. This was a violation of the Mann Act, the federal law passed in 1910 that

Indiana Industrial School for Girls, Indianapolis.

aimed to stamp out the problem of "white slavery" in the United States. Hazel's story demonstrates the range of women's agency in this period—how they took advantage of opportunities within a patriarchal cultural economy. It is a prime example of how laws that supposedly protect sex workers criminalize and punish them in practice.

At the turn of the twentieth century, many Americans were convinced there existed an international conspiracy to seduce and enslave (white) American girls, trapping them in a life of prostitution. Historian Mark Thomas Connelly has described the indignation and concern over "white slavery" as "intense, widespread, and often hysterical."[2] White slave narratives were especially popular in the early 1900s, and the 1910 Mann Act, which prohibited bringing women and girls across state lines to engage in "debauchery" or other "immoral purposes," was a product of this cultural and political moment.

At the start of the twentieth century, every American city of significant size had a district wherein prostitution was practiced more or less openly. San Francisco had the Barbary Coast; Chicago had the Levee; New York, the Tenderloin; and New Orleans, Storyville. Danville, a town just across the Indiana-Illinois border and a major railway intersection, also was known for having a red-light district.[3] The Danville Junction brought in travelers who enjoyed the town's saloons, supper clubs, and theaters. The working women of Danville were concentrated in the service and entertainment industries, which included a continuum of sex work that ranged from prostitution to providing services as escorts or companions. Sex work was bound up with other money-making ventures, like drinking and gambling, in the world of "vice." In Danville, for instance, workers known as "26 girls" were hired to sidle up to men in bars and encourage them to play dice, with the establishment "paying bonuses if the girls got men to spend more money."[4] Historians have emphasized the resourcefulness and agency of young women in this era who pursued sex work, while also stressing the limited economic choices available to them.[5]

Districts like the one at Danville were targets of middle-class social reformers who were concerned about the victimization of women and girls. In the 1910s, cities across the nation issued reports on white slavery as a social evil in their communities. White slave narratives of the early twentieth century paint a picture of the white slave as an innocent, presexual young girl who had been tricked into a life of prostitution. As Connelly explains, these narratives of white slavery followed predictable patterns:

> Typically, a chaste and comely native country girl would forsake her idyllic country home and family for the promise of the city. On the way, or shortly after her arrival, she fell victim to the swarm of panders lying in wait for such an innocent and unprotected sojourner. Using one of his vast variety of tricks, a promise of marriage, an offer to assist in securing lodging, or, if these were to no avail, the chloroformed cloth, the hypodermic needle, or drug-induced drink. The insidious white slavers would brutally seduce the girl and install her in a brothel, where she became an enslaved prostitute. Within five years she would end up in the potter's field unless she had the good fortune to be "rescued" by a member of a dedicated group fighting white slavery.[6]

In the popular imagination, the victim of white slavery did not choose a life of prostitution; it was imposed on her by clever men. Politicians seized on the proliferation of conspiracy theories about underground white slavery rings. It was an Illinois congressman, James Robert Mann, who was the lead author of the White Slave Traffic Act, aka the Mann Act, a law that promised a decisive response to the alleged crisis. But as legal scholar Michael Conant writes, "The Congressmen who drafted the Mann Act seem to have paid no attention to the possibility that some of the supposed victims, willing prostitutes, might also find themselves felons."[7]

Hazel France, née Moon, was born on May 18, 1890, and grew up in Vigo County, Indiana, near the Illinois border, not far from Danville. When she was fifteen years old, her mother brought her before the Vigo County judge for "being wayward and incorrigible." Her case records noted that Hazel "stays out late nights" and "persists in associating with men and girls of bad reputation."[8] The judge had her committed to the Indiana Girls' School, the juvenile facility located on the western outskirts of Indianapolis that would separate from the Indiana Reformatory for Women in 1907.[9] There, "girls from ten to eighteen years of age committed by the courts were confined at the school until they reached the age of twenty, unless released earlier by decision of the board of trustees."[10]

Hazel's behavior put her outside the bounds of acceptable femininity as defined by the criminal justice system of the time and as exemplified by a speech juvenile court judge Newton M. Taylor gave at the school in 1912: "A good woman means a good cook, a good housekeeper, a woman who is charitable and kind and who is able to obtain and hold the confidence and esteem of her husband."[11] While the school was supposed to reform young women, in fact it was deeply intertwined in networks of so-called vice, and girls circulated constantly between the facility and places like Danville, Illinois.

While on parole from the school between 1907 and 1911, Hazel encountered Hattie Black, the owner of the Danville Hotel.[12] In 1909, Hazel married a waiter named Roy France,[13] which did not prevent her and a female friend from running off to Chicago that same year with "William Lennot and William Marcel, an acrobatic team at a vaudeville house," after grabbing "all the ready cash their husbands had."[14] Little is known about Hazel's experience as a sex worker in Danville, but records show that she was returned to the girls' school for a few months in 1911, until she turned twenty-one and aged out of the institution.

I first became interested in Danville after seeing the town referenced in archival material from the girls' school. Along with a colleague, Lisa Hochstetler, I was examining the monthly reports of the girls' school superintendent during the 1910s. These documents made note of all the girls who entered and left the facility—girls "received" from various county courts, as well as "escapees," transfers, and girls returned to their families or "sent out on parole."

In July 1912, the superintendent reported that "two girls ran off from Cottage 8, went to Danville to a house of prostitution."[15] An Illinois newspaper reported that the escaped girls, Rhoda Schooler and Lulu Dilling, "were arrested in a disorderly house here" and that the girls "declared they would commit suicide if taken back." Schooler made good on this promise, ingesting poison she somehow was able to find at the police station.[16] She survived and, along with Lulu, was sent back to the girls' school, where they were subjected to hard labor. "They were returned to the School and are now excavating a ditch to run a water pipe line up to the hog pen," wrote the superintendent.[17]

A month later, the two girls were sent to court "to testify against young men who kept them in the city."[18] In this case, then, Lulu and Rhoda were situated as victims of the men's designs, despite the girls' fierce resistance to being confined at the school and their reputations as "wayward."[19]

Lulu and Rhoda were just two of several girls who moved between Danville, Illinois, and the Indiana Girls' School. In September 1912, three young men were charged with "having taken two girls who escaped from the Indiana Girls School at Clermont to a room," keeping them there for a week before buying them tickets for Danville.[20] In 1915, Vesta Hammer and Duva Fisher escaped the school and were found on a freight train in Danville. While detained by police, "they told of their extensive plans for escape from the institution, of their ride in a box car to Springfield, Ill., where they attended the state fair, and of their exciting ride on the engine from Decatur."[21]

As for Hazel, she was arrested in Indianapolis in January 1912, accused of having "purchased tickets for two girls," Emma Hudson and Lillian Brennan, who were "paroled inmates of the Indiana Girls' School at Clermont, and to have sent them to resorts at Danville."[22] Emma claimed that she and Lillian (who knew Hazel from the girls' school, as Hazel had just been released the previous year) arranged to meet Hazel on an Indianapolis street. Hazel asked the girls if they "would like to take a little trip," offering train tickets and cab fare to the Danville Hotel and

Faces White Slave Traffic Charges in Federal Court

HAZEL FRANCE ALIAS MOON

WOMAN ARRESTED AS WHITE SLAVE AGENT

Said to Have Induced Former State School Inmates to Go to Illinois.

Indianapolis Star, January 31, 1912.

assuring the girls that they "wouldn't have much to do and that everything was very nice."[23] Emma claimed it was only after their arrival that she learned the hotel was being used for "immoral purposes."[24] When Emma insisted on leaving, Hazel refused to return her clothes, which included a fur coat, a hat, a skirt, a pair of shoes made of black velvet, and underwear.[25]

For violating the Mann Act, Hazel would serve a two-month sentence at the Vermillion County Jail.[26] Hattie Black, the Danville Hotel owner, fared worse. She was charged with seven counts of transporting young women and girls "upon the line and rout of the Cleveland, Cincinnati, Chicago and St. Louis Railway Company . . . with the intent and purpose" that they "engage in the practice of prostitution in the said City of Danville" as well as for selling "intoxicating liquor, and conducting a disorderly, ill-governed place."[27] Knowing there was a warrant for her arrest, Hattie hid from the police. After an extensive search by local deputies and federal officers, Hattie was apprehended and sentenced to serve three years and three days at the Kansas State Penitentiary, a federal prison.[28]

The prosecution of Hazel France and her associates for white slavery in 1911 can be understood in the context of contemporary anxieties and legal developments concerning sex work and women's agency, themes that continue today in debates among scholars, sex workers, and advocates about human trafficking. The well-known images of male traffickers preying on women and young girls dating back to the late nineteenth century have been reinforced by the media, entertainment industry, international policy agendas, and academic literature. Critics of the notion of human trafficking have argued that the antitrafficking laws are merely the criminalization of sex work and that the discourse of victimhood ignores how sex workers make well-considered decisions to improve their economic position or quality of life.[29] Though both capitalism and patriarchy constrained the decisions available to Hazel, her story complicates the easy dichotomy of (male) victimizer and (female) victim, as she assertively pursued economic opportunity in the form of sex work for herself and encouraged other young women to do so as well.

If Hazel held Emma's clothes to prevent her from leaving the Danville Hotel, Hazel was guilty of taking advantage of others. However, more important than seeing Hazel as a victim or as a villain is recognizing the systems of power that her story reveals. The Mann Act, designed to protect "innocent" young women and girls, instead was used to control and punish sex workers, subjecting them to incarceration and the stigma of criminalization. In addition, the circulation of young women and girls between the juvenile facility and the Danville brothels demonstrates that the system of corrections did not oppose the criminalized world of sex work but existed in symbiotic relation to it. Even if the girls' school was "successful" in rehabilitating young women, its aim, we must recall, was to "make them into docile domestic servants or wives— not the autonomous subjects" that reformers of "prostitutes" "were *themselves* struggling to become."[30] For Hazel and her associates, the stigmatized cycle of sex work and incarceration was difficult to escape. Was this because once "fallen," it was difficult for a woman to ascend to the ranks of acceptable femininity? Perhaps risking prison was better than the alternative?

10

"Feeble-Minded" Women at Harper's Lodge

Molly Whitted

The Indiana School for Feeble-Minded Youth (ISFMY) opened in 1890 in Fort Wayne, Indiana, to house children with disabilities. "Feeble-minded" was a term used to describe people who were born through "faulty heredity" with what experts considered a below-average level of intelligence. Feeble-mindedness was considered an "incurable disease" that caused criminality, delinquency, and, in women, hypersexuality. In 1901, a law was passed dedicating $40,000 to creating a custodial department for adult women with a capacity of 134 at the ISFMY. There, the state of Indiana segregated for permanent custodial care women judged to be "feeble-minded." The story of these confined women is a vital and overlooked part of the history of eugenics in Indiana. Segregation was a legal and frequently used gendered eugenic tactic that preceded Indiana's better-known 1907 law mandating the forced sterilization of certain "defective" individuals. Incarcerated at the ISFMY for the whole of their reproductive years, hundreds of Indiana women suffered a fate that rivaled the indignity and horror of sterilization.

The eugenics movement emerged in the 1880s, when Sir Francis Galton coined the term, and was originally intended to optimize the genetic structure of the white populace through selective breeding. While straightforward in its biologic rationale and approach, eugenics became complexly and inextricably entangled in a variety of sociological, political, and scientific issues through its proponents' attempts to achieve a perfected physical and moral race. In the United States, eugenic ideas influenced legal policy, economics, and educational directives in the late nineteenth and early twentieth centuries.

Diverse scholars have examined the history of eugenics and its psychosocial and scientific consequences in the United States. In seeking to untangle the interactions among key eugenic players, practices, and policies throughout U.S. history, historians often focus their research on thematic or regional areas. Specific issues like the negative eugenic strategies, such as sterilization, marriage prohibition, deportation, and the nonconsensual segregation of women, that were employed all over the United States between the late nineteenth century and mid-twentieth century have all appeared in the historical narrative. Surgical sterilization is a common point of convergence among the subtopics explored by eugenic researchers and writers. This may be because of the abhorrent and permanent nature of a physically invasive surgical procedure that robbed people of their choice to have children.

The Indiana General Assembly is credited as being the first legislative body in the world to enact a eugenic sterilization law, in 1907, "making sterilization mandatory for certain individuals in state custody."[1] Many scholars, such as Alexandra Minna Stern, Molly Ladd-Taylor, Robert Osgood, Paul A. Lombardo, Elof Axel Carlson, and Jason Lantzer (just to name a few), have all extensively and thoroughly researched Indiana's eugenic history, with a primary focus on sterilization.[2] However, what is largely missing from their written work is the passage of an Indiana eugenic law that predated by six years the 1907 compulsory sterilization law. Further, the work of these scholars lacks any real analysis of the women themselves, the 1901 law, and the role of confinement as a eugenic tactic.

By way of exception comes the work of historian James W. Trent, which offers a more in-depth look at the history of custodial institutions created for the "feeble-minded."[3] Trent provides detailed reference to the ISFMY and the women confined there. However, while Trent's book does integrate the custodial adult female's housing and labor arrangements at the ISFMY, still, it lacks a quantitative or qualitative analysis of the women committed to the school.

Historian Alexandra Minna Stern provides some explanation of why this particular cohort of Hoosier women has remained obscure in the history of Indiana eugenics. After attempting to obtain details on a twenty-eight-year-old female inmate at the ISFMY who, in May of 1943, was coerced by the superintendent to consent to sterilization in order to be released from the school, Stern notes the difficulty of accessing information on these women:

> Given the spottiness of case files housed in the Indiana Archives and Records Administration and the strict confidentiality guidelines for patient records mandated by the 1996 Federal Health Insurance Portability and Accountability Act (HIPAA), it is unlikely that we will ever learn more about this young woman—what led to her commitment, how long she spent in Fort Wayne before her sterilization hearing, and how she fared upon release.[4]

After spending countless hours inside the Indiana Archives carefully examining every accessible document on the ISFMY, I can corroborate the bureaucratic obstacles that Stern encountered. Although these women were committed by the courts, considered "inmates," their individual case files are considered "patient files."

Under the Indiana legislature's interpretation of the 1996 Federal Health Insurance Portability and Accountability Act (HIPAA), their files are inaccessible to anyone who is not a direct descendant. This is a particularly unique catch-22 given that the sole purpose of segregating these women was to keep them from producing any descendants. Also inaccessible to me were individual women's court inquests. While these certainly are not considered protected documents under HIPAA guidelines, they are stored inside each woman's patient file. Fear of violating HIPAA laws kept the staff at the Indiana Archives hesitant to make them available to the public. This is unfortunate as they most likely would have been a valuable source of information. It is possible to obtain a copy of an individual's court inquest, given that the courthouse in a specified county still has them. However, to do that one must go to the county's courthouse and ask for a specific person's inquest. The problem with this approach is that the only place to find the women's names are in the U.S. census and in the ISFMY's minute books. Neither of these sources offers the county from which each woman came.

Despite these rather restrictive barriers, I was able to reveal a more detailed and in-depth qualitative and quantitative analysis of this seemingly forgotten subset of Indiana women by using the data from the U.S. census for the years 1910, 1920, and 1930. Moreover, I was able to unveil more about the experiences of these women through the use of primary documents from the Indiana Archives, such as the ISFMY's minute books and annual reports, contemporary news clippings, and handwritten correspondences from administrators, board members, and governors. Investigative reports of the institution by the Indiana Board of State Charities (BSC), the state agency founded in 1890 to organize and oversee Indiana's prisons, mental hospitals, and homes for "defectives," are another key resource. While it may be impossible to derive any absolute conclusion about these confined women without access to their patient files, we can better understand their place and importance in Indiana's history.

The scientific ideology at the turn of the twentieth century supposed that "feeble-mindedness" was an inherited and incurable disease, rendering the individual mentally underdeveloped at a level far below that of adult intelligence. Any immoral, criminal, or hypersexual behavior was attributed to the "disease" of "feeble-mindedness," which passed through inferior lineage from generation to generation. Women became the primary target for eugenicists and the BSC, as women were considered biologically responsible not only for the perpetuation of the fittest of our species but also for the maintenance of "female heterosexual virtuous norms."[5] Any woman who deviated from that precept was considered a threat to society, one that needed to be eradicated immediately lest she pollute future generations with her "faulty" genetics. No longer was saving or reforming "lost," "fallen," or "wayward" women a concern. Instead, eugenicists began to apply "advanced," for the time, sociological and scientific methods to control women's sexuality and reproduction via ethically questionable tactics to achieve class, racial, and genetic purity.[6]

The "feeble-minded" woman was considered the most dangerous of the defective types specifically because of her sexuality. Without the willpower to control her behavior or to maintain her virtuousness, she would certainly end up having sexual contact with unsuspecting upstanding men. Eugenicists feared that she would disrupt and corrupt proper society, spread venereal disease, or bear illegitimate children. The BSC addresses this concern in its *Fifth Report*:

[Feeble-minded women] are a heavy weight upon society, and in numberless instances have been the causes of demoralization and vice among the young men and boys. Lacking the intelligence and will-power to protect their own virtue, they easily fall into evil ways and become the source of temptation to others. . . . The presence of a woman such as has been described in a neighborhood may lower the moral standards of many young men and has been known to be the beginning of the ruin of many who otherwise might have remained moral and sober citizens.[7]

The notion that a normal woman would ever want to have sexual relations with any man other than her husband, and for any reason other than maternity, was incomprehensible to the conservative and traditional members of society. As sociologist Lisa Pasko explains, "Sexual purity became the ultimate marker of femininity, as mothers and fathers believed it solidified their daughters' chance for leaving the home, of maintaining a good reputation for the family, and of becoming a good wife and mother."[8] Based on this normative standard, any woman, especially a sex worker, who showed any sexual independence was assumed incapable of being in control of her primitive urges or mental faculties and so must surely be "feeble-minded," insane, or psychopathic. In fact, the sexuality of men considered "feeble-minded" was not generally called into question at all (unless his public behavior was sexually deviant in nature, i.e., homosexual, rapist, etc.). However, female "feeble-mindedness" was always associated with her morality and sexuality.[9]

Along with the alleged threat of the "feeble-minded" woman's immorality was the assumed detriment to the public purse she imposed through uncontrolled procreation. Her unruly reproduction only created more "feeble-minded," insane, and criminally inclined descendants who were thought to cost the state considerable dollars in aid, charities, and institutional costs. Many members of Indiana's BSC, along with reformers and crusaders, felt a strong need to check the moral depravity of the promiscuous woman. The BSC's *Fifth Annual Report* records the board members' pleas to Indiana legislators to "enact a law establishing an asylum for feeble-minded women":

It has long been undisputed that feeble-mindedness is in a large per cent of its cases inherited. Hundreds of feeble-minded women in Indiana are at that age at which they are likely to produce off-spring. It is beyond doubt that an appalling proportion of these children will be feeble-minded. Scores of feeble-minded women in the state are today the mothers of feeble-minded children. Illegitimacy must invariably be expected among a large per cent of feeble-minded women who become mothers. The presence of a single feeble-minded woman is often sufficient to seriously demoralize the peace and morality of a community. These women, wherever they may be, must be supported by the public. It were better to place them in a carefully managed State institution where they would be safe from the temptations and vice to which they are especially subject, and where their evil influence could not be exerted to injure the morals of others.[10]

With the earnest objective to quell the breeding of degeneracy throughout Indiana's populace, Amos Butler, secretary of the BSC from 1898 to 1923, proclaimed that "feeble-minded" women "should be kept separate and apart from the world . . . forever . . . prevented from reproducing their kind."[11] Indiana, however, was in no way a pioneer in the segregation of "feeble-minded" women as a eugenic strategy. In fact, Indiana eugenicists were inspired by other states' established means of isolating "feeble-minded" women. Butler commended those states for paving the way for Indiana's 1901 segregation law when he wrote the following:

A few states have established custodial institutions for the detention and care of feeble-minded women during the reproductive period. Here they have regular habits; their strength is employed in useful service and their passions are restrained. Forever they are separated from the world. One's feelings are those of gratitude to the states which have shown such wisdom.[12]

Finally, on March 8, 1901, Indiana governor Winfield Durbin passed a law making it legal to commit and confine women, exclusively, into a custodial institution for "feeble-minded" persons. These women were to be committed and confined to the institution for the whole of their childbearing years, from ages sixteen to forty-five, for noncriminal offenses. In fact, all it took to warrant this legal confinement was the accusation of being sexually immoral, rather than being in need of actual long-term custodial care. To have an adult female committed, any person could file a petition with the clerk of their county's circuit court. To be placed in a specialized facility for the "feeble-minded," the woman could not be "insane, pregnant, or helpless." She had to be "in good bodily health" and could not be "afflicted with any chronic or contagious diseases." She must also be a legal resident of the state of Indiana, as well as the county committing her, and be considered a "menace" to said community. To assess the threat a particular woman posed, the woman in question would be summoned by the court, examined by a physician, and questioned by a judge. The court would then question witnesses, and if the judge deemed her unfit, she would then be forcibly committed to the only custodial institution for the "feeble-minded" in Indiana at the time, the ISFMY in Fort Wayne.[13] Once inside the school, these women stayed imprisoned at the institution until they reached menopause and were no longer in danger of passing on their "faulty genes." Beginning in the late 1920s, the practice of sterilization opened the possibility for "early" release.

The twenty-two adult females initially committed to the ISFMY in 1901 resided in the Sunset Cottage, the custodial cottage that housed "girls of the upper and older grades" who had grown up in the ISFMY, until construction of the adult female custodial cottage was completed. A year later, Harper's Lodge opened and interned seventy adult females from thirty-seven counties across Indiana.[14] In 1903, members of the BSC applauded themselves for a job well done:

Ninety women who are not able to control themselves are there. Before their admission many of them had been the cause of social troubles and the spread of disease. Others were the mothers of a number of feeble-minded children, most of whom were illegitimate. Some were such depraved creatures that they were terrors to the communities where they had their homes. In their new home, which the state has provided, they are taught cleanliness and regular habits; are trained to work and are given employment. . . . These women do the washing, cleaning, household work and sewing. . . . Yet it costs little if any more to support them here in this manner than to permit them to remain in the poor asylums, where they lack employment and restraint and are perpetuating other generations of defectives whom we must support.[15]

By 1905, the BSC was already requesting more money from the state to expand housing for women at the ISFMY. Harper's Lodge had long exceeded its intended capacity. The school had a continuous waiting list. In 1907, the ISFMY annual report specified that Harper's Lodge was equipped with 126 beds for the adult females but had 139 women enrolled and 21 applications for adult females on file, "pending room."[16] The *Twenty-fifth Annual Report* of the ISFMY made clear that "these women are not committed with the thought that they at some future time be discharged as persons capable of caring for themselves."[17]

In 1909, another $60,000 (equivalent to $1,699,760.44 in 2020) was appropriated for the erection of another custodial cottage for women at the ISFMY.[18] The construction of this cottage was finished in 1911.[19] Despite their declarations that the newest custodial cottage would provide adequate space for "feeble-minded" adult women for years to come, the board of trustees of the ISFMY once again complained of overcrowding just one year later. In 1912, the board began entreating the state to build an entirely new facility, dedicated solely to the care of "feeble-minded" women of childbearing age. They claimed that all the beds for adult female residents would be filled within the year and that there were yet "more than 500 of this unfortunate class of child-bearing age to be found in the county infirmaries and jails of the State."[20]

"Feeble-minded" women at the ISFMY were classified into four divisions. Division A comprised the "brighter and more able-bodied class." Those in Division B were described as "a lower mental grade, physically strong, but mentally and morally weak." Sixteen of the seventy women were placed in Division B. Division C placements were deemed "the weaker ones." And Division D was composed of twenty "noisy, troublesome, and somewhat offensive" adult female inmates who were "needing to be kept apart from the rest as much as possible."[21] The descriptive classifiers used for these women by the staff at the ISFMY are very suggestive, with descriptions such as "troublesome" that might indicate the women's resistance to being held there. Classifying an entire division of women as "good workers" shows the school's need for and desire to have such a category and implies the intent to benefit from inmates' forced manual labor.

In the ISFMY's *Twenty-fourth Annual Report*, board managers gloat that by exploiting the girls' labor, they were able to "save three employees." Their job was to help and to teach the newly confined "feeble-minded" women how to "do more of their own work."[22] In a 1905 report entitled *Manual Training for Feebleminded Women*, Alexander Johnson gives his account of the first year inside the adult women's custodial cottage. Johnson recalls,

When the cottage was completed and the women were received, it was found necessary to send there some of the upper
grade girls of the school to do their housework. The girls had
been trained from childhood in the school and had grown up
capable, happy, industrious, and able-bodied, but the women
had had no such training and could not do even ordinary
housework. However, . . . at the end of the year . . . not only
were the women doing their own work, but four or five were
helping out in other places. They began by doing their own
laundry work, washing their hosiery and underclothes, and
after a while they took up other things. . . . They are also doing
a great deal of other work.[23]

He goes on to describe the women: "So about one-third of the feebleminded women . . . are practically self-supporting. Another
third can do some work, such as sweeping, dusting, and perhaps
even making the beds, and the other third are helpless, and the others must care for them."[24] This raises the question: Did the confined
women literally not know how to do "ordinary housework"? Or
did they simply refuse to do it in protest? What are the moral and
ethical implications of making women and girls, particularly those
with mental health challenges, "self-supporting" in a captive state?
    Using the U.S. census returns from 1910, 1920, and 1930 as an
additional means of establishing a profile of the women confined
at the ISFMY has provided much insight. For example, from 1901
until 1930 an estimated 1,380 Hoosier women were incarcerated at
the ISFMY.[25] Of these, 1,353 (98 percent) were recorded as white,
24 (1.7 percent) as Black, 2 (.14 percent) as "mulatto," and 1 was illegible. The average age at the time of committal was between sixteen and twenty-three years old. During the first thirty years of
operation, the youngest committed to the adult female custodial
department was sixteen and the oldest was fifty-nine. The "Marital Status" of these 1,380 confined women were entered as follows:

1,331 (96 percent) single, 29 (2.1 percent) married, 6 (.43 percent) divorced, and 14 (1 percent) widowed.

Under the "Place of Birth" category, a miscellany of geographic
locations were recorded. This category lists the women, forced to
live out their lives at the ISFMY in Fort Wayne, Indiana, as orig-
inating from three different countries (Canada, Germany, and
Wales) and from twenty-seven different U.S. states, including
two as having been born in Indian Territory. However, 27 women
were recorded as simply having been born in the United States or
"unknown." Still, the majority (1,127, or 81.7 percent) of the 1,380
women were listed as having been born in Indiana. Kentucky (31
women), Ohio (29 women), and Illinois (28 women) follow Indiana
in the succession of states with the highest numbers of women who
were born there.[26]

It is difficult to give an accurate average of the women's educational levels because of the extremely limited nature of information
recorded in the 1930 census. For instance, the 1930 census did not
record whether the women spoke English, and the census taker left
most of the entries blank in the combined category of "Able to Read
and Write." However, relying more heavily on the 1910 and 1920
census data, we can see that 506 (36.6 percent) women could read
and 449 (32.5 percent) could not, and that for 425 (30.8 percent) the
category was simply left blank. Additionally, 470 (34 percent) are
listed as able to write and 485 (35.1 percent) are listed as unable,
and that for 425 (30.8 percent) the category was left blank. It is unfortunate that roughly one-third of the confined "feeble-minded"
women's scholastic abilities went unrecorded; without it, it is impossible to discern whether these women were simply uneducated
or, as eugenicists alleged, "truly mentally deficient."

As mentioned, each decade's census has some slight variation
in data categories. For example, the 1910 census is the only one of
the three with entries recorded in the category labeled "Mother of

How Many Children." Under this category, only 35 women have comments regarding how many children they had given birth to and how many of those were still living. This section on maternity, along with the responses given, in the 1910 census is full of questionable incongruity. The 35 women who have a documented response in the "children" category include women from all four marital status options (single, married, divorced, widowed). The fact that this category comprises women with various marital statuses shows that the census taker posed the question of maternity to all the women committed to the school, regardless of marital status. If all 491 women were asked if they had any children, why did only 35 (7 percent) give a response, while the category was left blank for 456 (93 percent)? Of the 35 who gave a response, 29 (6 percent of the total) were mothers, though with such inconsistent data collection it is impossible to tell how many of the remaining were as well. This missing data is limiting, especially because the "rapid reproduction of illegitimate children" was what supposedly necessitated the confinement of Indiana's "feeble-minded" women. According to the BSC,

Observation has long ago shown that a large proportion of such females bear children, usually illegitimate and almost invariably deficient mentally. . . . The large number of children born of feebleminded mothers in the county poor asylums of Indiana proves that those institutions offer slight protection.

The BSC proceeds to present its biased observation as factual evidence:

There is hardly a poor house in this land where there are not two or more feebleminded women with from one to four illegitimate children each. There is every reason in morality, humanity, and public policy that these feebleminded women should be under permanent and watchful guardianship, especially during the childbearing age.[27]

A look at the category titled "Occupation" in the 1920 U.S. census reveals thirteen different types of designated job assignments that were distributed amongst the 723 women confined at the ISFMY that year. According to the job titles registered in this category, 1 woman worked in the "clothing room," 1 woman did the "darning," 11 women worked in the "dayroom," 53 did "dining room work," 46 did "dormitory work," 155 performed the "house work," 27 did "kitchen work," 73 did "laundry work," 7 did the "mending," 105 did the "polishing," 17 did the "scrubbing," 14 did the "sewing," and 1 did the "sweeping." Of the remaining, 210 women were listed as not being assigned an occupation, and 2 women's "occupations" were illegible.

A list of pieces made in the sewing room by the adult females offers some indication of the kind of dress the women were made to wear, along with the types of articles used in Harper's Lodge. Denim aprons, gingham dresses, drawers, underskirts, and white skirts were some of the clothing items sewn by the women delegated to do the sewing. Other piecework included comforts; table and toilet napkins; pillowcases and sheets; tablecloths; bath, kitchen, and roller towels; and union suits.[28]

Meanwhile, the state of Indiana continued to facilitate the passage of laws that aligned with the BSC's eugenic agenda. These additional eugenic laws did not target solely women as the 1901 custodial act did, but it shows Indiana's ongoing dedication to securing class and racial purity. In 1905, Indiana was one of the first states to enact a marriage regulation law.[29] This law, enacted by Governor J. Frank Hanly, "refused a marriage license to anyone who had been declared an 'imbecile, epileptic, of unsound mind.'" A marriage license was also to be refused to "any male . . . within five years an inmate of any county asylum or home for indigent persons, as well as to anyone with an incurable or transmissible disease."[30] In 1907, Governor Hanly signed into effect the world's first compulsory sterilization law. This law made it mandatory to surgically sterilize "confirmed criminals," "idiots," and "imbeciles" held in state institutions once two surgeons, appointed by the institutions, determined that the inmates should not procreate.[31] This first wave of forced sterilization in Indiana was short-lived, however, as Governor Thomas R. Marshall placed a moratorium on institutional eugenic sterilization in 1909. Governor Marshall felt the law was unconstitutional, and he threatened to discontinue funding to any institution that continued to perform the surgeries. In 1919, Governor James P. Goodrich attempted to bring sterilization back to Indiana state institutions, but in 1921 the Indiana Supreme Court officially repealed the original 1907 law, stating that it denied due process and was in fact unconstitutional.[32] After Governor Marshall's 1909 moratorium on involuntary eugenic sterilizations, segregation became the predominately used eugenic tactic in Indiana facilities like the ISFMY.

With the 1927 U.S. Supreme Court case *Buck v. Bell*, which supported states' ability to enact compulsory sterilization of the "unfit," sterilization was once again legal in Indiana, and it became the primary eugenic tool of the state. In 1927, Indiana governor Edward Jackson approved the revamped version of the 1907 sterilization law, "which granted the due process of law required by the Fourteenth Amendment, naming the courts as venues for appeal regarding sterilization decisions by the governing board of an institution."[33] Overcrowding and lack of funding called for sterilization as a prerequisite to early release from these facilities of confinement. After the 1927 sterilization act was passed, 1,500 sterilizations were performed at the ISFMY and another 500 performed at Muscatatuck (a second institution for the "feeble-minded" opened in 1920) between the years 1927 and 1974.[34] The American eugenics movement of the early twentieth century ended up being a very expensive and life-altering social science experiment, the cost of which was carried by those on whom it was performed. Indiana pioneered and cultivated the state-sanctioned violation of the constitutional and human rights of thousands of American women for over six decades.

I have focused my research on the state-ordered control placed over female agency in Indiana during the turn of the twentieth century. Women deemed "fallen," "wayward," and "feeble-minded" were under systematic attack in Indiana during this time period because of their rejection of contemporary norms, their economic- and class-based standing in the community, and their heightened sense of feminine agency. Progressive reformers, purity crusaders, and self-proclaimed eugenicists promoted social fears surrounding women's immorality, uncontrolled sexuality, and reproductive capacity to place collective pressure on Indiana lawmakers to categorically target "unmanageable" Hoosier women for confinement. This history of a negative, gender-specific, legal eugenic tactic in Indiana led me to investigate the ISFMY and the women segregated there.

Although the ISFMY opened in 1890 and did not close until 2007, I focused my attention on the first three decades after the 1901 law began to segregate women. Between 1901 and 1927, the permanent custodial confinement of women was the predominant eugenic strategy used in Indiana, despite the spotlight scholars place on sterilization as the primary tool. I would also argue, drawing from my lived experience of incarceration, that the involuntary, decades-long confinement of these women is just as contemptible as surgical sterilization, with equally traumatic effects.

PART III

Indiana's House of the
Good Shepherd

11

Sisters

Christina Kovats

As discussed in previous chapters, historians have long considered the Indiana Women's Prison, formerly known as the Indiana Reformatory Institution for Women and Girls, to be the first separate state prison for women in the United States. Thus, my colleagues and I were astonished to discover that there was already a women's prison in Indianapolis when the reformatory opened.

Early in our explorations, Michelle Daniel Jones examined the reformatory's original registries and analyzed the crimes for which the women had been convicted in the nineteenth century. She found that from the time of the prison's founding in 1873 until 1897, not a single woman had been incarcerated for prostitution or any other sex offense. Yet we had come across many accounts suggesting that Indianapolis residents in the 1860s, especially the elites, considered sex workers to be a substantial problem. Our early research seemed to indicate that prostitution was not a serious enough crime to warrant an extended prison sentence but rather "a few days' confinement" in the local jail. At least, that *was* our conclusion, until our

This chapter is based on "Indiana's Magdalene Laundry," a paper Christina Kovats wrote while incarcerated at the Indiana Women's Prison. It won the 2017 Peggy Seigel Award for best undergraduate paper in the state written on Indiana history. Her paper can be accessed at www.manchester.edu/docs/default-source/academics/by-major/history /kovats.pdf?sfvrsn=2.

friends at the Indiana State Library brought to our attention a 1967 article from the *Terre Haute Tribune.*

The article mentioned that a Catholic order of nuns known as the Sisters of the Good Shepherd was leaving Indiana. They had come to Indianapolis *nearly a century before* "to operate a correctional institution for women prisoners."[1] The sisters opened the House of the Good Shepherd (HGS) in Indianapolis in 1873 as a home for "fallen" women—and it *did* confine women convicted of sex offenses. Michelle Daniel Jones and another formerly incarcerated scholar, Lori Record, wrote an article challenging the idea that the Indiana Women's Prison was the first women's prison in the United States and arguing that Houses of the Good Shepherd were indeed prisons masked as convents.[2] They argued that

> if a prison is defined as a place of confinement for crimes and of forcible restraint, and if the persons committed to these places cannot leave when they want to and are, in fact, confined against their will, it becomes irrelevant whether the place is called a prison—or, instead, a refuge, correctional facility, house, penitentiary, or even laundry—if it operates as a prison. It is equally irrelevant if the facility is Catholic or Protestant, private or public. The operations and characteristics define a prison as a prison.[3]

According to this analysis, the Indianapolis HGS was, indeed, a prison. Furthermore, the Catholic-run facilities were much more numerous and important than state prisons for women in the nineteenth century. By 1900, there were only three state prisons for women—in Indiana, in Massachusetts, and in New York—whereas U.S. census data show there were already thirty-nine existing HGSs in the United States, making the amnesia concerning these prisons within American prison history even more egregious.[4] The conditions of confinement women and girls experienced in the laundries

were very similar to those of state-run prisons, with the main dif-
ferences being the type of religious indoctrination and the severity
of violence.

The Sisters of the Good Shepherd, members of a religious order
that originated in France, opened their first HGS in the United
States in Louisville, Kentucky, in 1843. The Indianapolis house was
the fifteenth established by the order in the United States, and it
opened five months *before* the Indiana Reformatory Institution for
Women and Girls.[5]

The origins of the HGS in Indianapolis not only revises our sense
of the trajectory of women's prison history but also provides fascinating insights into Catholic and Protestant relationships in postbellum Indiana. The number of Catholics in Indiana, primarily
of Irish and German origin, surged during the mid-1800s, though
overall numbers remained small. In the 1850 census, only 63 of the
2,032 churches in Indiana were Catholic.[6] In predominantly Protestant territory, Catholics, especially Irish Catholics, faced prejudice,
stigma, and hostility.[7] In Indiana, like much of the rest of the United
States in the mid-nineteenth century, this antagonism manifested
strongly in politics and social reform. Yet Catholics and Protestants
in Indianapolis eventually cooperated to address the "scourge" of
prostitution. It is possible that the Sisters of the Good Shepherd's
French origin and non-Irish identity served the order in establishing themselves in Indiana and in the United States.[8]

The story begins with the smallpox epidemic of 1855, which led to
a demand for a city hospital. The city council "took a decisive stand
for it, and lots were purchased and plans made for a building."[9]
But as the epidemic subsided, so did the urgency of this public
health measure. "The hospital was begun, but with the subsidence
of the alarm came indifference."[10] While the partially constructed
hospital lay idle, squatters took up residence. Soon the building
was "occupied by prostitutes and thieves."[11] Numerous ideas were
floated about what to do with the uncompleted building, including

"a proposition from the Catholic Church to conduct it as a hospital [which] was defeated, because of denominational objections."[12]

The hospital was finally completed during the Civil War, "when the necessities of the troops compelled its restoration to its proper uses,"[13] which involved expelling sex workers from the premises. In 1862, Mayor John Caven recommended the founding of a house of refuge where prostitutes and "abandoned women could be confined alone, and subjected to a discipline impossible in a common jail."[14] The following year, Stoughton A. Fletcher Jr., a wealthy businessman, proposed to donate seven acres of land to the city "if suitable buildings for a House of Refuge were put upon it."[15] As a member of one of Indianapolis's leading families, he contributed to (what he understood as) the betterment of the city in a number of ways, including promoting "the welfare and reformation of the unfortunate and the criminal."[16] Fletcher, a Protestant, initially gave the deed to the city for the Quakers to build the Home for Friendless Women.[17] The property and money donated were "to be used both as a refuge and reformatory school, and as a city prison for women."[18] Construction got as far as the foundation, when the contractor "broke down under the great advance in the cost of labor and materials, and abandoned it."[19]

Catholic efforts to find suitable property to open an asylum for "fallen" women accelerated after the end of the Civil War. Reverend August Bessonies, who was affiliated with both St. Peter's and St. John's Catholic churches, approached the city council in February 1866 and asked that the once-again abandoned city hospital be given to the Sisters of the Good Shepherd so they could open an institution for women.[20] He also requested that the House of Refuge, which remained unfinished on the old Stoughton Fletcher property, be given to them after it was completed to be used as a reformatory school for prostitutes.[21]

Two months later, council member Dr. Patrick H. Jameson argued in favor of Bessonies's proposal to take over the House of Refuge and encouraged others to support the "House for Abandoned Females." [22] The Sisters of the Good Shepherd pledged to finish construction and to have the building in full operation by December of that year. Councilman Dr. W. Clinton Thompson strongly opposed the idea and insisted that "the Home should be completed and used by the city, and not have our city prisoners farmed out to private corporations." To which Dr. Jameson retorted, "It matters little by whom the bad population of the city is taken care of, whether under the name of St John, the Good Shepherd, John Weasley, or John Knox." [23]

Tempers clearly ran high on the issue, so much so that Thompson and Jameson continued their exchange after the meeting. One journalist coyly implied as much by placing in brackets, "[Here a very unpleasant passage took place between Doctors Thompson and Jameson, in which personalities were freely used.]" [24] Another newspaper account was more explicit:

A most disgraceful occurrence took place last night immediately after the adjournment of the Council, which calls for the severest reprehension, for the honor of the city is compromised. An unpleasant and hot passage of words took place between Drs. Thompson and Jameson upon the paper presented by Father Bessonies, in reference to the Home for Desolate Females, which at the time was thought to be adjusted; but Dr. Thompson did not appear to be satisfied. Immediately upon the adjournment of the Council, Dr. Thompson walked to where Dr. Jameson was standing talking with the City Attorney, and addressed him. Dr. J supposed he was approaching to have the difficulty amicably adjusted, and such was our opinion, while standing within a yard of both gentlemen. Without any premonition, Dr. Thompson struck Dr. Jameson on the forehead, and both clinched. Jameson, although taken at a disadvantage, soon got his antagonist upon the knee, but they were soon

separated by the City Marshal and his assistant. Both gentlemen indulged in the grosest [sic] abuse, and Dr. Jameson threw
an inkstand at Dr. T., who attempted to retaliate by hurling one
of the heavy arm chairs, but was prevented.[25]

Perhaps because of the volatility of the issue, the city council did
not take up the idea of a Catholic-run city prison again until August
of 1869. According to press accounts, Councilman John S. Newman
expressed reservations because "Catholic institutions had refused
the right of visitation to officials of the law." Councilman Henry
Gimber countered that if the city were to send prisoners to the
House of the Good Shepherd, officials "would have the right to visit
and see how they were treated."[26]

Father Bessonies was asked to address the council on this matter.
His response was surprising to us. He reported that Sarah J. Smith,
who at the time was the Quaker leader of the Home for Friendless Women and the soon-to-be first superintendent of the Indiana
Reformatory Institution for Women and Girls, had "applied to him
to send these women to [the Houses of the Good Shepherd in] Cincinnati and Louisville, and that he had done so; but that he had
been imposing on the institutions there."[27] We were astonished to
realize that our Quaker reformers had been effectively cooperating
with Catholics for some time, despite the objection of some of the
city fathers. Smith's actions forced the hands of the men on the city
council, and eventually the following resolution was introduced:

Resolved, That the Mayor of the city of Indianapolis be directed to make a deed of conveyance to Stoughton A. Fletcher
(the donor of the ground) of the seven acres of land of ground
heretofore donated to the city for a Home for the Friendless,
lying south of the city, on condition that he make a conveyance of the same to the Sisters of the Good Shepherd, with the
understanding that they construct, within 5 years, a building

on the present location, to be used as a home for friendless females, and that such deed of conveyance shall include all improvements made on such land.[28]

The Catholics prevailed, and in 1873 Fr. Bessonies announced the
opening of the HGS on the land donated by Stoughton Fletcher.[29]
The vote was contentious and, as was the case in 1866, there were
heated arguments in the chamber. Councilman Thomas Cottrell
proclaimed "he did not care whether the Catholics or Protestants
got it" as long as the "public should be benefitted."[30] Councilman
Gimber agreed, calling the whole business a "'sectional' affair,"
noting that "certain members had been anxious to get rid of the
lewd women who infested the city, but now that the Sisters had offered to take them and keep them in prison, they were opposed to
it."[31] Mr. Newman objected, voicing fears that it would be difficult
for the council to know "whether those who were there were kept
by authority of law or against their will."[32] As we shall see in the
coming chapters, his concerns would prove prophetic.

12

Billy

Natalie Medley

In 1898, the *Indianapolis News* profiled the local Congregation of Our Lady of Charity of the Good Shepherd, also known as the Sisters of the Good Shepherd. The reporter conveyed a brief history of the order and its establishment in Indiana, outlining the sisters' mission "to reclaim fallen women, give a home to those who have reformed, and preserve young children, who might, as they grow older, be tempted." Inmates at the House of the Good Shepherd (HGS) followed a strict daily routine, which included times for prayers, meals, singing of psalms, and sewing and laundry work. The reporter asked one sister, "Can the inmates go away if they wished?" The sister responded, "The only chains we use are chains of kindness." [1] But the inmates were not free to leave the institution. In fact, the House of the Good Shepherd was a private prison that would operate in Indianapolis for nearly a century.

In the 1860s, the city of Indianapolis designated a parcel of land to serve as the site of a "House of Refuge and Reform for abandoned Females both prostitutes and those given to intoxication." [2] The city transferred the land to the Sisters of the Good Shepherd in 1873, and sisters soon arrived from Louisville, Kentucky (the location of the first HGS in the United States), and Angers, France (the order's headquarters) to found the Indianapolis HGS. [3] The sisters' mission was in exact alignment with the city's intentions for the land: they aimed to create "a place of retreat . . . for young women and girls, who, having entered a wrong way of living, or who were in some other moral danger, desired to do better and begin a new life."[4]

The first of these wards came in March 1873 and county authorities soon certified the house as "a suitable place for Judges to send females guilty of minor offenses."[5] Newspaper stories reveal that many young women were brought in for immoral behavior or for petty crimes. In 1883, sixteen-year-old Sadie Griffin was "locked up at the request of her friends, for safe keeping" because "she has led a very naughty life for a long time." Sadie "associates with worst kind of women, goes in saloons with strange men, and drinks freely," the *Richmond Item* explained.[6] Miss Etta Fry, sentenced by a judge in 1879, had a reputation for kleptomania;[7] Katie Governetta, admitted in 1889, had stolen a handkerchief. Though only ten years old, "the child is well known to the police, and was found some months ago sleeping at 2 o'clock one morning, on the steps of the Capital mill." At the time Governetta was placed in the HGS, her father was incarcerated in the Alabama penitentiary "where he was sent several years ago for shooting a woman."[8] One of few Black women taken to the house, Ina T. Sparks was sentenced to the HGS for thirty days in 1880 after assaulting a policeman with a hatchet. According to the newspapers, Sparks attacked the officer after he scolded her son for "throwing red ink from the windows upon passersby."[9]

Gender nonconformity and indigency were also causes for being sentenced to the HGS. In November 1877, a person described in the newspapers as a "weazen faced little tramp" known as "Billy" was sent to the HGS.[10] Presenting in court as a tobacco-chewing adolescent boy, this "queer fish" aroused the suspicion of the prosecutor, who guessed that "it" was a woman. At the threat of being strip-searched by police and jailed with male offenders, "Billy" revealed their given name, Ada Goodwin, and that they were nearly twenty years old and biologically female. The *Indianapolis News* reported that Goodwin, "finding she could not make a living . . . determined to be a man." According to the sisters' records, Billy made their living as a railroad worker and traveled widely.[11] When the sisters asked Billy about their mother, they replied, "I never had a Mother; my Aunt Lizzie raised me out in the woods."[12]

Agencies that aimed to protect children from neglect or exposure to vice made use of the HGS's services. The Indiana Board of Children's Guardians, for example, committed female juveniles to the institution beginning in 1889. Among the first was Jennie Golden, "a buxom lass of about fourteen years" whose mother ran "one of the most notorious and vile houses of ill fame in the city."[13] Priests and relatives instigated many commitments of underage children to the house. In 1874, for example, a Father Hamilton came to see a child he had placed under the sisters' care.[14] Soon after the HGS opened, a grandfather placed three of his grandchildren there. Two of the siblings remained in the house as Magdalene Sisters after reaching adulthood.[15]

The sisters systematically stripped inmates of their former identities through an enforced anonymity, which included the use of uniforms and the substitution of new names.[16] "Billy," for example, was given the name "Mary Angela," a name it does not seem Billy embraced. They are reported as saying to a priest who asked their name, "I don't know what it is now, when I was in the world they called me 'Billy!' Here they call me 'Mary Angela.' "[17]

From the very beginning, young people resisted confinement at the HGS. In July 1873, one of the first inmates, Laura Decker, filed an official complaint with the mayor of Indianapolis, accusing three police officers of kidnapping her and taking her to the HGS, where she was held against her will. Decker reported she was "fed upon stale food, forced to do penance for imaginary sins, and every means [was] tried to extort from her a belief in the Catholic Church." She also described forced labor and witnessing another girl "confined in a solitary room" with "her hands tied behind her . . . where food was thrown in like it would be to a hog." Father Bessonies, a local priest who helped establish the HGS in Indianapolis, stated in the sisters' defense: "She was brought to the Good Shepherds . . . where she was detained not by physical force but by moral suasion, until her mother asked for her release."[18] Laura's case was dismissed after she admitted to spending an evening "in the room of a saloon keeper" and she was personally reprimanded by the mayor of Indianapolis.[19] Her lawsuit provides a counternarrative to the sisters' assertions that "no one of age was detained against her will and those under age were there by consent of parent or guardian."[20]

In their own records, the sisters admitted to operating a prison during a brief span of time, from 1877 to 1881, when they accepted women sentenced by the City Court of Indianapolis.[21] The city allowed the sisters to take over the property with the understanding that the HGS would "receive Prisoners for half the price that the city was accustomed to pay for them," a measure that saved the city money, while allowing the sisters to establish their institution.[22] To fulfill this contract, the local police "made arrangement with the House of the Good Shepherd to board female prisoners for the city at the rate of $2.00 per week."[23] In August 1877, "five prostitutes" were sent to the establishment: "Hereafter prisoners of this description, when found guilty, will be given thirty days in this institution."[24] In documents preserved at the Indianapolis Archdiocesan Archives, the sisters described the 398 women who were accepted from the mayor's court during this four-year period as "prisoners," a group they considered distinct from the other "inmates" at the institution.[25]

The sisters recorded in the *Annals of the Good Shepherd in Indianapolis*, a yearly record of HGS activities, "Our dear Lord laid a severe Cross on our feeble shoulders in sending us these prisoners, some of whom were colored."[26] The sisters described the Black women as angry, threatening, and terrifying. The sisters' racism, as well as repeated acts of resistance from the prisoners, eventually led to the dissolution of the contract. For example, a group of five imprisoned Black women planned to escape the HGS, but their plan was revealed to the sisters by a white prisoner who overheard them. The sisters sent for the police, who took the conspirators to jail. Soon afterward, another group of prisoners, which included white and Black women, were foiled in their plans to kill Mother Ursula and take her keys. A third rebellion was quashed by the sisters' physician, Doctor Brennan, who attacked the women with a horsewhip.[27] Finding the women "very troublesome," the sisters terminated the agreement with the city by the end of 1881.[28]

It is evident from the sisters' records that they administered the prison at least somewhat separately from the main house.[29] But does that mean HGS "inmates" were not also, in a very real sense, "prisoners" as well? True, there are some important distinctions between the two groups. For example, "prisoners" were taken as payment for the debt incurred by the sisters for the property, whereas the monetary value secured for the "inmates" was the sisters' alone. Some "inmates" came to the house of their own volition (though even voluntary admissions were implicitly coerced by lack of other systematic structures that gave a woman protection, food, shelter, clothing, etc.). To further complicate the issue, many of the "inmates" were sentenced to the house by the courts, just as the "prisoners" were. "Prisoners" seem to all have had fixed, relatively short sentences, whereas "inmates" might be housed for an indeterminate length of time.

Regardless of the circumstances of commitment, both "inmates" and "prisoners" could be held against their will at the HGS, as is evident in multiple examples of escape both before and after the period between 1877 and 1881, when the city sent its prisoners. "Inmates" who escaped were subject to arrest and forcible return to the HGS by local or civil authorities. In the first year the house was open, 1873, the sisters and Father Bessonies complained that with no enclosure around the property, the inmates were difficult to keep in custody.[30] According to the sisters' own account, soon after the house opened, a girl named Molly, "tired of restraint," "jumped from the dormitory, upstairs," breaking several bones.[31] After the house was moved to its permanent residence on Raymond Street and "had a fence built around the property," escapes were still commonplace.[32] In 1894, the mother superior, Sister Mary of Saint Ursula, refuted allegations made by two girls who had escaped the house. The HGS "was really a prison, with a dungeon and barred windows," the girls said.[33] In 1897, an Indianapolis citizen penned an editorial in the *Indianapolis News* asking, "Why are those people allowed to hold persons without commitment? The sister superior says that they can leave at will. But if they could, why was it necessary for the girls to plan an escape?"[34]

The very architecture of the house revealed its carceral nature. "The rooms in the basement had been prepared as cells" and the windows were "small and barred."[35] These features did not disappear when the contract regarding the city prisoners ended. The design of the HGS incorporated principles of surveillance, classification, separation, isolation, and discipline, all representative of the "carceral enthusiasm" of the time.[36] Another feature, an on-grounds cemetery,[37] was a physical aspect that reinforced the notion that release would take place in the afterlife, not in physical freedom.

The sisters' approach to delinquent subjects was carceral, even if their work was spiritually benevolent. For example, while the sisters enforced their spiritual practices and psychology on the "prisoners" and "inmates" to ensure the salvation of their souls, they also recognized and supported the state's need to incarcerate and reform female bodies that were excessive to society. Working with the lawmakers who preferred these females to be out of sight, the contract with the city provided the sisters with legal incorporation, police and judicial authority, and the physical structure to incarcerate female delinquents.

To understand the sisters' mission, it is important to consider their vocation within the patriarchal church. The opportunities for women in the nineteenth century were few, and entering religious vocation secured autonomy outside of marriage while embodying the ideal of "chastity, piety and respectable womanhood."[38] Operating the House of the Good Shepherd was their moral authority, and the sisters enforced the women's subjugation to acceptable female behavior through forced labor and spiritual (psychological) restructuring.[39] The imprisoned woman would recognize that the power of her labor would reinstate her acceptable place in society.[40] Furthermore, the hierarchal separation of the women and girls by class, determined by moral deviancy and/or sexual immorality, and the promise of rising above subaltern standards of living, encouraged obedience. The women were provided fixed hours for work, sleep, meals, prayer, and recreation. They were not supposed to talk to one another, or risk isolation or physical punishment. The indoctrination by the religious overseers forced industry, good manners, and spiritual cognitive restructuring around notions of guilt, servitude, and penitence.

The laundry business inside the HGS furthered the sisters' mission of restoring women to assimilation in society while also profiting the order. In 1873, Father Bessonies wrote a letter to the editor of the *Indianapolis News* specifically stating the sisters' purpose:

The punishments now for females who are arrested in houses of ill fame is a fine, and if unable to pay it, as is generally the case, a few days confinement in the station house. . . . In fact it [*sic*] no punishment at all Idleness and laziness have led them to a life of shame and disgrace, and they are glad to have a chance to have a few days of rest in a place where they have nothing to

do but play, eat, and sleep, and from thence they go with a new
vigor to their former dens.

. . . They are afraid of being made to work. Let us then punish
them in that way, and make them earn their bread by the sweat
of their brow.[41]

Thus, the sisters' mission was not to alleviate hunger, poverty, or
unemployment for women but rather to take advantage of those
conditions.

Such treatment over time had debilitating, even disabling, effects. Remember "Billy," for example—the young "tramp" who was
brought to the HGS in 1877. The sisters wrote of Billy in the *Annals*,
"She was with us for a long time, but in her later years she became
feeble-minded." They ascribed Billy's decline to the "result of the
ill-spent years of her youth," that is, to the fact that, in their words,
Billy had once made "her way through the world [as] if she were a
man." But they also noted that Billy repeatedly expressed a wish
to "go out into the world again," a desire the sisters wrote off as a
mere "fancy" that would never come to pass.[42] Billy died at the HGS
in 1897, after over twenty years of confinement.

13

"Poor Stray Sheep"

Rheann Kelly

After establishing the House of the Good Shepherd (HGS) in Indianapolis in 1873, the Sisters of the Good Shepherd struggled to make ends meet. "Necessity compelled us to practice poverty in the strictest manner," the sisters recorded in the *Annals of the Indianapolis, Indiana House*, their chronicle of yearly activities.[1] The community offered some support, and the sisters collected donations, including cash but also material goods such as kitchen utensils, plows, pews, muslin, a coffee mill, bushels of coal, cords of wood, cows, chickens, hogs, and ducks. The most useful donations were those that afforded the nuns the capacity to sustain themselves financially, such as a sewing machine or "the necessaries for laundry work, such as tubs, washboards, and a small mangle."[2] In the early years, the sisters made their own clothes, took in washing, and tried their hands at bleaching hats and bonnets. They had a short-lived chair caning business, did tailoring and clothing altering, and tended their garden.[3]

Despite this industriousness, the house remained poor and the conditions of labor were difficult at best. The grounds were under construction for many years, as the sisters moved into one unfinished building and then another, upgrading their lodgings and workplaces slowly. Construction and renovation were often delayed and utilities sometimes shut off for lack of funds, exacerbating the difficulties and the feeling of precariousness and uncertainty.[4] In the beginning, lacking doors and windows, "the many crevices let in the bitter cold," especially in the laundry where the women were "worst off."[5] The sisters recorded extremely low temperatures in the laundry during the winter of 1874/75, and they reported that "the water freezing in the tubs before the clothes were out of them," "the ground floor was a sheet of ice," and "the water froze as it dripped from the clothes, or fell from the tubs to the floor." It was noted that a sister, having stood at the wringer "while one of the children was turning it," was unable to move, her shoes frozen to the floor. She needed that "child" to "heat a poker and run it around the soles of [the sister's shoes] so that she could get away."[6]

Clearly, the sisters' financial needs were as real as their sincere intentions to rescue "fallen" women and girls. Still, one wonders on balance what this meant for the experiences of the people living and working in the house. Although everybody worked, the labor was not equally distributed, particularly as the population grew. The institution divided its residents into different classes, with the sisters (nuns) at the top and the others arrayed below them according to age and perceived degree of sinfulness. Some classes were worked harder than others, and those assigned to the hardest labor suffered quite severely.

The *Annals*, along with financial records found among the sisters' records in the Archdiocesan Archives of Indianapolis, demonstrate how dependent on outside assistance the Indianapolis HGS was in its early years.[7] Good Shepherd houses in other U.S. cities sent donations to help their newest franchise get on its feet: bedclothes, some cash, and items to be sold at a fundraising bazaar, as well as a chest of tea and bouquets for the altar. A donated piece of property was valuable enough that the sisters sold it to pay the contractor for brickwork. The Chicago House of the Good Shepherd also sent an "out-sister," someone designated to work outside the convent itself, in the community. The out-sister was "welcome as the flowers of May" because she could be assigned to collect donations for the new building. Still, between the fruits of the out-sister's efforts, the generous donations from benefactors, the sale of the property, and the proceeds from the bazaar, the house took in only $290—an amount that could not, as they had hoped, defray expenses on the building.[8] What would turn out to enable the growth of the institution was monies earned through its residents' labor. In this pursuit, the sisters experimented with all sorts of potentially profitable enterprises, ultimately settling on sewing and laundry.

The sewing sector began in 1873, the sisters' first year in Indianapolis, with one sewing machine purchased on an installment plan and another donated by a Mrs. Tate.[9] Another machine was donated a few years later, in 1876.[10] Many people in the community commissioned sewing projects in this early period, and most of them were performed by the sisters themselves because at the time they had few "children," as they called their wards.[11] A benefactor commissioned them to sew for his clothing house, Gent's, providing "all the work we could do for the first year."[12] In 1875, they added work from the "New York Store," a dry goods store in Indianapolis, thanks to which, they noted gratefully, "we were liberally supplied with sewing."[13] The sisters noted that they began to make underclothes for "ladies and children," which the out-sister traveled the state to sell.[14] The sewing work brought in modest amounts of money at first, allowing them, for example, to turn the gas back on in 1873.[15] By 1892, they stayed "constantly busy trying to fill all the orders in the laundry department." They also did fine sewing and made shirts for stores.[16]

The laundry work also began almost as soon as the sisters set up at their first house in 1873. From the lectern, Father Bessonies, the priest who had urged the order to come to Indianapolis, exhorted members of the congregation to help the house by offering the sisters work.[17] A congregant soon obeyed, knocking on the door to offer some handwashing. Another soon followed, bringing two washtubs.[18] Having no facilities early on, the nuns did the washing in an outdoor shed. This would prove to be the beginning of a very profitable operation.[19]

The laundry expanded slowly during the first few years. In the first year, a nun from the nearby Sisters of Providence sent all the clothes from their boarders and "did all she could to procure washing from others."[20] In 1874, the HGS moved to its new, but still unfinished, building, where the workers could do laundry in the basement, hanging the clothes on the rafters to dry. There they began to do washing for a café attached to the Union Depot, a busy train station downtown.[21] The proprietor of the café helped them acquire tubs, washboards, and other equipment.[22] By 1882, the sisters had constructed a dedicated laundry facility that would eventually include a washhouse, ironing room, and packing room.[23] There they continued to do the washing by hand until 1885, when it appears they received their first washing machine.[24] In 1887, they built an additional level on to the laundry and added the highly profitable technology of steam.[25] Once the laundry was set up, it became "the basic source of income for the establishment."[26]

The division of labor in the HGS was strictly regulated according to the residents' status, or "class." When the Indianapolis house was first founded, there were only two classes of residents, sisters and penitents, also referred to as the Grande class. Eventually, a four-category system emerged, composed of Nuns, or Virgin Sisters, Grandes, Magdalens, and Preservates.[27]

The sisters were the leaders, the decision makers, and the most privileged of the four classes. In the early years of the Indianapolis house, the sisters worked alongside the other women there, as all labor was needed. They performed a range of duties, including the domestic work of cooking, cleaning, and tending the garden and the industrial labors of sewing and laundry. As new classes entered and expanded, the duties shifted. The nuns were able to assume an instructor's position, teaching the others and overseeing the work. By 1874, it was noted that there was one sister "caring for the washing and ironing-rooms" and another was the "mistress of sewing."[28] Other jobs the sisters retained at this time included baking the altar bread, cooking the meals, serving in the refectory, attending to the farm work, performing "general house-work," and being mistress of the children.[29] By 1903, a newspaper feature reported that the sisters' duties were "entirely that of managing the institution and directing work in the different classes."[30]

All the other residents at the house were subordinate to the sisters, as exemplified in the sisters' use of the term "children" for their charges of all ages.[31] Every "child" was expected to work, contributing to the development of the house and to the sustenance of the classes. The sisters claimed that talent, or lack thereof, would determine what work a resident was required to perform.[32] The finer tasks were reserved for those the nuns judged worthy: "Those who have the aptitude, and are considered deserving, are taught music, singing, stenography, embroidery, etc."[33] This designation of who was "deserving" indicates that the sisters may have used moral judgment and not an assessment of ability to assign tasks. In fact, in the sources I reviewed, only members of the Grande class are ever referenced as working in the laundry, the most grueling of positions. Likewise, members of the Magdalen and Preservate classes are shown to work in fine sewing and embroidery and are never mentioned in conjunction with the laundry.[34]

The Grande class, also referred to as the Penitent class, consisted of women and girls who had "wandered from the path of virtue, and are now trying to reform their characters and fit them for a more successful course in the world when they leave the shelter of the Convent."[35] The Grande class toiled in the laundry and with sewing. In 1903, a newspaper reported that the "work provided for the penitents is a garment-making factory, which is operated on contract work, and in a laundry, which a great deal of public washing is done."[36] By 1919, the Grande class was making men's union suits (long underwear) in a new sewing room.[37] The new room enclosed "everything one could wish for," such as baths, toilets, drinking water, lavatories, brooms, all on the same floor where they work, "so that there is no necessity for . . . leaving the sewing-room, until, dinner hour."[38]

Working in the laundry was hazardous. In 1888, while the steam laundry was being constructed and new machinery was being put into place, a woman from the Grande class, a "child" called Colette, put her hand in the mangle just as the steam was turned on. "Her screams were dreadful to hear." Her "whole hand was caught up above the wrist" and "had to be amputated with part of her arm." It is unclear why she did not remain in the house long after this accident. Following two other accidents, the mother superior "had all the machinery cased in with wire screens."[39]

The sisters anticipated that some of the penitents would stay for the remainder of their life. In 1889, a newspaper stated that "for the distressed women of the city," the HGS offered "a permanent home, where they may indicate by their future life their sincerity in a desire to lead a higher and nobler life."[40] This perhaps was beneficial to the house in that it secured free labor for the entirety of a woman's life.

A third class of women was the Magdalens. Once a woman had "fallen," she could not obtain the spiritually pure and virginal status required to become a sister. Yet some who had sinned, including some HGS residents from the Grande class, decided to devote themselves to the service of God in the religious life. As a compromise, "in order that they may become of service to the Church," the HGS allowed those who had resolved to live a better life to undergo a dedicatory process and become a Magdalen.[41]

The consecration process to become a Magdalen was arduous. The Magdalen-to-be, or postulant, received the holy habit, the "black dress of the Consecrated children."[42] After two years of prayer and penance, a postulant could pronounce her first vows, rendering her "dedicated to God by the vows of religion" and confirming her as a professed Sister Magdalen.[43] Once she was permitted to take vows, a Magdalen took them yearly until the tenth year, when she could take her final vow, which consecrated her to the cloister for the remainder of her life.[44]

Magdalens labored at difficult but highly valued tasks, "always under the immediate direction of one of the Sisters of the Good Shepherd. Their lives are devoted to prayer and penance, interspersed with hours of work, mainly embroidery, fine sewing, etc."[45] They made fancy articles and even painted. Their embroidery could be found "in the wealthiest homes."[46] According to a 1903 newspaper profile on the house, "The Magdalens, as a rule, are apt in needlework and in painting. Their schedule of hours for the day is much the same as that for the 'penitents,' except that at 3 o'clock they meet in their cloister chapel to repeat their offices, and at 6 o'clock they meet in the cloister for meditation. They do not converse more than is necessary, and they observe the spirit of contemplative service."[47]

Finally, the Preservate class was made up of younger girls, between the ages of ten and fifteen, who were not considered "fallen" but were in need of protection. They needed, or so the sisters thought, to be "raised properly" and to be "saved from ruin." Preservates came to the house from a range of conditions, "taken from the streets, from parents who were not capable of raising them properly, and from other sources of destitution."[48] The sisters prided themselves on the service they could provide to such girls, whose admittance to the HGS, they thought, would "make of them virtuous women" and would be a "sure prevention."[49]

The Preservates were not expected to remain permanently at the convent, unlike the "fallen women." The sisters intended to furnish the Preservates "a good home for a time, and prepare for them an honorable career."[50] The nuns claimed, therefore, that the Preservates attended school in the morning and busied themselves with sewing and other "similar handiwork" in the afternoon.[51] This class was established in 1889; prior to then, girls younger than fifteen years of age were not admitted into the house.[52]

Despite the increasing income from the laundry in the last decades of the nineteenth century, the Annals reveal that the house continued to experience a financial roller coaster of borrowing for construction, falling into debt, encountering difficulties, paying the debt, and then securing new loans. The sisters secured various loans over the years as their needs expanded. Their debt rose during developmental stages and fell as they paid off interest and capital with income earned through their work and donations. When they liquidated existing debt, they quickly secured new loans in the pursuit of continued growth. This cycle reveals the logic that guided their institution: building, not the devotional duties of charity and austerity but the growth imperatives of capital, yoked to spirituality through a sense of the morality, even the godliness, of labor.

In 1885, after eleven years of residence, the sisters commenced their first improvements to the house's physical structure. They took out a loan of $2,000 for the purpose of turning the attic into a "sleeping apartment."[53] In 1886, before the debt was paid, the mother superior was already planning the erection of another building, a monastery. There are discrepancies in the available records as to the final cost of the monastery, with estimates being between $30,000 and $40,000.[54] The monastery was a tremendous expense for the order. As they admitted in the Annals, the mother "had to plan and scheme for means to pay the erection of the building."[55]

In May 1887, with just $1,000 in hand, the sisters began building their terra-cotta monastery, which included a wing for the Magdalens.[56] Throughout the following month, the house received pledges amounting to "nearly one fourth of the amount necessary" to finish the building.[57] To fund the remaining amount, they took a bank loan of $15,000 at 6 percent.[58] It was at this time, the sisters noted, that a good benefactor suggested they add another story to the laundry and install a steam plant, "in order to accomplish more work, and be in a better position to liquidate our debt." [59] The sisters recognized that this development would improve their ability to do more and better work.[60] The development of the steam laundry at the house began in 1887, while the new monastery was under construction, and was completed in 1888.[61]

Construction of the steam laundry required substantial funds. The benefactor who had suggested its erection paid $3,000 for its construction.[62] A $25 monthly contribution from the county commissioners to buy coal also helped.[63] The Provincial House in Louisville lent the Indianapolis HGS $10,000 without interest, which the sisters called a "great charity." [64] They seem to have used this interest-free $10,000 loan as payment toward the $15,000 loan. Then the sisters borrowed again, mortgaging their property from another lender. Laundry work was central to the liquidation of the debt on their home, the sisters reported in 1887.[65] The steam laundry "netted a neat little amount" each month, and they soon secured "a very profitable trade," allowing them "to pay the interest and some small capitals promptly." [66]

In 1889, the sisters' monastery, including a chapel and a wing for the use of the Magdalens, was completed. At the dedication ceremony, the sisters held a door collection, charging 10¢ per person and 25¢ per family, plus accepting any other donations people chose to offer.[67] The door collection clearly did not cover the heavy debt on their new building, so the sisters solicited patronage of their needlework, which they planned to "continue through all seasons." [68] They also solicited "Laundry Trade" for their "St. Joseph's Laundry" as a means of supporting their many poor children.[69]

The sisters built and built. They added an infirmary to the

laundry building in 1895 and constructed a new boiler room after the old one was condemned in 1899.[70] Around this time, a third story was added above the laundry for use by the Grande class, whose area had been overcrowded.[71] The sisters did not specify the sources of funds for these expenses, but it was surely the same mix of labor, donations, and loans that financed all their projects. In 1900, the house was $30,000 in debt.[72] When Bessonies died in 1901, the attention his funeral brought to the house provoked a wave of new customers for laundry work, ensuring "the sustenance" of all house residents.[73] In 1905, the mother superior built an addition to the laundry and felt flush enough to install stained glass windows in the chapels and in the sanctuary.[74]

In the spring of 1906, the nuns constructed a new building for the Grande class, which was finished by December that same year.[75] In 1908, a permit was issued for a new convent that was to cost $20,000.[76] The sisters had not yet paid off the debt accrued for the Grande class building when they decided to defer their current debt and to begin building a three-story monastery for the Magdalens.[77] In April 1909, the Magdalen monastery (the Magdala) was finished.[78] That same year, to their "annoyance," they had to pay $923 for a sewerage tax, spending the "nest egg" they had hoped to use for another new building.[79]

While the HGS managed to expand, competitors in the laundry industry found their businesses in peril. They even adopted some of the abusive practices seen in the HGS in order to maintain profitability. In 1899, the proprietor of a local commercial laundry, who was facing criticism over the treatment of his employees, penned the following letter to the editor of the *Indianapolis News*:

In reference to working, or overworking the girls in the laundries, I wish to say this: How can you expect me to do otherwise? The Sisters of the Good Shepherd come in direct competition with me. They canvass from house to house for laundry work, have a large number of girls to whom they pay nothing whatever, whom they compel to do men's work, and keep them at it all hours. Besides, they pay no taxes on their buildings, machinery or their business. This is the sort of competition I must meet. If my competitors, the House of the Good Shepherd, are made to pay taxes, I shall feel justified in doing more for our girls. As it is, we must meet pauper labor.[80]

The unpaid labor of HGS inmates ensured the house's competitive place in the local laundry business.

Women and girls came to the HGS voluntarily and involuntarily and through a multitude of avenues. Some women clearly arrived there voluntarily, showing up at the door needing assistance or riding back with the out-sister from her collection tours. The sisters reported that on the very day the order arrived, February 26, 1873, "a poor woman . . . her old shawl dragging in the mud" ran to them, becoming their "first sheep of the fold in Indianapolis."[81] Another "poor stray sheep," as the sisters characterized her, presented herself at their door in 1874 and remained there until her death a few years later.[82] In 1879, an "old lady" came to them "seeking a quiet home, and as we had no Out-Sister . . . we were delighted to have her come. She was quite a help. She went to market for us, and did much of the outside work . . . she went around from door to door, selling fancy and useful articles. She was a very saintly person, inclined to be austere to herself. When she was home she helped in the kitchen."[83] In 1881, a woman claimed that the Virgin Mary appeared to her in a dream and guided her steps to the HGS. The sisters noted that the woman "asked to be received into the house," then noticed that one of her hands was "crippled." She had been born with one of her hands having "no fingers at all." She worked in the laundry, and it was noted that "to her we owe the real establishment of the ironing-room" and that she was "a beautiful ironer, and taught many of the children how to do good work."[84] In 1895, "a young girl applied for admission to the Grande Class. She was in the last stages of consumption and scarcely able to walk. She was admitted."[85] In 1921, an officer brought a girl to the house. She had gone to him for help, telling him that "he could take her to the Good Shepherd. . . . Her mother was a dope-fiend, her father in the penitentiary." She was admitted into the house.[86] These voluntary commitments seem to have been the exception, though they were noted in some detail in the *Annals*. Clearly, favorable details were more interesting to the writers of such reports.

Involuntary commitments were more common at the HGS. As Natalie Medley explores in chapter 12, women were brought to the HGS by police and were sentenced to the house by the courts. Moreover, between the years 1877 and 1881, prisoners were committed by the city of Indianapolis to the HGS. Family members and clergy also placed young women and girls there. To cite just a couple examples, in 1875, a woman was placed there by her father. She escaped and was brought back by city authorities.[87] In 1895, a woman addicted to morphine was brought by her husband to join the Grande class.[88]

No matter the mode of entry, a resident's labor and revenue were immensely important to the survival and growth of the house. The sisters sought out new admissions, particularly valuing those who could contribute their labor. While it is apparent that the young women and girls endured extreme working conditions, perhaps more insidious were the manipulations of people and situations that seemingly contradict the moral and religious standard the sisters claimed to exemplify. A few examples stand out from the sisters' own records.

In 1877, the out-sister badly wanted to go to the novitiate in Louisville to prepare for receiving the "coveted treasure—the white habit." To appease the out-sister, the mother superior of the house told her that she could go only "when she would succeed in collecting a certain big sum of money to help us with our work here." The mother, not wanting to lose her services as an out-sister, quoted an amount she thought to be so enormous that the out-sister, with the means she had of receiving it, would never succeed in collecting it. The mother superior showed "unbounded surprise" when the sister achieved the required amount and lamented her leaving as an "immense sacrifice."[89] Thus, the out-sister was only allowed to finish her religious training when her labor and income were no longer critical to the house.

Another example is from 1907. When developing the new building for the Magdalens, a city ordinance was passed requiring all large buildings to be fireproof, necessitating the use of steel and the minimal use of wood. Because of an oversight on the part of ordinance officials, the architect commissioned to build the Magdalene monastery did not receive notice of this ordinance. Since the fault was with the ordinance officials, the HGS did not have to follow the updated codes. "Under the new code, requiring a fire-proof building, we would have had to expend four times the amount that the old way cost us." The sisters were ecstatic: "Was this not a miraculous escape for us?" That the sisters counted this a "very Providential matter" indicates that they were not interested in safety, only in the development of space for their labor force at minimal expense. For an order supposedly devoted to the "protection" and "preservation" of young women and girls, such calculations are striking.[90]

Finally, in the spring of 1908, a doctor came to the HGS to treat a child who was ill. He "promptly fulfilled his duty and reported a case of Diphtheria to the city authorities." With that the health officer placed a blue card, meaning quarantine, on their front door. "This meant ostracism and an immense loss," for the house would not be allowed to traffic their laundry. The mother superior was "panic-stricken" and "pleaded with the man of law to spare [them]" and allow them to resume their business. The health officer, a "big-hearted Irishman" whose sister was a superior in a convent in England, was sympathetic to the sisters' plight. Nonetheless, he dutifully refused the sisters' request to reopen.

But the sisters were in luck. The *Annals* recorded, "Fortunately for us the child had died during the night . . . and her mother arriving from a distance, took the body away, before morning." They pleaded with the Irish health officer to remove the quarantine, and he reported to the Indianapolis Board of Health that the child "was dead and buried, and no symptoms appeared. . . . Perfect isolation, etc.!" The sisters thought the officer provided an "act of charity" when he "elaborated the circumstances to a degree!!!" in telling the main office that that the six-year-old had been isolated, that the house "was reeking with disinfectants," and that the sisters "depend on charity, and their daily income of customer work and washing. . . . They and their children would starve if quarantined." The sisters knew the health officer was lying for them. After this they looked on him as a "real benefactor."[91] The sisters were less concerned with the child's life than with their income, though they

Girl Loses Arm in Wringer

An 18-year-old Indianapolis girl lost her right arm this morning when it was accidentally caught in a wringer of a washing machine.

She was identified by police as Mary Louise Acton, who lives at the Sisters of Good Shepherd Home, 111 W. Raymond. The St. Joseph laundry in which she was working is adjacent to the home.

A police report said the girl's arm was torn off below the elbow.

She was rushed to St. Vincent's Hospital in a city ambulance where her condition is described as fair.

Indianapolis Star, May 8, 1951.

did note that the child had "received private baptism," so her soul, presumably, was secured.

The order claimed to be devoted to the care of desperate women and girls in the community. Their need for profit and expansion was based in the belief that they were the "greatest charity of all charities" and "the desire to succeed at all costs."[92] That is surely why they allowed terrible labor conditions to prevail throughout the institution. It was the extraction of maximum profit from the inmates that allowed the sisters to continuously expand capacity, taking in more and more "children." The HGS, including its laundry operations, remained operational until the 1960s.

14

Minnie and Mamie

Lara Campbell

On February 12, 1907, twenty-six-year-old Mamie Smith filed a $25,000 lawsuit against the House of the Good Shepherd (HGS) in Indianapolis, alleging she was held there against her will for six years.[1] Mamie claimed that the sisters who ran the house prevented her from communicating with friends on the outside and provided her with no education. Further, Mamie's time in the house had transformed the "strong and healthy girl" into "a physical wreck."[2] Forced to perform unpaid labor in the laundry, she contracted rheumatism working without rest on cold, damp floors. Mamie said she remained in the house so many years "only because the walls were too high for her to scale."[3] In 1906, Mamie did manage to escape. She filed her lawsuit against the HGS the following year.

In 1925, another former Indianapolis HGS inmate, Minnie Morrison, wrote a memoir titled *Awful Revelations of Life in Convent of Good Shepherd*. She aimed to "enlighten people with facts of what is really going on in our beautiful America today."[4] Born in 1897, her childhood was unstable. From the age of three she was raised by her grandmother. But when her grandmother died, the juvenile court placed her in an orphanage, the Indianapolis Children's Guardian Home. She was adopted by several families but was always returned to the Guardian Home.[5]

When Minnie was ten, a case worker took her to the HGS: "I will never forget the creepy feeling I had when that door to the convent opened by those unseen hands," Minnie wrote.[6] The girl was stripped of her clothes and, worse, stripped of her real name and identity. A sister told her, "We change all the girls' names here, and so your name will be Teresa Shepherd."[7] Served food with roaches, forced to work in the laundry, and beaten, Minnie soon realized that she was trapped.[8]

As my colleagues argue, institutions like the Indianapolis HGS should be considered the first separate prisons for women in the United States. Mamie's and Minnie's stories help us to understand how these prisons affected the young women who were held at these institutions. These narratives provide evidence of abusive conditions inside the institution but also give us examples of young women and girls who refused to conform. Both Minnie and Mamie escaped the convent and made public the horrors they were subjected to inside it. Although both bravely spoke up, their voices have not been properly heard. Their contemporaries and many historians have dismissed their stories as anti-Catholic propaganda.

During the opening decades of the twentieth century, the United States witnessed a tremendous outpouring of books, pamphlets, journals, and newspapers promoting anti-Catholic themes.[9] Self-proclaimed activists like Louis Joseph King traveled all over the United States to advance conspiracy theories about "the takeover of America by Catholic boogie men."[10] Catholic clerics and lay spokespeople wrote rebuttals to these attacks, waged legal battles charging publishers for slanderous remarks, and produced large sums of money to neutralize anti-Catholic propaganda.[11]

Some of this material attacked the houses kept by the Order of the Good Shepherd and similar institutions. Newspapers and magazines ran cartoons depicting girls imprisoned. They also portrayed convents as impenetrable fortresses outside the bounds of the law and American values. They penned grotesque accounts of life within convent walls to fuel charges of Catholic enslavement of innocent girlhood and femininity. In April 1914, for example, the anti-papal newspaper *The Menace* reported that two teenage girls had escaped from a Santa Barbara convent. A four-day chase by police ended when the fugitives "collapsed from exhaustion."[12] The article condemned the "torture and suffering inflicting upon innocent girlhood in these hell holes of iniquity."[13] While anti-Catholic sentiment certainly produced exaggerated accounts of the crimes committed in convents and similar places, some of the scandalous tales also harbored truth.

Historian James H. Madison describes Minnie Morrison's 1925 memoir as a "modest Indiana version" of the "anti-Catholic stories [that] often appeared in print in the form of lurid escaped nun tales."[14] Although many anti-Catholic narratives were likely "fake news," it is important that we do not dismiss all testimonies as mere conspiracy theories. Historians like James Smith and Rie Croll have revealed the disturbing histories of Magdalene Laundries in multiple countries, including Ireland and Canada. In 2011, the United Nations Committee Against Torture recommended an investigation of the Irish state's responsibility for the wrongful imprisonment and systematic abuse of young women and girls in such facilities.[15] In this light, Minnie's story deserves reexamination.[16]

According to her memoir, Minnie arrived at the Indianapolis HGS in 1907 and soon found that her new home was a sweatshop. Not tall enough to see over the ironing board, Minnie had to stand on a wooden box to iron her quota of five hundred handkerchiefs a day.[17] The girls received one clean dress a month and clean underwear every two weeks. They were slapped, punched, and flogged with sewing machine belts. Minnie witnessed many residents beaten so violently they lost consciousness.[18] She recalled a dungeon where the girls were kept for weeks if they disobeyed.[19]

Some of Minnie's claims seem improbable. She remembered, for example, catching a glimpse of a man trapped underneath the floor:

I was one of the girls who were sent over to clean the parlors. As we were brushing the rugs, we heard what we thought was a groan. We could not think where it came from, but it seemed very plain. All at once, a section of the floor under my feet began to move downward. I jumped back just in time. This trap door moved down only just a little way, and we looked through the cracks, and just below I saw a man's head. He looked up and said, "My God, let me out of here."

Just then Mother Priscilla came in the door, and said, "What are you girls doing in here?" I said, "Mother, there is a man down there." She called me a little liar, and came over there and boxed my ears. Then she sent me back to the class room. I was never sent over to help clean the parlors again.

I have always thought this man was the one she referred to when she said that the Devil had taken him down through the floor.[20]

She also claimed that as punishment for wearing rings, a nun strapped her to a water pipe and burned her with a hot poker while the engineer held her down. Four of her fingers were severely burned where the sister used the poker to melt Minnie's rings. Forced to work despite this injury, the wounds did not heal. After three weeks, the sisters finally sent Minnie to a hospital where her fingers had to be amputated. Minnie was told to lie and tell the other inmates that her hand had been caught in a machine.[21]

While Minnie's claims seem extreme, the sisters' own records corroborate them. According to the HGS *Annals of the Indianapolis, Indiana House*, "in 1916, one of our dear children, through her own fault, had her hand crushed in the mangle of laundry." The sisters performed countless acts of penance and prayer, the nuns reported, but "man proposes and God disposes," so several of the girl's fingers had to be amputated. The *Annals* contain an interesting disclaimer: "The girl made a written statement acknowledging that she did the deed of her own accord, but we feel that in some years hence she will try to blame the convent for it. This has been our experience of the gratitude for what is done for the uplift of many who are placed under our care." [22]

The date of this ghastly trauma suggests that Minnie was the girl whose injury was documented in the *Annals*, as does Minnie's account of an attestation she was forced to sign:

While I was so sick that I did not know what I was doing, the Sisters from HGS brought me a paper and pencil, and said that I would write on this paper that I would never sue this institution for damages, and that I had run my hand through a mangle by carelessness. While I was half unconscious, I signed this paper. I was so nervous that the Sister held paper and helped me to write it. I really did not know what I was signing at the time. [23]

After nearly fourteen years of psychological, emotional, and physical abuse at the HGS, Minnie escaped in 1920 by taking one of the nun's keys and jumping over the fence into the path of a policeman, who assisted her with transportation. [24]

Newspaper accounts of escape attempts, many of them involving great risk, indicate that the HGS was holding women and girls against their will. On February 17, 1894, according to the *Indianapolis News*, Grace House and Laura Larsh escaped from the HGS in Indianapolis: "The girls told of stories of cruelty at the House of the Good Shepherd; said it was really a prison, with a dungeon and barred windows; that inmates were whipped with a strap on the naked flesh and punished in various cruel ways." Sister Vincent, responding to the charges against her, "acknowledged having struck Grace House, but denied catching her by the hair. She says that she slapped her because she was impudent one day in the refectory." Sister Angelo claimed amnesia, saying "she did not think she had ever struck anyone of the girls; she might have done so, but she could not remember." As for the dungeon, the mother superior, Sister Mary of St. Ursula, admitted, "This was built for a prison you know. . . . Some of the cells are down in the basement, but they are not dark and they are seldom used for places of punishment."[25] Perhaps the man whose moans Minnie reported hearing beneath the floorboard was in one of these cells.

The escape stories are numerous. Ella Noon, aged twenty-two, tragically died from a fall while trying to escape from the HGS in 1897. She hung from a windowsill by her hands and dropped, striking her spine on the roof.[26] When a journalist from the *Indianapolis News* investigated, the mother superior insisted that no adult was detained against her will, and the underage girls were there by consent of a parent or guardian. Furthermore, she objected to any "cross-questioning" about the incident.[27] The *Pharos-Tribune* reported that the mother superior was "reticent," saying little except that Ella's death was a "willful accident."[28]

In 1906, sixteen-year-old Mary Burke suffered a compound fracture of her left leg after jumping from a second-story window onto the sidewalk.[29] In 1907, Marie Miller and Ethel Darbyshire, both aged thirteen, "scaled a high fence and then boarded a traction car for Muncie."[30] In 1908, sixteen-year-old Katherine Nickum apparently judged her only hope to be to plummet sixty feet out of a third-story window. She was found unconscious and suffered a fractured ankle.[31] Stella Nickolick and Helen Shikoski, both aged fourteen at the time of their escape attempts, tried to flee the HGS in 1918 and 1926, respectively. That so many young women and girls risked their lives to run from the house makes clear the HGS was not a safe space.[32]

Resistance to confinement at the HGS also took the form of lawsuits, as in the Mamie Smith case that opened this chapter. Born Mamie Sullivan in April 1881 in Terre Haute, Indiana, her mother died during her birth, leaving her father to raise her. She was baptized by family friend Reverend Schnell, from St. Patrick's Church. As a teenager, Mamie butted heads with her father. They quarreled about her short-lived marriage at the age of eighteen and over an accusation of theft by her employer. Unable to control Mamie, her father brought her to the HGS in Indianapolis in 1899. After her 1906 escape, Mamie took refuge with the Brickert family in Indianapolis and married one of their relatives, Gustav Smith, in 1907.[33] It was around this time that Mamie filed her lawsuit against the HGS.

The sisters acted quickly and energetically to refute Mamie's charge of wrongful imprisonment. They hired Sydney B. Davis, an attorney who assured them they were being "unduly nervous."[34] He considered Mamie's claims a bluff and predicted she would demand money to settle the issue quietly. The sisters wrote to Mamie's father and stepmother, priest, and associates in an attempt to dig up dirt on her to compel her to drop the claim.[35] As it became clear that the suit would be heard in court, the sisters sought counsel from other houses in the Midwest that had faced similar challenges. A representative of the HGS in Detroit, Michigan, informed the Indianapolis mother superior that they had recently been defeated in court regarding a comparable claim of wrongful imprisonment: "The lawyers and jurors on the opponents' side were Freemasons, A.P.A.s & oddfellows; it is not surprising that God's work should suffer at their hands."[36] The HGS also consulted the attorney for the Louisville sisters of the Good Shepherd, who assured the Indianapolis HGS that "we have had so many suits of this character to defend . . . (all of which we have won)."[37]

In their records, the sisters of the Good Shepherd dramatically describe the lawsuit and subsequent trials as a "heavy shadow"[38] and a "laden cross which heaven deigned send us."[39] After many delays, the case finally went to trial in 1910. The sisters lamented that many of them, including the mother superior, had to "appear in the public court . . . and listen to the abuse and ridicule of everything sacred to our holy religion."[40] Apparently, the sisters considered testifying in court a fate worse than death: "An old Outdoor Sister had also been summoned, but she had happily gone to her eternal reward."[41]

A curious public crowded into Marion Circuit Court to watch the proceedings. "The case is attracting much attention and yesterday afternoon every available chair in the courtroom was occupied and nearly 100 persons were standing in the lobby," a newspaper reported early in the trial.[42] E.W. Brickert, the uncle of Mamie's new husband and a self-proclaimed Baptist preacher, was Mamie's attorney. Brickert was virulently anti-Catholic and believed the church enslaved innocent American girls "to enrich some heartless corporation."[43]

On May 11, 1910, Brickert called Mamie to the stand. Her testimony focused on the relentless dehumanization and lack of freedom she experienced at the HGS. She recalled that she was not allowed to call herself Mamie during her six years inside the house and instead was given the name " 'Clara' and the number, 'Cross P. 16' . . . the 'Cross P' standing for Cross Penitent class." She described her first escape attempt. She fled the HGS through the engine room, wearing the "plain and apparently much worn and faded gown of light blue flannel" the sisters made her wear. The dress was displayed before the jury. She found refuge in the home of the Brickert family near the convent. They protected her for several days until the police came to retrieve her.[44]

Brickert called other witnesses who supported Mamie's narrative. A young woman who had been confined along with her sister at the HGS described the meager food, the long work hours, and the lack of education at the house. She also remembered the nuns' inhumanity: "Her sister died at the convent, the witness said, and she was never able to learn where the body was buried. After her marriage she stated she attempted to find where the body was and was given $10 by a sister. This, she said, she supposed was to keep her quiet."[45]

For their part, the HGS lawyers called witnesses who attested that the institution was clean and well run. Among those witnesses was the president of the Marion County Board of State Charities, "who said she has visited the home often during the last ten years and that it has always been properly conducted."[46] Their strongest line of defense was to undercut Mamie's claims that she had been personally mistreated. They argued that Mamie had exhibited no signs of distress and was even "trusted around the farm," meaning she had freedom of movement to move about the "outside parlors" and even deliver messages "down the road."[47] "No other girl seemed to be as devoted, generous and handy," they affirmed.[48]

In a dramatic flourish, the defense lawyers produced a set of letters they claimed Mamie had written to her father while she was confined at the HGS, letters whose existence "was a complete surprise to the attorneys for the plaintiff."[49] The letters seem to be written by a young woman who was content and appreciative, especially of the special events the sisters organized for holidays.[50] Some of Mamie's family members, including her father and stepmother, confirmed the authenticity of the letters and the fact that Mamie had never reported being mistreated in the home and even "seemed affectionate toward the sisters at the time she left."[51]

Used as exhibits in the trial, these handwritten letters remain among the sisters' preserved files on the case. While the letters appear cheerful, there is an undertone of desperation. The author repeatedly conveyed how much she longed to be with her family: "I would give anything in the world to see you."[52] If Mamie did write these letters, interpreting their meaning is far from straightforward, despite the HGS's attempt to do so in court. Under extreme stress, and knowing the sisters would read the letters, she may have been pretending contentment to gain the sisters' trust in the hope they would release her. It is also possible that the sisters told Mamie exactly what to write, as in the case of Minnie Morrison's coerced statement. However, during the trial, Mamie denied having written the letters at all, and her lawyer declared them to be forgeries.[53]

While the letters might have sunk Mamie's case, it was the testimony of Father Francis Gavisk, rector of St. John's Catholic Church and vice president of the Society of the Good Shepherd, that would prove most damning for the HGS. Gavisk affirmed that when the "inmates" entered the HGS, they were stripped of their real names and kept under constant guard: "there is a high wall and fence about the grounds and . . . inmates are not permitted to leave."[54] They were not allowed visitors and were not paid for their work. He also admitted there was no education for the inmates and that all mail was subject to the strictest supervision.[55] Father Gavisk was also seen prompting witnesses by shaking or nodding his head as they presented their testimony. Moreover, another witness, an Evansville banker and president of the Vanderburgh County Board of Children's Guardians who had attested to the cleanliness and well-regulated nature of the home, admitted under cross-examination that the sisters paid him $50 for his testimony.[56]

Mamie was vindicated after the two-week trial; she won her case against the HGS and was awarded $4,000.[57] The HGS sisters and their allies saw the verdict as a product of prejudice, claiming the jurors were "bigoted non-Catholics."[58]

Mamie did not enjoy her victory for long. The HGS quickly sought and obtained an appeal, citing witnesses who claimed to have seen "some of the jury talking to . . . enemies of our cause."[59] The judge granted a new trial; in his view "the preponderance of evidence was against the plaintiff."[60] In response, Mamie's lawyer contacted Father Gavisk, warning him that they planned to pursue the appeal aggressively: "You know that it will be much worse than the last time. I know that reporters from some strong religious journals will attend the trial through out and report it and editorials will be written on it, which will not injure *us* in the least." [61]

The second trial was held in the Superior Court of Marion County before Judge Vinson Carter in April 1911. Again, crowds gathered to watch the proceedings. One newspaper observed that "the number of women among the spectators was noticeable." [62] We have less information about the course of the second trial, but it appears that two former inmates testified they had no recollection of mistreatment and they were grateful to the sisters for helping them. [63] The *Indianapolis Star* reported that "on cross-examination the defense compelled Mrs. Smith to go into the details of her past life" in an attempt to undermine her credibility as a witness. [64] The jury spent hours deliberating and, after receiving additional instructions from the judge, returned a verdict in favor of the HGS. [65]

The Mamie Smith trial demonstrates the tenacity of the sisters' self-preservation. Their seething hatred for anyone they deemed "enemies" of the house can be seen plainly in the gleeful description of health problems suffered by one of Mamie's attorneys after the trial, which they considered a form of "retribution":

He gradually became a raving maniac! At first he was not dangerous, and they tried to keep him at his own house, tying him to a chair out on the porch, when he would need air. His tongue would not remain in his mouth, but hung out in a repulsive way. Passers-by would upbraid him, and ask if he remembered how he had used his tongue to revile the Sisters of the Good Shepherd? His case was sad in the extreme. Finally, he had to be put away to keep him secure. His tongue, even after his fearful death, hung out of his mouth down on his chest! Does this example not recall the words of St. Hilary: "Woe to him who lays a finger upon the spotless Spouse of Christ!" And another saying: "That no one ever yet persecuted the Catholic Church who did not come to a terrible end." [66]

The interests of the HGS came before the protection of any individual woman or girl. If the sisters really believed Mamie had fallen "into the hands of companions of the worst type," why didn't they express concern for her well-being? Instead, they sought to destroy her credibility and reputation. In the construction of their defense, the sisters presented Mamie in contradictory ways, sometimes as responsible and content and other times as easily manipulated and out of control, according to their own interests in the moment. We have little of Mamie's own words, but the record shows that her testimony remained consistent. Setting her story alongside the stories of other escapees and survivors reveals patterns. As someone with great empathy for Mamie Smith, as someone who knows what it means to have your credibility questioned because of the taint of criminality and incarceration, I wonder how differently history might be written if we take women's claims seriously.

Conclusion

Michelle Daniel Jones

This history of women and girls incarcerated in various institutions in the state of Indiana shows the value of excavating subjugated knowledge by those who have the shared experience of incarceration. The women and girls in this book experienced sexual and gendered violence, physical abuse, deprivations, isolation, experimentation, and torture at the hands of religious and secular individuals who believed that homes, laundries, reformatories, prisons, and other carceral institutions were the best options of refuge and reform. These many stories of state-sanctioned violence display how during a time of great precarity for women and girls, reformers legitimated the use of duress and abuse against them in the name "better outcomes."

The erosion of options for poor women at the close of the Civil War saw the proliferation of various carceral institutions explicitly designed to hold and house women and girls as the primary response to a surplus population problem. Lack of employment, racism, and the sexual and cultural constraints common to all women left some with theft, fraud, and sex work as their only options for survival. The state's response to poor, disenfranchised, disabled women and girls was to incarcerate them. The state and reformers built prisons and other institutions to house women and girls separate from congregate incarceration with men. The taint of criminality from detention in these institutions penalized these captives and limited their possibilities when they got out, compounding the harm already done. Many prison officials directed women into domestic labor, continuous incarceration, and marriage as viable solutions. Others preyed on them for sexual exploitation and profit. Officials in these carceral institutions were constantly burdened with how to make their institutions economically viable and, all too often, they extracted labor from women and girls in order to make their institutions function. Capitalism, religion, gender, and concepts of domesticity further limited their lives and agency. But women and girls met these challenges with resilience and tenacity, as seen in these stories. Reading these stories alongside dominant narratives offers a more complete account of Indiana women's carceral history and a more complex interpretation of white benevolent reformers. As Avery Gordon and Janice Radway said, "The power relations that characterize any historically embedded society are never as transparently clear as the names we give them imply."[1]

The state works to suppress and make invisible mass torture in carceral institutions like those highlighted in this book. Citizens cooperate with state violence and denials of state violence when we choose not to see and not to believe the stories of incarcerated women. A remaining and urgent question is: How much violence enacted upon incarcerated women is enough for the citizens for whom the system acts to demand and enact change?

By the nineteenth century, the growth of cities, blurred class lines, and personal and political changes in ideological perspectives on crime and criminality changed the state's approaches to social control. Self-policing was a thing of the past. By the late eighteenth century, old methods of punishment for crime, such as the public viewings of gallows and stocks, were thought barbaric and antiquated.[2] Sweeping efforts throughout the United States and in Indiana sought to make the punishment for crime humane and "incarceration seemed more humane than hanging and less brutal than whipping."[3]

Criminal justice extended beyond merely punishing crimes to include detention as a tool to "clean" and purify the social order, addressing perceived failings in families and the "faulty organization of society."[4] This new mandate combined with the state's increasing power for detention and with violence within prison systems to legitimize dehumanization and inequality.[5]

We show in this book how religious organizations like the Sisters of the Good Shepherd, who created Magdalene Laundries in the United States, and religious leaders like Rhoda Coffin and Sarah Smith, who created Protestant institutions like the Home for Friendless Women and the Reformatory Institution for Women and Girls, ran their facilities similarly. The presence of linen tablecloths and vases with flowers didn't create a safer or more humane prison for women and girls. What the women and girls experienced in these institutions is historically important in shaping attitudes toward female sexuality, identity, and societal reintegration that live on today. These institutions focused on controlling, silencing, and experimenting on the vulnerable and the marginalized. In fact, the initial premise of these institution is false: that to be reformed, redeemed, or helped, especially if labeled "fallen" or deviant, women must be incarcerated. The premise is false because it rests on the sexist idea that women must be removed from homes and society to prevent them from tainting "good" soldiers and "good" men or to keep them from being a burden on others. This premise has no regard for the structural inequities affecting women, especially during the period after the Civil War.

This project confirmed in many ways what we were living out in prison ourselves: that gender-responsive carceral systems criminalize the sexuality of women and girls and facilitate their silencing and disappearance, especially when coupled with religion. Operations are often corrupt because these heterotopic spaces of secrecy are without the real oversight and transparency needed to balance the unequal power dynamics. Therefore, what we now know about the first prison for women and what we already know about our own experience is that these spaces proliferate with gendered and sexual violence. This project also affirmed what we also knew intimately: a nonviolent woman-run correctional facility serving women is imaginary. We must be careful, then, with the latest gender-responsive programming.[6] We have to be careful when criminologists, sociologists, and the like focus on "reforming" or "tweaking" the existing system given that gendered and sexual violence is embedded in the ideology and operations of these institutions and that solutions to address the structural formations in society that feed women into the carceral state are not robust and comprehensive. As this project shows, the building of carceral institutions to house women and girls led to an increase in the number of women and girls imprisoned.

These strengthened carceral institutions captured women and girls, criminalizing their bodies and subjecting them to temporal and physical separation, confinement, and violence.[7] Maintaining their bodies in prisons, jails, laundries, and reformatories galvanized capitalism. The captured body requires shelter, food, water, clothing, soap, handcuffs, gates, uniforms, medicine, toilet paper, mattresses, blankets, and more. State institutions needed revenue to maintain the systems of incarceration, and capital markets responded, delivering financing and profits.[8] The symbiosis of profits for capitalists and power for the carceral state continued to adapt and strengthen through the decades examined in this book, and it continues today.

Women represent the fastest-growing populations in prisons today. In 1978, there were 121 women incarcerated in the entire state of Indiana; in 2015, there were 2,540.[9] Almost all incarcerated women, 90 to 95 percent, suffer trauma directly related to our charges and convictions. Women suffer without adequate access to health care, programming, and educational opportunities. We are also subjected to epistemic, gendered, and sexualized violence that combines with the ongoing racialized criminalization of who we are. This project demonstrates that this has been the condition of women's lives since the emergence of the carceral state. Any #MeToo movement or any movement for women's justice that does not include incarcerated women and girls is shortsighted and ignorant of history and incarceration's lasting effects on women.

In addition to carceral institutions, many ideologies and state practices relating to women and their children derive from carceral logics, including surveillance, classification, and punitive responses for labeled failures. Like carceral institutions, these practices consistently fail the women and children they seek to serve. No matter the progressive legacy of establishing institutions for women, girls, and boys, the legacy of these carceral institutions is tainted at best and corrupt at worst. Not completely benevolent, nor malevolent, reformers' "calling" to "save" and the results of their work raise two crucial questions: who is a criminal and what constitutes a criminal act?

In the methodology section, I discuss our approach to excavating this history. Collectively, my colleagues and I centered our experiences of incarceration, using our lived realities as one lens through which to read the archives. By privileging our experiences, we do not mean to suggest that nonincarcerated persons should not do this work. As Professor Ruth Wilson Gilmore has said, "Geography does not equal consciousness." Just because someone is in prison does not mean they have the capacity or consciousness to reflect on and to mobilize their experience for liberation. Rather, what we mean is that one's positionality, mentally, emotionally, and physically, affects how a person interacts with and gleans understanding from an archive. In the traditional academy, our lived experience of incarceration is not privileged. Often it is suppressed. Nevertheless, as we have shown here, our historical scholarship offers a glimmer of the possibilities for history when subjugated knowledge is centered. As incarcerated and formerly incarcerated scholars, we are just as intensely engaged with the archives, just as theoretically informed, and just as relevant to contemporary issues as any scholar. Our goal for this project is to counter epistemic violence, the violent extinguishment of our right to be knowers of our own lived experience, of our right to our own intimate understanding of the nature of the carceral environments in which we live/lived, and of our right to mobilize that knowledge for change. In this book, we have mobilized our lived experience of incarceration and our consciousness to counter the dominant narratives of women in Indiana's carceral institutions.

Whiteness is not an unnamed category in this volume. In the Victorian mindset, criminality degenerated the white race and stigmatized its members. Often these "fallen" women and girls were already tainted with poverty or with their immigrant or racial status. In 1870, the U.S. census reported the female population in Indiana to be composed of 810,530 (98.53 percent) white women, 11,975 (1.45 percent) African American women, and less than 1 percent Indigenous women.[10] African American women were incarcerated nearly thirty times more than their population in the state.[11] Indiana was a state primarily populated with white people, and it created carceral institutions to capture African Americans as well as to police whiteness and to protect the boundaries of white respectability.[12] The primary work of Indiana's women's carceral institutions was to manage the white "criminal" class and to stave off the degeneration of the white race. State-sanctioned violence was part of the overall methodology for achieving that goal. Nonetheless, the young African American boys and girls in the Quaker-led Indianapolis Asylum for Friendless Colored Children—the first of its kind in the state—had experiences similar to those of the incarcerated women and girls in the reformatory: compelled memorization of scripture, mandated silence during meals, enforced discipline and regimentation, and coerced acceptance of "good" Christian values, all of which were prioritized over "fire protection measures, medical care, play space" in an asylum where "rooms for the children" were "dark and foreboding" and "unpleasant in every particular," according to the New York Bureau of Research.[13] And like the reformatory's ticket-of-leave system, the Asylum for Friendless Colored Children also instituted a practice of indentured servitude that placed African American children in the home of a "master," who agreed to "provide clothing, lodging, education and food for the apprentice." Such conditions put some children at greater risk and many were abused.[14] The history of well-intentioned white women and men reformers, even pioneering reformers, must be told as holistically as possible to disrupt narratives that their work was wholly benevolent. Additional critical research on institutions like the Asylum for Friendless Colored Children is urgently needed across the United States.

While women and girls of color face more violence, sexual or otherwise, than do their white counterparts, and while their experiences are quantitatively different from those of white women and girls, at the intersection of crime, imprisoned white women experience sexual violence in many of the same ways imprisoned women of color do. Carceral institutions legitimize violence against all women, criminalize their sexuality, rob them of their agency, and declare them, per Andrea Smith, "inherently rapable" and "inherently violable." Together, both white and African American women and girls found themselves targeted for reeducation, religious indoctrination, domestic labor, and marriage through the constant threat of violence, practices that continue to have implications for the present.[15]

We hope this research and analysis challenges the systemic separation of incarcerated and nonincarcerated persons. It is a false dichotomy. Distinguishing the 70-plus million people with criminal records from those without becomes suspect when those who evade conviction do so largely because of their financial status, race, sex, and class. In addition, in a country marked by extreme economic inequality, who is a criminal and what is a crime are not driven solely by morality or harm but also by financial status, access to resources, race, sex, and class. Finally, incarceration and jailing affects us all, and very few people in the United States have zero connection to the criminal legal system. The current carceral system touches lives in countless, often tragic, ways. It behooves us to dismantle and transform a carceral system that from its origin damages us more than it repairs us.

We have to be prepared to tackle and counter dominant narratives that leave us out and make the sufferings of women invisible, the sufferings of the poor invisible, the sufferings of people of color invisible. The stakes are too high because although "women represent a small fraction of all incarcerated people, women's prison populations have seen much higher relative growth than men's since 1978. Nationwide, women's state prison populations grew 834% over nearly 40 years—more than double the pace of the growth among men." [16]

Further, if efforts don't counter the original purpose, premise, and operations of these facilities, then such efforts simply reinscribe the carceral state. We must be critical, then, when historians and other scholars tout their scholarship as definitive. We as scholars must ask pointed questions of race, sex, gender, and even criminality of the scholarship. We, many of us people of color disenfranchised by race, sex, class, and criminality, must epistemically privilege our lived experiences to solve the challenges we face living in this country. It is on us to critique, analyze, and ultimately rewrite the dominant narratives that have prevailed in leaving out lived experiences of women, girls, people of color, the poor, and the incarcerated. It is in this way that our research can create change, because from the first women's prison to the current state of women's growing incarceration, we have failed to learn the critical lesson that women are best served with structural and community supports and are not ever, *ever* served by prisons, laundries, reformatories, or other institutions of social control.

Afterword

Elizabeth Nelson

There's something alluring about the idea of an all-woman renegade prison history collective writing a book.

I admit that allure is part of the reason I find myself here, as co-editor of this collection, despite having little experience of incarceration myself. As a historian of psychiatry who studies institutions of confinement like mental hospitals, I was thrilled that my expertise allowed me to lend support to a project as exciting as this one. The scholarship in this volume exposes the gendered violence at the origins of the United States' system of mass incarceration and represents a vanguard of historical scholarship produced by incarcerated people themselves. It also charts new territory for histories of human subjects research in medicine, as well as histories of eugenics and reproductive justice.

This book should prompt readers to consider the symbiotic relations grounding the development of institutions in so-called modern America: the interconnections between the carceral and the medical, for example, and the knitted relationships among a variety of public and private establishments in the late nineteenth and early twentieth centuries, including prisons, poorhouses, brothels, orphanages, asylums, hospitals, and homes for "fallen" women.

I suggest we also take a critical look at how educational institutions such as colleges and universities interact with prisons today, as these relationships can sometimes become too comfortable. In my short time in this field, I've witnessed growing excitement about the possibilities of prison education and have been privy to growing partnerships between prisons and institutions of higher education that are often well meaning. However, the perceived "sexiness" of such programming (along with the financial motivations brought about by recent Pell Grant reforms) should give us pause.

The Indiana Women's Prison History Project is badass. These scholars are badass. But we shouldn't get lost in the word "prison."

Michelle Daniel Jones presents a new term here: "the *embodied observer*, one who views the archive from the position of the captive, from the inside of their experience."

The authors' lived experience as prisoners does give them incomparable insight into the history of incarcerating women in Indiana. But that experience belongs to them. Only they can claim it. We must not credit "the prison" for this book or use it as a defense of "prison education." We also shouldn't be so entranced that this book was written by lady murderers and thieves inside the slammer. This isn't *Chicago* the musical.

In addition, while we celebrate the triumph this book represents and the remarkable accomplishments of these scholars, we should remember that writing this book has not set its authors free from stigma, from surveillance, from difficulties accessing housing and employment, from intimate partner violence, from addiction, from post-traumatic prison disorder, from the heartbreak of being separated from and reunited (or not) with their children. And of course, for those still inside, writing this book has not freed them from incarceration itself. Higher education in prison uncoupled from the work of abolition is a red herring.

Don't get me wrong. I am all for education inside prison, but the meat of it must be separated from the so-called rehabilitative logic of the prison itself. The prison did not provide the foundation for the writing of this book, even if it was possible to negotiate with prison administrators for limited access to necessary resources.

The prison did not grant these authors opportunities to pursue higher education after release; these are pathways that these scholars and their allies carved out for themselves. Operating the Indiana Women's Prison History Project as part of the prison's higher education programming was an act of strategy, a shell game that involved certain risks. The writing of this book was at heart a clandestine and subversive operation; in the acts of researching, thinking, and writing, the authors claimed moments of fugitivity that are part of the long game of liberation. This is a book that was created *in* a prison, but it is not *of* it.

I am not fundamentally opposed to programs that offer opportunities to earn college degrees that can make a real difference in the life trajectories of (post)incarcerated people. But we must remember that any "higher education" that happens inside a prison happens despite the fact that it is happening inside a prison. That is not to say one doesn't learn something very fundamental and very shocking about the world by being in one, even as a visitor. And there is something about the stillness of the air in a prison and the austerity of it that makes the classroom crackle. I too am tempted to romanticize it!

But the fact is this book was an enormous pain in the ass to put together because we had to field each scholar's research requests, ferry in loads of scanned documents from multiple libraries and archives, and then try to keep track of them. This was necessary because the authors of this book were being kept in a cage. An immense pastoral cage with a chapel in the center.

What this group of scholars was able to achieve despite such conditions is astonishing. As co-editor, I take responsibility for any mistakes that are bound to be in this volume; moreover, I am unabashedly proud of this work.

Elizabeth Nelson, PhD
Paris, France
June 2022

Acknowledgments

It requires a lot of folks to support the work of incarcerated scholars. We acknowledge and thank all the faculty who came to the prison to teach and challenge us and to shape the history project. Most notably, we acknowledge Kelsey Kauffman, Elizabeth Nelson, Micol Seigel, Alex Tipei, Lesley Neff, Alex Lichtenstein, Eliza Brown, Sharon Maes, Meg Galasso, Emmalon Davis, Ougie Pak, Robert Schneider, and Charlene Fletcher Brown. A range of professors, students, archivists, and others have inspired and/or enabled our ability to research, write, and present our work, namely Marlon Bailey, Lorraine Boissoneault, Dale Chock, Ken Colburn, Vivian Deno, John Dittmer, Barbara Fister, Wendy Gamber, Thomas Hamm, Elizabeth Hinton, Pippa Holloway, Mariam Kazanjian, Talitha LeFlouria, Eli Meyerhoff, Julie K. Motyka, Khalil Gibran Muhammad, Marcus Rediker, Lorna Rhodes, Eric Sandweiss, Peggy Seigel, Andrea Smith, Caleb Smith, James M. Smith, Heather Thompson, Lisa Timothy, Katherine Tinsley, Vassiliki Tsitsopoulou, and Mary Xiao. Professor Gamber also very kindly reviewed an early draft of this book.

Several amazing student interns helped us in obtaining research, editing drafts, visiting the prison, providing logistics and overall support: Monica Deck, Peper Langhout, Marlen Huesca, Jerome Bingham, and Madeline Stull.

We received so much support in research from the Indiana Archives and Records Administration and the awesome Vicki Casteel. She knows where everything is; she is truly gifted and talented in finding rare information. Chandler Lighty of the Indiana Historical Bureau gave us boxes of free books on Indiana history. The amazing

Monique Howell at the Indiana State Library supported our work early on and was our primary contact with research assistance and was the one who retrieved the original picture of Sarah J. Smith from the prison and digitized it for this book. Librarian and author Barbara Fister filled our research requests from Minneapolis.

At the prison, numerous education staff and prison leadership supported our research: providing space to organize the archive and time on the computers and lending support so we could present at live conferences. We thank and acknowledge Steven McCauley, Carol Foster, Mary Saegesser, James Evans, Randy Marcy, Lora Schmalfeldt, Bruce Lemmon, Jan Davis, Velma Simpson, Tammy Atwood, and Brandi McNeal. We also thank Martha Rainbolt for her leadership of the Pre-College Program at the Indiana Women's Prison, of which the History Project was a part, and all the volunteer teachers for the program.

Much love to Andy Eisen, Pamela Cappas-Toro, and the scholars of the Community Education Project at the Tomoka Correctional Facility, who have been key partners in pioneering original historical research written by incarcerated people themselves, as well as our new friends at Operation Restoration in Louisiana.

We deeply appreciate Diana O'Hara and Joycelyn Dolliole, both survivors of U.S. Magdalene Laundries, who shared their stories with us.

We also acknowledge all those who supported the development and presentation of *The Duchess of Stringtown*: Gigi Jenewein, Bryan Fonseca, Anna Deavere Smith, Stephanie Schneider, Elena Araoz, and Virginia Grise.

We also acknowledge those organizations that awarded the Indiana Women's Prison History Project for our work, namely the Indiana Historical Society, the Indiana Academy of the Social Sciences, the American Association for State and Local History, the Goshen College Peggy Seigel Writing Competition, the American Studies Association, and the American Historical Association. We are also grateful for those institutions that gave us the opportunity to present our work and the news media that told our stories: Indiana University and Indiana University–Purdue University Indianapolis (Gary Curto and Steve Egyhazi for videoconferencing support), the Indiana Association of Historians, Hoosier Women at Work, the American Studies Association, the American Academy of Religion, the American Historical Association, *Perspectives Magazine* (Seth Denbo, Allen Mikaelian, and Shatah Almutawa), the Making and Unmaking Mass Incarceration Conference (Garrett Felber), the Prison to School Pipeline Conference at the Indianapolis Boner Center (Sue Hyatt), the Correctional Medicine Student Outreach Program at Indiana University School of Medicine, the Organization of American Historians (Hajni Selby), *Abolitionist Journal*, the *Journal of Prisoners on Prisons*, the National Conference on Higher Education in Prison, Platform: Arts and Humanities Research Laboratory at Indiana University (Micol Seigel), Bloomington, the DePauw University *Prindle Post* (Sandra Bertin, Christiane Wisehart), the National Council on Public History and the *Public Historian* (Julie Peterson), *American Public Media* (Samara Freemark), *Sick: A WFYI Podcast* (Britanni Howell and Jake Harper), and *Slate* (Rebecca Onion).

We are so thankful for the team at The New Press, Ellen Adler, Sarah Swong, Julie Enzer, and Marc Favreau, for all of their support in believing in our work and pulling off this book.

Lastly, we are so appreciative of the Art for Justice Fund, the Indiana Humanities Council, and IUPUI's Center for Translating Research into Practice, whose generous contributions enabled Dr. Nelson and her students to support the incarcerated scholars in completing and sharing their work. Many folks at IUPUI lent support in various ways to this project, including Emily Beckman, Judi Izuka-Campbell, Ray Haberski, Mary Price, Marianne Wokeck, Nancy Robertson, Edith Millikan, and Eric Hamilton.

The old adage "it takes a village" is apt and we thank you all.

Notes

Preface

1. Erving Goffman defined "total institutions" as isolated spaces where people's lives are confined, tightly administered, and reshaped, such as prisons, asylums, boarding schools, and convents. Erving Goffman, *Asylums: Essays on the Social Situation of Mental Patients and Other Inmates* (New York: Anchor Books, 1961).

2. The cast included Shirwanda Boone, Connie Bumgardner, Lara Campbell, Michelle Jones (Daniel), Danielle Green, Leslie Hauk, Lisa Hochstetler, Jeneth Hughes, Rheann Kelly, Heather Lace, Melinda Loveless, Nan Luckhart, Natalie Medley, Dominique Parks, Irene Price, Anastazia Schmid, Heather Shaw, Tiara Shelton, Cindy White, and Michelle Williams.

Methodology: "We're Doing a New Thing"

1. Linda Tuhiwai Smith, *Decolonizing Methodologies* (New York: St. Martin's Press, 1999), 5.

2. Nicholas Wolfinger, "On Writing Fieldnotes: Collection Strategies and Background Expectancies," *Qualitative Research* 2, no. 1 (2002): 86–87.

3. Donald Andrews and James Bonta, *The Psychology of Criminal Conduct* (United Kingdom: LexisNexis/Anderson, 2010); James McGuire, *Understanding Psychology and Crime: Perspectives on Theory and Action* (Berkshire: McGraw-Hill, 2004); John J. Dilulio Jr., *Governing Prisons: A Comparative Study of Correctional Management* (New York: Free Press, 1987); C.T. Lowenkamp, E.J. Latessa, and A.M. Holsinger, "The Risk Principle in Action: What Have We Learned from 13,676 Offenders and 97 Correctional Programs?" *Crime and Delinquency* 52, no. 1 (January 2006): 77–93; J. Petersilia, "Influencing Public Policy: An Embedded Criminologist Reflects on California Prison Reform," *Journal of Experimental Criminology* 4, no. 4 (2008): 335–56; Todd Clear, *Harm in American Penology: Offenders, Victims, and Their Communities* (New York: State University of New York Press, 1994); Elliot Currie, *Confronting Crime: An American Challenge* (New York: Pantheon Books, 1985); Elliot Currie, *Crime and Punishment in America*

(New York: Macmillan, 1998); James Irwin and John Austin, *It's About Time: America's Imprisonment Binge* (Belmont, CA: Wadsworth, 1994); Joan Esherick, *Prisoner Rehabilitation: Success Stories and Failures* (Broomall, PA: Mason Crest); Shadd Maruna, *Making Good: How Ex-Convicts Reform and Rebuild Their Lives* (Washington, DC: American Psychological Association, 2001); David Farabee, *Rethinking Rehabilitation: Why Can't We Reform Our Criminals?* (Washington, DC: AEI Press, 2005); Steven Michael Teles and David Dagan, *Prison Break: Why Conservatives Turned Against Mass Incarceration* (Oxford: Oxford University Press, 2016); Ann Chih Lin, *Reform in the Making: The Implementation of Social Policy in Prison* (Princeton, NJ: Princeton University Press, 2002).

4. Chicago Beyond, *Why Am I Always Being Researched: A Guidebook for Community Organizations, Researchers, and Funders to Help Us Get from Insufficient Understanding to More Authentic Truth*, Equity Series, vol. 1, Chicago Beyond, chicagobeyond.org/researchequity/.

5. Smith, *Decolonizing Methodologies*, 4.

6. Jamie Barlowe Kayes, "Reading Against the Grain: The Power and Limits of Feminist Criticism of American Narratives," *Journal of Narrative Technique* 19, no. 1 (Winter, 1989): 130–40; Liz Clarke and Trevor R. Getz, *Abina and the Important Men: A Graphic History* (New York: Oxford University Press, 2011).

7. Joy James, ed., *Imprisoned Intellectuals: America's Political Prisoners Write on Life, Liberation and Rebellion* (Lanham, MD: Rowman and Littlefield, 2003), 28.

8. Patricia Hill Collins, "Learning from the Outsider Within: The Sociological Significance of Black Feminist Thought," in *Beyond Methodology: Feminist Research as Lived Research*, ed. M.M. Fonow and J.A. Cook (Bloomington: Indiana University Press, 1991), 36–38.

9. Collins, "Outsider Within."

10. Smith, *Decolonizing Methodologies*, 2.

11. Smith, 3.

12. Khalil Gibran Muhammad, "Where Did All the White Criminals Go?" *Souls* 13, no. 1 (2011): 72–80; Mary De Ming Fan, "Disciplining Criminal Justice: The Peril amid the Promise of Numbers," *Yale Law and Policy Review* 26, no. 1 (Fall 2007): 38–39, 50, 54–56; Jock Young, *The Criminological Imagination* (Cambridge, MA: Polity Press, 2011).

13. Mary Coffin Johnson, *Rhoda M. Coffin, Her Reminiscences, Addresses, Papers and Ancestry* (New York: Grafton Press, 1910).

14. Michel Foucault, *Discipline and Punish: The Birth of the Prison* (New

York: Vintage Books, 1979); Rudi Visker, *Michel Foucault: Genealogy as Critique*, trans. Chris Turner (London: Verso, 1995).

15. Michel Foucault, *"Society Must Be Defended," Lectures at the Collège De France, 1975–1976*, trans. David Macey (New York: Picador, 2003), 10.

16. "Sarah J. Smith: A Modern Friend," *American Friend* 7, no. 2 (First Month 11, 1900): 31–32.

17. Foucault, *"Society Must Be Defended,"* 6–12.

18. Collins, "Outsider Within," 39.

19. Erving Goffman, "On Fieldwork: Editor's Introduction," *Journal of Contemporary Ethnography* (1989): 129.

20. James R. Cochran, "The Epistemic Violence of Racism: Hidden Transcripts of Whiteness," 2001, www.academia.edu/665931/The_Epistemic _Violence_of_Racism.

21. Gayatri Spivak, "Can the Subaltern Speak?" in *Marxism and the Interpretation of Culture,* ed. Cary Nelson and Lawrence Grossberg (London: Macmillan, 1988), 282–83.

22. Miranda Fricker, "Forum on Miranda Fricker's Epistemic Injustice: Power and the Ethics of Knowing," *Theoria* 23, no. 1 (January 2008), 69–71.

23. Anastazia Schmid, "Community Engaged Research and Epistemic Injustice" (presentation to the Association for the Study of Higher Education Conference on Community-Engaged Research, Indianapolis, 2018).

24. Michelle Jones (Daniel), "Biographic Mediation and the Formerly Incarcerated: How Dissembling and Disclosure Counter the Extended Consequences of Criminal Convictions," *Biography: An Interdisciplinary Quarterly* 42, no. 3 (November 2019).

25. Hugh Gusterson, "Studying Up Revisited," *PoLAR* 20, no. 1 (May 1997), 116.

26. Cathy MacDonald, "Understanding Participatory Action Research: A Qualitative Research Methodology Option," *Canadian Journal of Action Research* 13, no. 2 (2012), 34–50, pdfs.semanticscholar.org/3b78/ecfe 0b4a0a7591d2ea068c71e8ea320ff451.pdf.

27. Michelle Fine and Maria Elena Torre, "Critical Participatory Action Research: A Feminist Project for Validity and Solidarity," *Psychology of Women Quarterly* 43, no. 4 (2019), 433–44; Michelle Fine and Maria Elena Torre, *Essentials of Critical Participatory Action Research* (Washington, DC: American Psychological Association, 2021).

28. Michelle Fine and Maria Elena Torre, *Critical Participatory Action Research: Conceptual Formations* (Washington, DC: American Psychological Association, 2021).

29. Harrie J. Banka, *State Prison Life: By One Who Has Been There* (Cincinnati: C.F. Vent, 1871), 11.

30. Banka, 11.

31. Banka, 12.

32. Banka, 13.

33. The conditions of the men and women at Jeffersonville that Harrie Banka revealed were corroborated by several historical references, memoirs, the legislative committee investigating Jeffersonville, and the media.

34. C. Wright Mills, *The Sociological Imagination* (New York: Oxford University Press, 1959), 195.

1: Sallie and Eva at Indiana's First Prison, Jeffersonville

1. J. Harrie Banka, *State Prison Life: By One Who Has Been There* (Cincinnati: C.F. Vent, 1871), 154–56. "Sallie" is often a nickname for Sarah, and Banka identifies Sallie as "Sallie M." The only Sallie or Sarah incarcerated with Banka and who had a last name starting with *M* was Sarah Morgan.

2. See Methodology section for more discussion on Harrie J. Banka.

3. Banka, *State Prison Life*, 145, 151–54.

4. Banka, 151–52.

5. Estelle Freedman, *Their Sisters' Keepers: Women's Prison Reform in America, 1830–1930* (Ann Arbor, MI: University of Michigan Press, 2000), 14.

6. Freedman, 81.

7. Banka, *State Prison Life*, 156.

8. Banka, 169. "You will remember, Mr. Deputy F——r, that fir the first three months or more of your official career, your family did not take up their residence at this place. Well sir, I should like to ask you where you lodged during that winter? . . . Allow me to refresh your memory. Do you remember cell No. ——, in the female department? . . . Do you remember a fair young girl, the occupant of that cell? . . . you were a constant lodger in that little dungeon . . . Sallie herself will testify to the fact."

9. Banka, 169–70.

10. L.A. Williams, *History of the Ohio Falls Cities and Their Counties: with Illustrations and Biographical Sketches*, vol. 2 (Cleveland, OH: L.A. Williams, 1882), 464, archive.org/stream/historyofohiofal02will/historyofohiofal-02will_djvu.txt.

11. Emma Lou Thornbrough, *Indiana in the Civil War Era, 1850–1880* (Indianapolis, IN: Indiana Historical Bureau and Indiana Historical Society, 1965), 585–86. In convict leasing, incarcerated people are leased out

to a contractor for a period of time for a cost. "From the beginning it was the practice to lease the Jeffersonville prison to the highest bidder at three-year intervals, thus leaving the prisoners to the mercy of a superintendent who was interested in getting as much personal gain from the contract as possible."

12. Williams, *History of the Ohio Falls Cities*, 465. "The sick and disabled were neglected as if the consideration of life weighed lightly in the balance against the few cents daily necessary for their maintenance. The cells and corridors were foul, damp, and unwholesome; swarms of vermin infested every corner, and thus overwork, cruelty, starvation, filth, the pistol and lash of the guard, all contributed to a wholesale murder of the weak, and to brutalizing the strong beyond the hope of redemption here or hereafter."

13. Pamela Bennett and Shirley S. McCord, *Progress After Statehood: A Book of Readings* (Indianapolis, IN: Indiana Historical Review, 1974), 386. Report by Dorothea Dix was published in the *Indiana Daily State Journal*, January 7, 1846.

14. Garry J. Nokes, *Images of America: Jeffersonville, Indiana* (Charleston, NC: Arcadia, 2002), 12.

15. Banka, *State Prison Life*, 279; Thornbrough, *Indiana in the Civil War Era*, 585–86.

16. Thornbrough, *Indiana in the Civil War Era*, 585–86; Banka, *State Prison Life*, 282.

17. Thornbrough, *Indiana in the Civil War Era*, 585.

18. Banka, *State Prison Life*, 280–81; Thornbrough, *Indiana in the Civil War Era*, 586.

19. Banka, *State Prison Life*, 282.

20. Banka, 286.

21. Thornbrough, *Indiana in the Civil War Era*, 588.

22. Banka, *State Prison Life*, 297.

23. Jacob Piatt Dunn and G.W.H. Kemper, *Indiana and Indianans: A History of Aboriginal and Territorial Indiana and the Century of Statehood*, vol. 2 (Chicago, IL: American Historical Society, 1919), 1014.

24. Mary Coffin Johnson, *Rhoda M. Coffin, Her Reminiscences, Addresses, Papers and Ancestry* (New York: Grafton Press, 1910).

25. Johnson, 87–88.

26. Johnson, 151.

27. Banka, *State Prison Life*, 142.

28. See Methodology discussion on Banka.

29. Banka, *State Prison Life*, 119.

30. Banka, 83–84, 224.

31. "The Prison at Jeffersonville," *Cincinnati Daily Enquirer*, March 1, 1869; Estelle Freedman, *Their Sisters' Keepers: Women's Prison Reform in America, 1830–1930* (Ann Arbor, MI: University of Michigan Press, 2000), 60.

32. Banka, *State Prison Life*, 171.

33. Banka, 171.

34. Banka, 172.

35. Banka, 172–73.

36. Banka, 173.

37. Indiana General Assembly, *Report of the Committee on Prisons Together with the Evidence of the Officers and Others Before the Committee at the Southern Prison* (Indianapolis, IN: Alexander H. Conner State Printer, 1869).

38. Dunn and Kemper, *Indiana and Indianans*, 1014.

39. Banka, *State Prison Life*, 239.

40. "The Jeffersonville Penitentiary," *Courier-Journal*, October 29, 1868.

41. Banka, *State Prison Life*, 165.

42. Banka, 167.

43. Banka, 221.

44. "The Prison at Jeffersonville."

45. Banka, *State Prison Life*, 240–41.

46. Banka, 243.

47. "Indiana State Prison Horrors," *New York Times*, March 14, 1869.

48. "A Model Female Prison," *Greencastle Press*, December 22, 1875.

49. *Report of the Committee on Prisons, Together with the Evidence of the Officers and Others, Before the Committee at the Southern Prison* (Indianapolis, IN: Alexander H. Conner, 1869), 7.

50. *Report of the Committee on Prisons*, 12–14.

51. *Report of the Committee on Prisons*, 10.

52. *Report of the Committee on Prisons*, 8.

53. The spelling of Lawrence S. Shuler's last name is inconsistent in our source material; at times it is rendered as "Schuler."

54. "The Indiana Penitentiary: Convict Life as It Is in the State Prison South," *Daily Inter Ocean*, May 22, 1869.

55. Banka, *State Prison Life*, 312–14.

56. Banka, 304–5; 308–9.

57. *Testimony in the Southern Prison Investigation Transmitted to the House, March 6, 1875* (Indianapolis, IN: Sentinel Company, 1875), 51.

58. "The Prison Embroglio: Investigation of the Charges of Malfeasance

and Misfeasance in the Indiana Penitentiary," *Courier-Journal*, May 27, 1871. For more about Mrs. Clem, please see Wendy Gamber, *The Notorious Mrs. Clem: Murder and Money in the Gilded Age* (Baltimore, MD: Johns Hopkins Press, 2016).

59. *Testimony in the Southern Prison Investigation*, 15–19, 24–28, 39–40, 47.

60. *Testimony in the Southern Prison Investigation*, 25.

61. *Testimony in the Southern Prison Investigation*, 5–6.

62. Dunn and Kemper, *Indiana and Indianans*, 1014.

63. Registry provided by the Indiana Archives on Jeffersonville.

2: Rhoda and Sarah—Toward the Home for Friendless Women

1. E.C. Wines, ed., *Transactions of the Third National Prison Reform Congress Saint Louis, Missouri, May 13–16, 1874: Being the Third Annual Report of the National Prison Association of the United States* (New York: National Prison Association of the United States, 1874), 305.

2. "Memorial of Sarah J. Smith," *Minutes of Indiana Yearly Meeting* (Richmond, IN: Nicholson Brothers, 1887), 116.

3. "Sarah J. Smith: A Modern Friend," *American Friend* 7, no. 2 (First Month [January] 11, 1900).

4. "Memorial of Sarah J. Smith," 117.

5. "Sarah Smith," United States Index to Passenger Arrivals, Atlantic and Gulf Ports, 1820–1874, database with images, FamilySearch.org, accessed March 13, 2018, familysearch.org/ark:/61903/1:1:KDRZ-J39, Sarah Smith, 1849; citing Immigration, NARA microfilm publication M334 (Washington, DC: National Archives and Records Administration, n.d.); FHL microfilm 418,323.

6. "William McLaughlin age 37 and Abigail McLaughlin age 35 and their children, Mary Jane, age 15, William age 13, Sarah age 9, Ann Maria age 7, Amanda Ellen age 2, Manerva, age 1 and two other adult women." "United States Census, 1850," database with images, FamilySearch.org, accessed December 19, 2020, www.familysearch.org/ark:/61903/1:1:MHV6 -NQY, Sarah Smith in household of William McLaughlin, Milton, Wayne, Indiana, United States; citing family, NARA microfilm publication (Washington, DC: National Archives and Records Administration, n.d.).

7. Elizabeth Comstock (1815–91) traveled the United States ministering and providing aid to marginalized populations. U.S. census data reports that for a time Elizabeth lived in the home of Sarah Smith.

8. "Memorial of Sarah J. Smith," 118.

9. Rosemary Skinner Keller, Rosemary Radford Ruether, and Marie Cantlon, *Encyclopedia of Women and Religion in North America* (Bloomington:

Indiana University Press, 2006), public.ebookcentral.proquest.com/choice /publicfullrecord.aspx?p=273932.

10. Rhoda Coffin, "Women's Prisons: Reformatories, Police, Matrons" (address before the National Prison Congress, Detroit, MI, 1885).

11. Wines, *Transactions of the Third National Prison Reform Congress*, 305.

12. Mary Coffin Johnson, *Rhoda M. Coffin, Her Reminiscences, Addresses, Papers and Ancestry* (New York: Grafton Press, 1910).

13. Johnson, 76; Thomas D. Hamm, *The Transformation of American Quakerism: Orthodox Friends, 1800–1907* (Bloomington: Indiana University Press, 1988), 46. Coffin stated, "No so-called Christian work should ever be allowed to interfere with the relation of or duties as husband and wife to each other and this is extended to the family relation, which is God-ordained, entered into by our own free will and choice. Her home was the showplace, the refuge and haven from the travails of the outside world and the site of the Indiana renewal movement that changed the trajectory of American Quakerism."

14. Rhoda Coffin died in 1909. Her memoir was published in 1910 by Mary Coffin Johnson. The dedication reads: "Dedicated to the memory of Rhoda M. Coffin by her family with the kind regards of Charles Coffin."

15. "My daily work was soon done and then commenced the tedious part. I had nothing to do; I sewed for Mother Coffin . . . commenced to read all the Friend's books. . . . I did this not from inclination but because I thought it a duty. It was weary work; I would read until tired, then lie down and take a nap, then go to reading again." Johnson, *Rhoda M. Coffin*, 56–57.

16. Nancy Hewitt, *Women's Activism and Social Change: Rochester, New York, 1822–1872* (New York: Cornell University Press, 1984), 39.

17. Hewitt, 39.

18. Hamm, *Transformation of American Quakerism*, 47.

19. Bruce Dorsey, *Reforming Men and Women: Gender in the Antebellum City* (New York: Cornell University Press, 2002), 7.

20. Ellen D. Swain, "From Benevolence to Reform: The Expanding Career of Mrs. Rhoda M. Coffin," *Indiana Magazine of History* 97, no. 3 (September 2001): 196.

21. Johnson, *Rhoda M. Coffin*, 70–73. She was also involved in and led various Quaker organizations, including Bible studies, reading societies, and the Friends Sabbath School.

22. Swain, "From Benevolence to Reform," 194.

23. Dorsey, *Reforming Men and Women*, 12.

24. Dorsey, 25.

25. Anne Boylan, *The Origins of Women's Activism: New York and Boston, 1797–1840* (Chapel Hill: University of North Carolina Press, 2002), 218.

26. Boylan, 211.

27. Andrea Smith, *Conquest: Sexual Violence and America Indian Genocide* (Boston: South End, 2005), 5, 15–16.

28. Dorsey, *Reforming Men and Women*, 13, 25.

29. Nancy Cott, *The Bonds of Womanhood: "Women's Sphere" in New England, 1780–1835* (New Haven, CT: Yale University Press, 1997), xix–xx. "Women's sphere was not a separate sphere . . . woman's work was extrinsic to capitalist industrialization but essential to it."

30. Lori Ginzberg, *Women in Antebellum Reform* (Wheeling, IL: Harland Davidson, 2000).

31. Kathryn Kish Sklar, *Women's Rights Emerges Within the Antislavery Movement, 1830–1870* (Boston, MA: Bedford/St. Martin's Publishing, 2000), 2.

32. Nancy A. Hewitt, *Women's Activism and Social Change: Rochester, New York, 1822–1984* (New York: Cornell University, 1984), 22; Sklar, *Women's Rights Emerges*, 2.

33. Ginzberg, *Women in Antebellum Reform*, 6–7.

34. Sklar, *Women's Rights Emerges*, 12.

35. Sklar, *Women's Rights Emerges*, 12.

36. Barbara Leslie Epstein, *The Politics of Domesticity: Women, Evangelism, and Temperance in Nineteenth-Century America* (Middletown, CT: Wesleyan University Press, 1981), 6.

37. Epstein, *Politics of Domesticity*, 50. Lucretia Mott (1793–1880) was a Quaker abolitionist, speaker, and writer who worked tirelessly with William Lloyd Garrison and the Anti-Slavery Society and later with the women's rights movement with Elizabeth Cady Stanton. Elizabeth Cady Stanton (1815 –1902) was a suffragist, abolitionist, speaker, and writer who led the nascent women's rights movement in the United States.

38. Epstein, 66–67.

39. Ginzberg, *Women in Antebellum Reform*, 11.

40. Sklar, *Women's Rights Emerges*, 73.

41. Cott, *Bonds of Womanhood*, 69.

42. Ginzberg, *Women in Antebellum Reform*, 9; Cott, *Bonds of Womanhood*, 64.

43. Anne McClintock, *Imperial Leather: Race, Gender and Sexuality in the Colonial Conquest* (New York: Routledge, 1995), 85, 162. Integral domestic workers performed all the laborious and dirty duties necessary to advance the image of a "proper" home and to permit the wife a life of

leisure. Nevertheless, choosing not to be a wife of leisure did not negate the need to appear as one. It is extremely crucial to note the contradictory nature of the "proper" home: it simultaneously had to be devoid of the evidence of work and had to have the appearance of work done.

44. Cott, *Bonds of Womanhood*, 98.

45. Cott, 70.

46. Susan Hill Lindley, *"You Have Stept Out of Your Place": A History of Women and Religion in America* (Westminster, KY: Westminster John Knox Press, 1996), 54–55.

47. "Portrayed as women's fulfillment, motherhood manifested itself in self-denial. The correct rearing of children required habitual command over one's won passions." Cott, *Bonds of Womanhood*, 91.

48. "Influence unlike virtue, did not have centuries of invested meaning in republican and Protestant thought." Dorsey, *Reforming Men and Women*, 38.

49. Cott, *Bonds of Womanhood*, 197.

50. Cott, 199.

51. Dorsey, *Reforming Men and Women*, 43.

52. James H. Madison, *Hoosiers: A New History of Indiana* (Bloomington: Indiana University Press, 2014), 135 and 165; Ellen Skinner, *Women and the National Experience: Primary Sources in American History* (Boston, MA: Addison-Wesley, 1996), 93.

53. Estelle Freedman, *Their Sisters' Keepers: Women's Prison Reform in America, 1830–1930* (Ann Arbor: University of Michigan Press, 2000), 14, 90.

54. Madison, *Hoosiers*, 165.

55. William Robeson Holloway, *Indianapolis: A Historical and Statistical Sketch of the Railroad City, A Chronicle of its Social Municipal, Commercial and Manufacturing Progress, with Full Statistical Tables* (Indianapolis, IN: Indianapolis Journal Print, 1870), 125.

56. Holloway, 195.

57. Helen Lefkowitz Horowitz, *Rereading Sex: Battles over Sexual Knowledge and Suppression in Nineteenth Century America* (New York: Vintage Books, 2002), 68.

58. Charles Richmond Henderson, Papers, [Box 2, Folder 10], Special Collections Research Center, University of Chicago Library https://socialwelfare.library.vcu.edu/corrections/friends-quakers-prison-reform/. In 1867, the representative boy of the Indiana Yearly Meeting of Friends, held in Richmond, appointed a committee of six "to organize a system

for the Reformation of Juvenile offenders and the improvement of Prison Discipline."

59. Hamm, *Transformation of American Quakerism*, 60; Johnson, *Rhoda M. Coffin*, 59–60, 79, 82. Arguably, the repression by church elders was part of Rhoda and Charles's motivation to work outside the Quaker church. From cleaning the meetinghouse without elder permission to holding prayer meetings with younger Quakers in their home with permission but against church traditions, Charles and, especially, Rhoda faced much opposition and ridicule from the Quaker church.

60. Susan Hill-Lindley, *You Have Stept Out of Your Place: A History of Women and Religion in America* (Louisville, KY: Westminster John Knox Press, 1996), 13.

61. Epstein, *Politics of Domesticity*, 9.

62. Johnson, *Rhoda M. Coffin*, 57–58.

63. Johnson, 85–87.

64. Hamm, *Transformation of American Quakerism*, 46–47, 49–52, 58–61. This move was part of a shift that changed American Quakerism through what is now called the "renewal movement."

65. Johnson, *Rhoda M. Coffin*, 215.

66. Johnson, 215. The HMAW, while not orthodox, did serve to heal some of the division in the Quaker church between the older and younger members, as older members were welcomed.

67. Johnson, 217. Coffin stated, "With an intense burning in my soul for the advancement of the work, and all absorbed in the purpose, and fearing that I was about to break the rules of the Church, I knelt down by one of the benches in the porch, and, taking an old envelope and a pencil, wrote, 'A meeting will be held this afternoon at 3 o'clock in this room for the purpose of organizing a Women's Home Mission Association.' "

68. Hewitt, *Women's Activism and Social Change*, 41–43.

69. Dorsey, *Reforming Men and Women*, 13.

70. Dorsey, 25.

71. Dorsey, 35–36.

72. Johnson, *Rhoda M. Coffin*, 218.

73. Holloway, *Historical and Statistical Sketch*, 126.

74. Hewitt, *Women's Activism and Social Change*, 67.

75. Freedman, *Their Sisters' Keepers*, 23.

76. "Memorial of Sarah J. Smith," 116.

77. Holloway, *Historical and Statistical Sketch*, 195; Johnson, *Rhoda M. Coffin*, 88–89.

78. Holloway, *Historical and Statistical Sketch*, 195; Johnson, *Rhoda M. Coffin*, 88–89. Sarah had been part of the Whitewater Meeting since she and her husband moved to Richmond in 1846. Both were present at Rhoda Coffin's wedding.

79. Swain, "From Benevolence to Reform," 199.

80. Mary Raddant Tomlan and Michael A. Tomlan, *Richmond, Indiana: Its Physical Development and Aesthetic Heritage to 1920s* (Indianapolis, IN: Indiana Historical Society Press, 1993), 63.

81. Johnson, *Rhoda M. Coffin*, 146

82. Johnson, 145.

83. Johnson, 146.

84. Holloway, *Historical and Statistical Sketch*, 197; Charles Coffin, "Influence of Friends in the Development of the Life of the State of Indiana." The state constitution allowed for the creation of benevolent institutions.

85. Margaret Hope Bacon, *Mothers of Feminism: The Story of Quaker Women in America* (San Francisco: Harper and Row, 1986), 143; Johnson, *Rhoda M. Coffin*, 145–46.

86. Hewitt, *Women's Activism and Social Change*, 68. These identities, structured within organization and institutions, provided a relatively autonomous framework within which women could locate themselves, either as new members of the community or as members of new social or economic groups within the community.

87. Lori Ginzberg, *Women and the Work of Benevolence: Morality, Politics and Class in the Nineteenth-Century United States* (New Haven, CT: Yale University Press, 1990), 74.

88. Johnson, *Rhoda M. Coffin*, 95.

89. Freedman, *Their Sisters' Keepers*, 14.

90. William Page, "Prison Reform IX: Treatment of Prisoners," *Fort Wayne News*, January 30, 1897.

3: Belle at the Home for Friendless Women

1. "City Drift: The Home of the Friendless Affair," *Sentinel* (Indianapolis, IN), December 8, 1873, 1.

2. "City Drift."

3. "City Drift"; "Mysterious Doings: A Dark Transaction at the Home of the Friendless," *Indianapolis Daily Sentinel* (Indianapolis, IN), December 7, 1873, 4; "Another Unfortunate Death of a Well Known Young Lady of Lawrenceburgh," *Lawrenceburgh Register* (Lawrenceburgh, IN), December 11, 1873.

4. The surname of the home's matron is variously given in accounts as Brower, Brawer, Brewer, and Brauer. She is also variously referred to as "Miss" and "Mrs." Because the board of managers, which employed her, referred to her as "Miss Brower," I have used that spelling and title.

5. "City Drift."

6. "Mysterious Doings."

7. William Robeson Holloway, *Indianapolis: A Historical and Statistical Sketch of the Railroad City, a Chronicle of Its Social, Municipal, Commercial and Manufacturing Progress, with Full Statistical Tables* (Indianapolis, IN: Indianapolis Journal Print, 1870), 126, 196.

8. "The Home for Friendless Women: The Matron's Statement in Reference to the Sentinel's Stories Published Yesterday," *Indianapolis News* (Indianapolis, IN), December 8, 1873.

9. "Mysterious Doings."

10. "City Drift"; "Investigated," *Indianapolis Daily Sentinel* (Indianapolis, IN), December 13, 1873.

11. "Another Unfortunate Death."

12. "City Drift."

13. According to "City Drift," the sisters planned to place the baby in an orphanage but eventually to raise it. "Investigated" states the baby was still at the home when the hearing took place.

14. "Mysterious Doings."

15. "Mysterious Doings" (emphasis in original).

16. "Mysterious Doings."

17. "Mysterious Doings."

18. "Mysterious Doings."

19. "More 'Wool,' " *Indianapolis Daily Sentinel* (Indianapolis, IN), December 11, 1873.

20. "Mysterious Doings."

21. "Mysterious Doings."

22. "More 'Wool.' "

23. "Investigated."

24. "Mrs. Margaret M. Todd Dead," *Indianapolis Journal* 49, no. 80 (March 21, 1899); "Thomas H. Sharpe Dead," *Indianapolis News*, February 13, 1893, 6.

25. "Investigated."

26. Ettie Ward is referred to as Edith Ward in some accounts.

27. "Investigated."

28. "Investigated."

29. "Investigated."

30. "City News: The Home for the Friendless," *Indianapolis News* (Indianapolis, IN), December 12, 1873.

31. "City Drift."

32. "Investigated."

33. "Investigated."

34. "Investigated."

35. "Investigated."

36. "Investigated."

37. "City News."

38. "Investigated."

39. "Investigated."

40. "The Vindication of Miss Brauer," *Indianapolis News* (Indianapolis, IN), December 13, 1873.

41. "Articles of a Voluntary Charitable Association Called 'The Indianapolis Home for Friendless Women,' " a handwritten volume of minutes dating from February 21, 1867, to February 4, 1875. The volume is held by the Indiana Historical Society as part of its Indianapolis Retirement Home Records (collection M 0519). See entry dated December 4, 1873.

42. Howard Zinn, *A People's History of the United States* (New York: Harper and Row, 1980); Robert V. Robinson and Ana-Maria Wahl, "Industrial Employment and Wages of Women, Men, and Children in a Nineteenth-Century City: Indianapolis, 1850–1880," *American Sociological Review* 55, no. 6 (December 1990): 912–28; Samuel Bernstein, "American Labor in the Long Depression, 1873–1878," *Science and Society* 20, no. 1 (1956): 59–83; Ruth Sidel, *Keeping Women and Children Last: America's War on the Poor* (New York: Penguin Books, 1996).

See also Robert V. Robinson, "Making Ends Meet: Wives and Children in the Family Economy of Indianapolis, 1860–1920," *Indiana Magazine of History* 92, no. 3 (September 1996): 197–234; Wendy Gamber, "A Gendered Enterprise: Placing Nineteenth-Century Businesswomen in History," *Harvard Business History Review* 72 (Summer 1998): 188–218.

43. Kali Gross, *Colored Amazons: Crime, Violence, and Black Women in the City of Brotherly Love, 1880–1910* (Durham, NC: Duke University Press, 2006); Timothy J. Gilfoyle, *City of Eros: New York City, Prostitution, and the Commercialization of Sex, 1790–1920* (New York: W.W. Norton, 1992).

44. Estelle B. Freedman, *Their Sisters' Keepers: Women's Prison Reform in America, 1830–1930* (Ann Arbor: University of Michigan Press, 1981), 14. For more on this topic, see Sharon E. Wood, *The Freedom of the Streets:*

Work, Citizenship, and Sexuality in the Gilded Age (Chapel Hill: University of North Carolina Press, 2005); Helen Lefkowitz Horowitz, *Rereading Sex: Battles over Sexual Knowledge and Suppression in Nineteenth-Century America* (New York: Vintage Books, 2003).

45. John Peter Altgeld, *Our Penal Machinery and Its Victims* (Chicago: A.C. McClurg, 1886).

46. Sidel, *Keeping Women and Children Last*; Freedman, *Their Sisters' Keepers*; Horowitz, *Rereading Sex*.

47. Elaine Pagels, *The Origin of Satan: How Christians Demonized Jews, Pagans, and Heretics* (New York: Random House, 1995); Rey Chow, *The Protestant Ethnic and the Spirit of Capitalism* (New York: Columbia University Press, 2002).

48. Herbert G. Gutman, "Work, Culture, and Society in Industrializing America: 1815–1919," *American Historical Review* 78, no. 3 (June, 1973): 531–88.

49. Nicole Hahn Rafter, *Partial Justice: Women, Prisons and Social Control*, 2nd ed. (New York: Routledge, 2017), 29–32; Freedman, *Their Sisters' Keepers*, 46, 51, 69–70.

50. "Grave Charges," *Indianapolis News* (Indianapolis, IN), May 20, 1872.

51. Holloway, *Historical and Statistical Sketch*, 126, 196.

52. *City of Indianapolis v. Indianapolis Home for Friendless Women*, 50 Ind. 215 (1875), Supreme Court of Indiana.

53. "Mysterious Doings."

54. "We know these people, and we know their characters and we know them to be earnest, intelligent, and conscientious Christian women, zealously striving to live lives of usefulness, the very last persons who would attempt to conceal or condone a wrong." Untitled editorial [beginning "The Sentinel of yesterday contained more than a column about The News"], *Indianapolis News*, December 15, 1873.

4: Sally and the Women and Girls at the Reformatory

1. *Second Annual Report of the Board of Managers of the Indiana Reformatory Institution of Women and Girls, Year Ending, January 1, 1874* (Indianapolis, IN: Sentinel Company, 1874), 7.

2. *Second Annual Report of the Board of Managers*, 8. The first three-person board of visitors comprised Hon. Conrad Baker, Indianapolis; Rhoda Coffin, Richmond; Addison Roache, Indianapolis.

3. *Second Annual Report of the Board of Managers*, 8.

4. *First Report of the Board of the Indiana Reformatory Institution for Women and Girls* (Indianapolis: R.J. Bright, 1871), 8–9.

5. A short list includes: Brinton Howard, *Friends for 300 Years: The History and Beliefs of the Society of Friends Since George Fox Started the Quaker Movement* (New York: Harper, 1952); Jacob Piatt Dunn and G.W.H. Kemper, *Indiana and Indianans: A History of Aboriginal and Territorial Indiana and the Century of Statehood*, vol. 2 (Chicago: American Historical Society, 1919); Margaret Hope Bacon, *Mothers of Feminism: The Story of Quaker Women in America* (San Francisco: Harper and Row, 1986); Norval Morris and David J. Rothman, *The Oxford History of the Prison: The Practice of Punishment in Western Society* (New York: Oxford University Press, 1995); Nicole Hahn Rafter, *Partial Justice: Women, Prisons, and Social Control*, 2nd ed. (New Brunswick: Transaction Books, 1997); Estelle Freedman, *Their Sisters' Keepers: Women's Prison Reform in America, 1830–1930* (Ann Arbor: University of Michigan Press, 2000); E.C. Wines, *State of Prisons and Child-Saving Institutions in the Civilized World* (Cambridge, MA: John Wilson, 1880).

6. E.C. Wines, ed., *Transactions of the Third National Prison Reform Congress Saint Louis, Missouri, May 13–16, 1874: Being the Third Annual Report of the National Prison Association of the United States* (New York: National Prison Association of the United States, 1874), 304–6.

7. Mary Coffin Johnson, *Rhoda M. Coffin, Her Reminiscences, Addresses, Papers and Ancestry* (New York: Grafton Press, 1910), 155.

8. Johnson, 150–51.

9. J. Harrie Banka, *State Prison Life: By One Who Has Been There* (Cincinnati: C.F. Vent, 1871), 140, 376.

10. Johnson, *Rhoda M. Coffin*, 155.

11. "A Model Female Prison," *Greencastle Press*, December 22, 1875.

12. Johnson, *Rhoda M. Coffin*, 156.

13. Johnson, 155–56; "A Model Female Prison."

14. For example, *Fourth Report of the Indiana Reformatory Institution for Women and Girls, Year Ending December 31, 1875* (Indianapolis: Sentinel Company, 1876), 10.

15. Johnson, *Rhoda M. Coffin*, 155–56; "A Model Female Prison."

16. "The president visited the prison frequently and issued orders of his own." Rafter, *Partial Justice*, 31.

17. Rafter, 31.

18. Jacob Piatt Dunn and G.W.H. Kemper, *Indiana and Indianans: A History of Aboriginal and Territorial Indiana and the Century of Statehood*, vol. 2 (Chicago: American Historical Society, 1919), 1017.

19. Johnson, *Rhoda M. Coffin*, 157.

20. Johnson, 157–59.

21. Johnson, 158.

22. Rhoda Coffin, "System of Discipline Suited to a Female Prison," in *Transactions of the Fourth National Prison Congress Held in New York, June 6–9, 1876, Being the Report of the National Prison Association of the United States, for the Years 1874 and 1875*, ed. E.C. Wines (New York: National Prison Association of the United States, 1877), 423.

23. Rhoda Coffin, "Women's Prisons: Reformatories, Police, Matrons" (address before the National Prison Congress, Detroit, MI, 1885), 85.

24. Freedman, *Their Sisters' Keepers*, 62.

25. *Fourteenth Annual Report of the Managers of the Indiana Reformatory Institution for Women and Girls Year Ending October 1885* (Indianapolis: Wm. B. Burford, 1886), 6; *Twelfth Annual Report of the Managers of the Indiana Reformatory Institution for Women and Girls, Ending October 31, 1883* (Indianapolis: Wm. B. Burford, 1884), 2; *Thirteenth Annual Report of the Board of Managers of the Indiana Reformatory Institution for Women and Girls*, 2; *Forty-First Annual Report of the Board of Trustees of the Indiana Women's Prison and the Fifth Annual Report of the Correctional Department of the Indiana Women's Prison for the Year Ending September 30, 1912* (Indianapolis: Wm. B. Burford, 1913), 4.

26. Freedman, *Their Sisters' Keepers*, 62; Rafter, *Partial Justice*, 31; Johnson, *Rhoda M. Coffin*, 157–59.

27. *Sixth Annual Report of the Board of Managers*, 5.

28. Freedman, *Their Sisters' Keepers*, 62.

29. Coffin, "Women's Prisons"; Coffin, "System of Discipline," 424; Smith in Wines, *Transactions of the Third National Prison Reform Congress*, 305.

30. "The Reformatory: Mrs. Sarah Jane Smith, the Superintendent, Presents Her Case to the Committee," *Indianapolis Journal*, February 5, 1881.

31. Ellen D. Swain, "From Benevolence to Reform: The Expanding Career of Mrs. Rhoda M. Coffin," *Indiana Magazine of History* 97, no. 3 (September 2001): 190.

32. Wines, *Transactions of the Third National Prison Reform Congress*, 303; Wines, *State of Prisons*, 169.

33. Johnson, *Rhoda M. Coffin*, 150.

34. Coffin, "System of Discipline," 571.

35. Bacon, *Mothers of Feminism*, 143. It is also likely that James's poor health and age factored into this dynamic.

36. *Third Report of the Indiana Reformatory Institution for Women and Girls, Year Ending December 31, 1874* (Indianapolis: Sentinel Company, 1875), 13.

37. "Upon recommendation of the Superintendent and after due consideration, on motion it was ordered that Fanny Wagoner, Vanderburg Co. be released on Ticket of Leave and sent out to a home found for her by the Superintendent. Also that Ella Green, Vigo Co. be released on Ticket of Leave and sent out to a home found for her by the Superintendent." *Minute Book No. 2 Reformatory Institution for Women and Girls*, April 7, 1879, 227.

38. "The Reformatory: Mrs. Sarah Jane Smith."

39. For example, Allen County sent four people to the reformatory for a charge of $116.78 due for the period ending December 1, 1874, which is roughly $2,345.63 or $714.12 per person today.

40. "The Power of the Gospel on the Fallen," *American Friend* 1 (1880): 24.

41. *Minute Book No. 4*, November 3, 1885.

42. *Minute Book No. 4*, March 15, 1886.

43. *Third Annual Report of the Indiana Reformatory Institution*, 13.

44. Michelle Jones, "Incarcerated Scholars, Qualitative Inquiry, and Subjugated Knowledge: The Value of Incarcerated and Post-Incarcerated Scholars in the Age of Mass Incarceration," *Journal of Prisoners on Prisons* 25, no. 2 (2016): 102–3.

45. *Twelfth Annual Report of the Indiana Reformatory Institution*, 12.

46. *Twelfth Annual Report of the Indiana Reformatory Institution*, 13.

47. Wines, *Transactions of the Third National Prison Reform Congress*, 304; "A Model Female Prison"; *Second Annual Report of the Board of Managers*, 26.

48. *Eleventh Annual Report of the Managers of the Indiana Reformatory Institution for Women and Girls, Year Ending October 31, 1882* (Indianapolis: Wm. B. Burford, 1882), 15.

49. *Fourth Report of the Indiana Reformatory Institution*, 10.

50. Rafter, *Partial Justice*, 174.

51. Registry of the Indiana Reformatory Institution for Women and Girls. Compiled from Indiana Archive Records, 2017.

52. Michelle Jones and Lori Record, "Magdalene Laundries: The First Prisons for Women in the United States," *Journal of the Indiana Academy of the Social Sciences* 17, no. 1 (2014): 166–79; William Robeson Holloway, *Indianapolis: A Historical and Statistical Sketch of the Railroad City, a Chronicle of Its Social, Municipal, Commercial and Manufacturing Progress, with Full Statistical Tables* (Indianapolis: Indianapolis Journal Print, 1870), 1196; "Sisters of the Good Shepherd," *Evening News*, February 25, 1873. The Indianapolis (1866) and Richmond (1868) Homes for Friendless Women and the House of the Good Shepherd (1873) received convicted prostitutes.

53. Freedman, *Their Sisters' Keepers*, 18.

54. *Second Annual Report of the Indiana Reformatory Institution*, 16; *Fourth Annual Report of the Indiana Reformatory Institution*, 11.

55. Wines, *Transactions of the Third National Prison Reform Congress*, 84.

56. Helen R. Harris, "A Visit to Indianapolis in 1877," *Journal of the Friends' Historical Society* 10, no. 1 (First Month [January] 1913): 13.

57. *Minute Book No. 2*, May 5, 1879.

58. *Minute Book No. 2*, September 1, 1879.

59. Wines, *Transactions of the Third National Prison Reform Congress*, 305.

60. *Seventh Report of the Managers of the Indiana Reformatory Institution for Women and Girls, Year Ending October 31, 1878* (Indianapolis: Indianapolis Journal Company, 1878), 18.

61. An issue that would not subside until the girls were removed to their own location in 1909. "Brevier Legislative Reports. Indiana Legislature, 1881," *Indianapolis Journal* (1881): 225.

62. *Eighth Report of the Managers of the Indiana Reformatory Institution for Women and Girls, Year Ending October 31, 1879* (Indianapolis: Douglass and Carlon, 1879), 6.

63. See Wendy Gamber, *The Notorious Mrs. Clem: Murder and Money in the Gilded Age* (Baltimore: Johns Hopkins University Press, 2016).

64. "The Female Reformatory," *Indianapolis Journal*, January 13, 1881. In this investigation, the legislative committee interviewed over seventy witnesses over a six-to-eight-week period. The fact that this document is missing from the archives is frankly amazing, especially since both the old Jeffersonville legislative committee investigations are available.

65. "The Reformatory: An Investigation of Charges of Cruelty Commences by the Legislative Committee," *Indianapolis Journal*, January 25, 1881.

66. "Investigation of Charges of Cruelty," *Indianapolis Journal*; Anastazia Schmid, "Sexual Conquest in Nineteenth Century Institutions: Dr. Theophilus Parvin's Captive Patients and His Connections in Medical Science" (presentation, American Historical Association, January 2016).

67. "Investigation of Charges of Cruelty," *Indianapolis Journal*; "Another Andersonville: Investigation of the Indiana Female Reformatory," *Cincinnati Commercial Tribune*, January 28, 1881; "The Ducking Tub," *The People* (Indianapolis, IN), January 29, 1881; "Christian Punishment," *The People* (Indianapolis, IN), February 5, 1881.

68. Freedman, *Their Sisters' Keepers*, 24.

69. "Inside," *Chicago Tribune*, January 28, 1881.

70. "What Is Supposed to Have Been General Streight's Statement to Legislative Committee," *The People* (Indianapolis, IN), January 29, 1881.

71. "Inside."

72. "The Hospital for the Insane," *Indianapolis Saturday Review*, January 29, 1881.

73. "Inside."

74. "Female Reformatory," *Indianapolis Journal*, January 13, 1881.

75. "Hospital for the Insane."

76. Justin E. Walsh, *The Centennial History of the Indiana General Assembly, 1816–1978* (Indianapolis: Select Committee on the Centennial History of the Indiana General Assembly, Indiana Historical Bureau, 1987), 252.

77. Walsh, *Centennial History*, 252–53.

78. "Inside." Historian Wendy Gamber chronicled the life of Mrs. Clem in *The Notorious Mrs. Clem*.

79. "Another Andersonville."

80. "Inside."

81. "Inside."

82. "Christian Punishment."

83. "Investigation of Charges of Cruelty."

84. "Christian Punishment."

85. "Christian Punishment."

86. "Investigation of Charges of Cruelty."

87. "Investigation of Charges of Cruelty."

88. "The Reformatory: Mrs. Sarah Jane Smith, the Superintendent, Presents Her Case to the Committee," *Indianapolis Journal*, February 5, 1881.

89. *Minute Book No. 3*, January 7, 1881.

90. "No subordinate officer should have the power to inflict punishment." Coffin, "System of Discipline."

91. Coffin.

92. Coffin, 424.

93. Coffin, 424.

94. "Mrs. Sarah Jane Smith."

95. April Haynes, *Riotous Flesh: Women, Physiology, and the Solitary Vice in Nineteenth-Century America* (Chicago: University of Chicago Press, 2015), 12.

96. Haynes, 12.

97. Helen Lefkowitz Horowitz, *Rereading Sex: Battles over Sexual Knowledge and Suppression in Nineteenth-Century America* (New York: Vintage Books, 2003), 68.

98. "Mrs. Sarah Jane Smith."

99. Aka Mary Jane Schweitzer.

100. "Nearing the Close of the Reformatory Investigation. The Story as Told by a Better Class of Prisoners," *Sentinel*, February 9, 1881.

101. "Mrs. Sarah Jane Smith."

102. Haynes, *Riotous Flesh*, 10–13.

103. David Rothman, *The Discovery of the Asylum: Social Order and Disorder in the New Republic*, rev. ed. (Boston: Little, Brown, 1990), 15–19.

104. "State Reform School and Women's Prison," *Richmond Indiana Palladium*, March 7, 1874.

105. *Minute Book No. 2*, April 7, 1879.

106. *Minute Book No. 2*, May 5, 1879.

107. *Minute Book No. 2*, June 2, 1879.

108. "Mrs. Sarah Jane Smith."

109. James E. Rhoades, ed., "A Women's Prison," *Friends' Review: A Religious, Literary and Miscellaneous Journal, 1877–1878* (Philadelphia, 1878), 31:219.

110. "Mrs. Sarah Jane Smith."

111. "At Last: The Reformatory Investigating Committee Thinks It Has Got Enough," *Indiana State Sentinel*, February 23, 1881.

112. "Reformatory Investigating Committee."

113. "Reformatory Investigating Committee."

114. "Reformatory Investigating Committee."

115. "Nearing the Close."

116. "Nearing the Close."

117. Rafter, *Partial Justice*, 172.

118. "Not Guilty," *Indiana State Sentinel*, March 2, 1881.

119. "Brevier Legislative Reports. Indiana Legislature, 1881," *Indianapolis Journal* (1881): 225; "Female Reformatory."

120. "Brevier Legislative Reports," 225.

121. "Laws Governing and Controlling the Indiana Women's Prison," *Forty-First Annual Report of the Board of Trustees of the Indiana Women's Prison and the Fifth Annual Report of the Correctional Department of the Indiana Women's Prison for the Year Ending September 30, 1912* (Indianapolis: Wm. B. Burford, 1913), 41.

122. "Brevier Legislative Reports," 225.

123. "Interest Legislation," *Indiana State Sentinel*, February 5, 1881, 16.

124. "Indianapolis, IN," *Chicago Tribune*, June 7, 1883, 27.

125. "The fact is mentioned in the hope that no successor may have to pass through the same ordeal at the suggestion of some dissatisfied officer or ungrateful inmate confined for murder; perjury or theft, and ready to swear to anything for a ride to the city, or a few hours spent in the company of the opposite sex." *Tenth Annual Report of the Managers of the Indiana Reformatory Institution for Women and Girls, Year Ending October 31, 1881* (Indianapolis: Wm. B. Burford, 1882), 13.

126. E.C. Wines, ed., *Transactions of the Third National Prison Reform Congress Saint Louis, Missouri, May 13–16, 1874: Being the Third Annual Report of the National Prison Association of the United States* (New York: National Prison Association of the United States, 1874), 306. Sarah Smith's methods, at least on paper, included "special care in sickness, little acts of kindness," "commendation and encouragement," and "firmness and steadiness in the administration of discipline." The results being "a well-regulated family; good religious influence; rules willingly obeyed; duties cheerfully performed; little punishment necessary; the use of tobacco dispensed with . . . [along with] the religion of Jesus, [would] subdue the most hardened."

127. "Nearing the Close."

128. "Mrs. Sarah Jane Smith."

129. For example, Wines, *State of Prisons*; Harris, "Visit to Indianapolis in 1877," 13.

130. "It is said that Mrs. Sarah Smith who has been superintendent of the Indiana Prison and Reformatory for Women and Girls from the beginning, is preparing to resign, a step made necessary by continued ill-health and increasing infirmities." *Fort Wayne Daily News*, November 23, 1883.

131. *Fourteenth Annual Report of the Managers of the Indiana Reformatory Institution for Women and Girls, Year Ending October 31, 1885* (Indianapolis: Wm. B. Burford, 1886), 5.

132. "Obituary," *Steuben Republican*, April 27, 1887, 4.

133. Henry Hartshorne, ed., "Anecdote of Sarah J. Smith," *Friends' Review: A Religious, Literary and Miscellaneous Journal* 1885–1886 (Philadelphia, 1886), 39:391; "A Noble Life: Death of Sarah J. Smith, the Well-known Quaker Philanthropist," *Daily Inter Ocean*, December 19, 1885; *Minutes of Indiana Yearly Meeting of Friends Held in Richmond, Indiana* (Indianapolis: Nicholson and Bro., 1887), 116–20; "Memorial of Sarah J. Smith"; "Sarah J. Smith—A Modern Friend," *American Friend* 7, no. 2 (First Month [January] 11, 1900): 31.

134. *Minute Book No. 4*, May 6, 1884.

135. *Minute Book No. 4*, May 7, 1884.

136. *Minute Book No. 4*, February 25, 1885.

137. *Minute Book No. 4*, March 15, 1886.

138. *Minute Book No. 4*, March 15, 1886.

139. *Minute Book No. 4*, March 2, 1886.

140. "Indiana Women's Reformatory," *Indiana State Sentinel*, August 31, 1887.

141. "The   Female   Reformatory: Newspaper   Comment   Upon

Mrs. Rhoda M. Coffin's Resignation," *Sentinel*, April 7, 1881; "Trouble Among the Reformatory Lady Managers," *The People*, April 9, 1881.

142. "The Female Reformatory: Mrs. Rhoda M. Coffin, the President, Sends In Her Resignation as a Member of the Board of Managers," *Indianapolis Journal*, April 5, 1881.

143. "Trouble Among the Reformatory Lady Managers."

144. "The Female Reformatory: Newspaper Comment."

145. "The Female Reformatory: Mrs. Rhoda M. Coffin, the President, Sends In Her Resignation as a Member of the Board of Managers," *Indianapolis Journal*, April 5, 1881.

146. "The Female Reformatory: Newspaper Comment."

147. "Trouble Among the Reformatory Lady Managers."

148. "Trouble Among the Reformatory Lady Managers."

149. "The Female Reformatory: Newspaper Comment."

150. "The Female Reformatory: Newspaper Comment."

151. Ginzberg, *Women and the Work of Benevolence*, 74.

152. "The Female Reformatory: Newspaper Comment."

153. Thomas D. Hamm, *The Transformation of American Quakerism: Orthodox Friends, 1800–1907* (Bloomington: Indiana University Press, 1988), 220.

154. "Prominent Women Are Both Called on the Same Day," *Richmond Palladium and Sun Telegram*, September 29, 1909.

155. "Prominent Women."

156. Stephanie Shields, "Gender: An Intersectionality Perspective," *Sex Roles* 59 (2008): 307.

157. Rafter, *Partial Justice*, 13, 49.

158. Chandan Reddy, *Freedom with Violence: Race, Sexuality, and the U.S. State* (Durham, NC: Duke University Press, 2011), 58.

159. Michel Foucault, *Language, Counter-Memory, Practice: Selected Essays and Interviews*, trans. Donald Bouchard and Sherry Simon, ed. Donald Bouchard (Ithaca, NY: Cornell University Press, 1977).

160. Michel Foucault and Jay Miskowiec, "Of Other Spaces," *Diacritics* 16, no. 1 (Spring 1986).

161. Foucault and Miskowiec, "Of Other Spaces."

162. "Prison Town: Paying the Price," Real Cost of Prisons Project, www.realcostofprisons.org.

163. Foucault and Miskowiec, "Of Other Spaces."

164. Foucault and Miskowiec, "Of Other Spaces."

165. William Page, "Prison Reform IX: Treatment of Prisoners," *Fort Wayne News*, January 30, 1897.

166. J. Harrie Banka, *State Prison Life: By One Who Has Been There* (Cincinnati: C.F. Vent, 1871), 152.

167. Horowitz, *Rereading Sex*, 106.

168. "A Model Female Prison," *Greencastle Press*, December 22, 1875.

169. "A Model Female Prison."

5: Jennie and the Economics of the Reformatory

1. "The Official Registry of the Indiana Reformatory Institution for Women and Girls," 1873–1884, Indiana Women's Prison, Indiana Archives and Records Administration.

2. *Third Report of the Indiana Reformatory Institution for Women and Girls* (Indianapolis: Sentinel Company, 1875), 12. For itemized annual accounts and eleven-year totals by county, see Molly Whitted and Michelle Williams, " 'But I Only Wanted Them to Conform': A Detailed Look into the Initial Cohort of Girls at the Indiana Reformatory Institution for Women and Girls between 1873 and 1884," *Midwest Social Sciences Journal* 22 (2019): 184–86.

3. *Second Report of the Indiana Reformatory Institution for Women and Girls* (Indianapolis: Sentinel Company, 1874), 27.

4. *Second Report*, 28.

5. *Fifth Report of the Indiana Reformatory Institution for Women and Girls* (Indianapolis: Sentinel Company, 1877), 23.

6. *Fifth Report*, 21.

7. *Fifth Report*, 23.

8. *The Revised Statutes of Indiana Containing also the United States and Indiana Constitutions and an Appendix of Historical Documents, Collated and Annotated by James S. Frazer, John H. Stotsenburg and David Turpee, Commissioners* (Chicago: E.B. Myers, 1881).

9. *Fifth Report*, 14.

10. "The Close of the Reformatory Investigation," *Indiana State Sentinel*, February 9, 1881, 5.

11. *Second Report*, 13; *Seventh Report of the Indiana Reformatory Institution for Women and Girls* (Indianapolis: Sentinel Company, 1877), 14.

12. *Report of the Board of Managers of the Indiana Reformatory Institution for Women and Girls* (Indianapolis: R.J. Bright, State Printer, 1871), 12.

13. *Fifth Report*, 17.

14. *Fifth Report*, 17.

15. *Ninth Report of the Indiana Reformatory Institution for Women and Girls* (Indianapolis: Sentinel Company, 1881), 8.

16. *Seventh Report*, 14.

17. *Eleventh Report of the Indiana Reformatory Institution for Women and Girls* (Indianapolis: Sentinel Company, 1883), 11.

18. *Second Report,* 16.

19. *Eighth Report of the Indiana Reformatory Institution for Women and Girls* (Indianapolis: Sentinel Company, 1880), 45.

20. *Thirteenth Report of the Indiana Reformatory Institution for Women and Girls* (Indianapolis: Sentinel Company, 1885), 64.

21. "Female Convicts: How They Are Treated in the Indiana State Reformatory," *Sentinel,* September 25, 1890.

22. *Thirteenth Report,* 65–66.

23. *Fifth Report,* 26–27; *Seventh Report,* 22; *Thirteenth Report,* 65.

24. "Nearing the Close of the Reformatory Investigation," *Sentinel,* February 9, 1881.

25. *Third Report,* 17. The importance of religion is shown by the board's decision to refuse reformation to those unwilling to embrace the faith. In one instance, Amelia Stout, a girl from Marion County who was younger than sixteen years of age, arrived at the institution on May 15, 1876, only to be "Liberated by the Board on account of Poor Faith" five months later. See "Official Registry."

26. *Third Report,* 13.

27. *Fifth Report,* 17.

28. *Eighth Report,* 12.

29. *Eighth Report,* 12.

30. *Thirteenth Report,* 10.

31. *Third Report,* 12.

32. Estelle Freedman, *Their Sisters' Keepers: Women's Prison Reform in America, 1830–1930* (Ann Arbor: University of Michigan Press, 1984), 94.

33. *Sixth Report of the Indiana Reformatory Institution for Women and Girls* (Indianapolis: Sentinel Company, 1878), 7.

34. *Fifth Report,* 14.

35. *Fifth Report,* 15.

36. *Eighth Report,* 12.

37. *Ninth Report,* 8.

38. *Third Report,* 30–31.

39. *Fifth Report,* 48.

40. *Seventh Report,* 9.

41. *Eleventh Report,* 17.

42. Ellen D. Swain, "From Benevolence to Reform: The Expanding Career of Mrs. Rhoda M. Coffin," *Indiana Magazine of History* no. 97 (September 2001): 190–217, 214.

43. *Coffin v. United States*, 156 U.S. 432 (1895); *Clinton Weekly Age* (September 17, 1897): 3.

44. As the sociologist Kai Erikson observes in his study of seventeenth-century Puritan life in Massachusetts, there is often a fine line between the behavior a society deems deviant and the behavior a society deems acceptable or even exemplary. "Behavior which qualifies one [wo]man for prison may qualify another for sainthood." Kai T. Erikson, *Wayward Puritans: A Study in the Sociology of Deviance* (New York: John Wiley and Sons, 1966), 23.

6: Mary Jane and Dr. Parvin at the Reformatory

1. "The Reformatory: An Investigation of Charges of Cruelty Commences by the Legislative Committee," *Indianapolis Journal*, January 25, 1881, 8.

2. "Investigation of Charges of Cruelty," *Indianapolis Journal*. "Mrs. Smith" here refers to Sarah Smith, then superintendent of the reformatory.

3. D.P. Hall, "Our Surgical Heritage," *American Journal of Surgery* 115 (March 1968): 427–28, 428.

4. Theophilus Parvin, *The Science and Art of Obstetrics*, 3rd ed., carefully rev. (Edinburgh: Young J. Pentland, 1895).

5. William H. Parish, "In Memoriam. Theophilus Parvin, MD, LLD," *Transactions of the American Gynecological Society* 24 (1899): 511–14, 514.

6. Dr. W.B. Fletcher, cited in G.W.H. Kemper, "Theophilus Parvin," *A Medical History of the State of Indiana* (Chicago: American Medical Association, 1911), 324–27, 326.

7. Kemper, "Theophilus Parvin," 326.

8. Deirdre Cooper Owens, *Medical Bondage: Race, Gender, and the Origins of American Gynecology* (Athens: University of Georgia Press, 2017), 48.

9. Ojanuga Dorrenda, "The Medical Ethics of the 'Father of Gynecology,' Dr. J. Marion Sims," *Journal of Medical Ethics* 19, no. 1 (March 1993): 28–31.

10. Sims, cited in G.J. Barker-Benfield, *The Horrors of the Half-Known Life: Male Attitudes Towards Women and Sexuality in Nineteenth-Century America* (New York: Routledge, 2000), 89.

11. Tears between the vaginal walls and bladder causing incessant leakage of urine from the vagina.

12. Barker-Benfield, *Horrors of the Half-Known Life*, 89.

13. Cooper Owens, "Irish Immigrant Women and American Gynecology," in *Medical Bondage*.

14. Barker-Benfield, *Horrors of the Half-Known Life*, 96.

15. Barker-Benfield, 83–84.

16. "The Sims Statue Unveiled: A Heroic Figure in Memory of the Great Surgeon," *New York Times* (October 21, 1894), 16.

17. David M. Oshinsky, *Worse Than Slavery: Parchman Farm and the Ordeal of Jim Crow Justice* (New York: Free Press Paperbacks, 1996); Alex Lichtenstein, *Twice the Work of Free Labor: The Political Economy of Convict Labor in the New South* (London: Verso, 1996). The "convict" was in many ways identical to a disposable leased-out enslaved person: a human commodity profitable to both the state and the private corporation. Convicts, disproportionately Black, including Black women, were leased to work in terrible conditions. Eventually the barbaric treatment of those convicts created public opposition, and Black and white convicts alike were relegated to the prison, where both the "criminal" and their treatment were hidden from the general public.

18. Matthew J. Mancini, *One Dies, Get Another: Convict Leasing in the American South, 1866–1928* (Columbia: University of South Carolina Press, 1996).

19. Also see medical experimentation in Oshinsky, *Worse Than Slavery*; Allen M. Hornblum, Judith L. Newman, and Gregory J. Dober, *Against Their Will: The Secret History of Medical Experimentation on Children in Cold War America* (New York: Palgrave Macmillan, 2013); and Harriet A. Washington, *Medical Apartheid: The Dark History of Medical Experimentation on Black Americans from Colonial Times to the Present* (New York: Doubleday, 2006).

20. H. Tristram Engelhardt Jr., "The Disease of Masturbation: Values and the Concept of Disease," *Bulletin of the History of Medicine* 48, no. 2 (Summer 1974): 234–48, 248.

21. "All-Male White House Health Bill Photo Sparks Anger," *BBC News*, March 24, 2017.

22. Salamishah Tillet, "Forced Sterilizations and the Future of the Women's Movement," *Nation*, July 9, 2013.

23. Andrea Smith, *Conquest: Sexual Violence and American Indian Genocide* (Durham, NC: Duke University Press, 2005), 81–82.

24. Courtney R. Hall, "The Rise of Professional Surgery in the United States: 1800–1865," *Bulletin of the History of Medicine* 26, no. 3 (May–June 1952), 250.

25. Hall is not alone in her blatant disregard of these particular facts, and Sims has had defenders. Cf. Regina Markell Morantz, review of *Horrors of the Half-Known Life*, by G.J. Barker-Benfield, *Bulletin of the History of*

Medicine 51, no. 2 (Fall 1977): 307; and L.L. Wall, "The Medical Ethics of Dr. J. Marion Sims: A Fresh Look at the Historical Record," *Journal of Medical Ethics* 32, no. 6 (June 2006): 346–50.

26. Cooper Owens, "Afterword," in *Medical Bondage*.

27. Nadja Sayej, "J. Marion Sims: Controversial Statue Taken Down but Debate Still Rages," *Guardian*, April 21, 2018; Barron H. Lerner, "Scholars Argue over Legacy of Surgeon Who Was Lionized, Then Vilified," *New York Times*, October 28, 2003. See also Sara Spettel and Mark Donald White, "The Portrayal of J. Marion Sims' Controversial Surgical Legacy," *Journal of Urology* 185 (June 2011): 2424–27.

28. Cooper Owens, *Medical Bondage*, 5.

29. Cooper Owens, 6.

30. See each "Physician's Report" from the annual *Report of the Indiana Reformatory Institution for Women and Girls*, 1874 (second report) to 1885 (fourteenth report) (Indianapolis: Sentinel Company; Douglass and Carlon; Wm. B. Burford).

31. Women's medical concerns, gynecological disorders, pregnancies, births, sexually transmitted diseases (STDs), etc., are not documented in any of the original annual reports or physician's notes until a female physician took charge of the institution's medical department in 1886. Despite none of the female physicians being gynecologists or obstetricians, their reports are far more illuminating of such issues than are Parvin's, who at the time was one of the nation's leading ob-gyns. From 1886 to 1900, female physicians took charge of the reformatory's medical practice. It is of interest to note the way these physicians' notes differ from Parvin's. Most of the female doctors record the full names of patients, provide more detailed accounts of births and deaths, often include the names (and sometimes the race) of the babies and/or women, and note venereal diseases and subsequent deaths. In 1890, Dr. Mary Smith noted "an operation for removal of warty growth around the anus was done on October 29." No further details are provided, yet this is far more than what Parvin offered in the prison reports, as he failed to record any surgical procedures he performed there. From 1892 to 1898, Dr. Sarah Stockton presided as physician. She practiced at Central State Hospital for the Insane before and after her term at the reformatory. Her physician's notes provide much greater detail than do the reports of those who came before her, and included notes on pregnancies, STDs (particularly syphilis), uterine problems, menstrual disturbances, and psychological disorders, some of which caused their sufferers to be transferred to the Hospital for the Insane. See each "Physician's Report" from the annual *Report of the Indiana Reformatory Institution*

for Women and Girls, 1886 (fifteenth report) to 1901 (thirtieth report) (Indianapolis: Wm. B. Burford).

32. See each "Physician's Report" from the annual *Report of the Indiana Reformatory Institution for Women and Girls,* 1874 (second report) to 1885 (fourteenth report).

33. Theophilus Parvin in *American Practitioner,* cited in H. Hall, "Sulphate of Cinchonidia," *Cincinnati Lancet and Observer* 19 (1876): 72–74, 74.

34. Theophilus Parvin, "Typhoid Fever in the Indiana Reformatory," *American Practitioner* 21 (1880): 329–42, 334–35.

35. Parvin, "Typhoid Fever," 335.

36. Theophilus Parvin, "An Illustration of Xenomenia," *Transactions of the American Gynecological Society* 1 (1876): 135–36.

37. See "Physician's Report" (p. 49) and "Superintendent's Report" (p. 14) from the *Eighth Report of the Indiana Reformatory Institution for Women and Girls* (Indianapolis: Douglass and Carlon, 1879).

38. Margaret Conrads–Prisoner Number 127. "IWP First 300 Prisoners" Excel spreadsheet. Department of Correction, Indiana Women's Prison, Indiana Archives and Records Administration.

39. Theophilus Parvin, "Notes of Practice at the Indiana Reformatory for Women and Girls," *American Practitioner* (October 1875): 193–200, 198–99.

40. "The Reformatory: Mrs. Sarah Jane Smith, the Superintendent, Presents Her Case to the Committee," *Indianapolis Journal,* February 5, 1881.

41. According to Michel Foucault, nineteenth-century protection of wealth was tied to rigorous morality. Foucault states, "It was necessary to constitute the populace as a moral subject and to break its commerce with criminality, and hence to segregate the delinquents and to show them to be dangerous not only for the rich but for the poor as well, vice ridden instigators of the gravest social perils" (p. 41). This instilled paradigm of thinking has remained necessary for the continuation, and indeed the expansion, of the carceral state. See Michel Foucault interview by J.J. Brochier, "Prison Talk," in *Power/Knowledge: Selected Interviews and Other Writings 1972–1977,* ed. Colin Gordon (New York: Pantheon Books, 1977).

42. "Mrs. Sarah Jane Smith."

43. Hiram Corson, A. Nebinger, R.L. Sibbet, "Report on the Propriety of Having an Assistant Female Superintendent for the Female Department of Every Hospital for the Insane Under Control of the State," in *Transactions of the Medical Society of the State of Pennsylvania* (Philadelphia: Collins, 1878), 174.

44. See "Superintendent's Report" from the *Eleventh Report of the Indiana Reformatory Institution for Women and Girls* (Indianapolis: Wm. B. Burford, 1882), 15.

45. *Eleventh Report*, 17.

46. Engelhardt, "Disease of Masturbation," 247.

47. Theophilus Parvin, "Hygiene of the Sexual Function: A Lecture Delivered in the Regular Course at Jefferson Medical College of Philadelphia, November 7, 1883" (Philadelphia: Wm. F. Fell, 1884), 7.

48. Theophilus Parvin, "Nymphomania and Masturbation," *Medical Age* 4, (1886): 49–51, 49.

49. Parvin, "Nymphomania and Masturbation," 50.

50. "Nearing the Close of the Reformatory Investigation," *Sentinel*, February 9, 1881.

51. Parvin, "Hygiene of the Sexual Function," 8.

52. "Mrs. Sarah Jane Smith."

53. "Mrs. Sarah Jane Smith."

54. "Nearing the Close."

55. "Investigation of the Indiana Female Reformatory," *Cincinnati Commercial Tribune*, January 28, 1881.

56. Parvin, "Notes of Practice," 197.

57. "Investigation of Charges of Cruelty"; "Reformatory Investigation: The Edwins Committee Holds Its First Meeting for Inquiry into the Truth of Charges," *Indianapolis News*, January 25, 1881.

58. Helen Wilson, *The Treatment of the Misdemeanant in Indiana, 1816–1936* (Chicago: University of Chicago Press, 1938); Wendy Gamber, *The Notorious Mrs. Clem: Murder and Money in the Gilded Age* (Baltimore: Johns Hopkins University Press, 2016).

59. "Mrs. Sarah Jane Smith."

60. Parvin, "Notes of Practice," 196.

61. Parvin, "The Third Stage of Abortion," *Obstetric Gazette* 3 (July 1880): 1–5.

62. Parvin, "The Third Stage of Abortion," 4–5.

63. "Mrs. Sarah Jane Smith."

64. J. Clifton Edgar, "The Manikin in the Teaching of Practice Obstetrics," *New York Medical Journal* 52 *(July–December 1890)* (New York: D. Appleton, 1890), 701–9, 705–6.

65. Edgar, "The Manikin," 705. Dr. Edgar also produced a textbook in 1903, *The Practice of Obstetrics*.

66. Edgar, 706.

67. Edgar, 708–9.

68. Brandy Schillace, "Of Manikins and Machines: The Evolution of Obstetrical Phantoms," Dittrick Museum of Medical History blog, October 15, 2013.

69. J. Harrie Banka, *State Prison Life: By One Who Has Been There* (Cincinnati: C.F. Vent, 1871), 238.

70. Susan Lederer, "Experimentation on Human Beings," *OAH Magazine of History* 19, no. 5 (September 2005): 20.

71. L. Song Richardson, "When Human Experimentation Is Criminal," *Journal of Criminal Law and Criminology* 99, no. 1 (Winter 2009): 101.

72. Alice Walker, *Possessing the Secret of Joy* (New York: Simon and Schuster, 1997), 288.

7: Johanna Kitchen—The Grand Lady of Stringtown

1. Jacob Piatt Dunn, *Greater Indianapolis: The History, the Industries, the Institutions, and the People of a City of Homes*, illustrated (Chicago: Lewis, 1910), 1:434.

2. "Those Dead Babies," *Indianapolis News*, April 3, 1872.

3. "Pitiful (Drunken Teen)," *Indianapolis News*, September 2, 1872.

4. "An Indianapolis Sensation: How Subjects Are Procured for the Dissecting Table: Negroes Murdered. Horrible Revelations," *Conservative*, March 25, 1870.

5. "A Religious Skirmish," *Indianapolis News*, December 17, 1870.

6. "An Indianapolis Duchess," *Cincinnati Enquirer*, February 15, 1872.

7. "An Indianapolis Duchess."

8. "The End of a Spree" *Indianapolis News*, October 4, 1871; "Man Robbed," *Indianapolis News*, August 6, 1870; *Indianapolis News*, June 10, 1872.

9. *Indianapolis News*, December 29, 1870.

10. *Indianapolis News*, December 29, 1870.

11. "Substantial Improvement," *Cincinnati Enquirer*, January 13, 1872.

12. *Indianapolis News*, January 13, 1872.

13. *Indianapolis News*, May 9, 1870.

14. *Terre Haute Daily Gazette*, July 7, 1871.

15. *Indianapolis News*, March 4, 1871.

16. *Indianapolis News*, April 19, 1872.

17. "The Sunday School Work," *Indianapolis News*, June 17, 1872.

18. *Indianapolis News*, January 27, 1874.

19. "Pleasant Valley Stringtown," *Fayette County Herald*, May 11, 1876.

20. "Death of the Duchess of Stringtown," *Indianapolis News*, February 7, 1872.

21. Hedges was commonly involved in investigations of death

believed to be foul play, yet he regularly ruled in favor of natural causes, at least as far as the Stringtown cases were concerned. An argument can be made that the coroner found little merit in investigating the death of a sex worker or, perhaps more likely, that those in positions of power pressured him to disguise murder as "natural causes" or not to investigate.

22. "Death of the Duchess of Stringtown," *Indianapolis News*, February 7, 1872.

23. "Death of the Duchess of Stringtown."

24. "Death of the Duchess of Stringtown."

25. "Death of the Duchess of Stringtown."

26. "Death of the Duchess of Stringtown."

27. "Death of the Duchess of Stringtown."

28. "Pleasant Valley Stringtown," *Fayette County Herald*, May 11, 1876.

8: *The Duchess of Stringtown* Play

1. "A Solemn Scene," *Indianapolis News*, February 12, 1872.

2. "The Grand Duchess," *Indianapolis Journal*, February 8, 1872.

3. "Death of a Noted Character," *Indianapolis People*, February 11, 1872.

9: Hazel at the Indiana Girls' School

1. U.S. Marshall's Office, form no. 491. *The United States v. Hazel France*. Case no. 2047, General Record 6, p. 407, United States Court, Eastern District of Illinois, National Archives at Chicago, National Archives and Records Administration.

2. Mark Thomas Connelly, *The Response to Prostitution in the Progressive Era* (Chapel Hill: University of North Carolina Press, 1980), 115.

3. Janet Duitsman Cornelius and Martha LaFrenz Kay, " 'Sin City' and Its Reformers," in *Women of Conscience: Social Reform in Danville, Illinois, 1890–1930* (Columbia, SC: University of South Carolina Press, 2008).

4. Cornelius and Kay, 124.

5. Cornelius and Kay, 124.

6. Connelly, *Response to Prostitution*, 115–16.

7. Michal Conant, "Federalism, the Mann Act, and the Imperative to Decriminalize Prostitution," *Cornell Journal of Law and Public Policy* 5, no. 2 (Winter 1996): 110.

8. Hazel Moon–Prisoner Number 1473. Department of Correction, Girls' School 1873–1935, ICPR Digital Archives, Indiana Archives and Records Administration.

9. Hazel Moon–Prisoner Number 1473.

10. Clifton Phillips, *Indiana in Transition: The Emergence of an Industrial*

Commonwealth: 1880–1920 (Indianapolis: Indiana Historical Bureau and Indiana Historical Society, 1968), 488.

11. "Urges Respect for Work," *Indianapolis Star*, April 8, 1912, 2.

12. United States of America: SS. Eastern District of Illinois. *The United States v. Hattie Black*, Case no. 2048, General Record 6, p. 408, 434, Complete Record 7, p. 413.

13. Roy France, Terre Haute, Indiana, City Directory, 1906; U.S. City Directories, 1822–1995; Ancestry.com; Vigo County, Indiana, *Index to Marriage Record 1840–1920*, County Clerk's Office, Book 26, p. 189.

14. "Tell Their Wives Walking Is Good. And Cruel Terre Haute Men Refuse to Send Money to the Runaways," *Richmond Palladium (Daily)*, November 28, 1909, 1.

15. Superintendent's Monthly Reports, Girls' School Indiana, July 1912, Policy Files and Correspondence, Box 47 of 52, Indiana Department of Correction, Indiana Archives and Records Administration.

16. "Takes Poison When Caught," *Waukegan News-Sun*, August 7, 1912, 2.

17. Superintendent's Monthly Reports, Girls' School Indiana, July 1912.

18. Superintendent's Monthly Reports, Girls' School Indiana, September 1912.

19. Lulu, for example, had been confined at the school after being caught with a married man, who was then arrested for "having contributed to the girl's delinquency." After his wife filed for divorce, the man told reporters, "The money I spent on [Lulu] I don't regret, for I certainly had a good time out of it." "Not to Fight Divorce," *Champaign Daily News*, April 30, 1909, 11.

20. "Held on Story of Girls," *Indianapolis Star*, September 29, 1912, 40.

21. "Girls Captured When Riding on Engine Pilot," *Indianapolis News*, September 24, 1915, 1.

22. "Woman Arrested as White Slave Agent," *Indianapolis Star*, January 31, 1912, 3.

23. "Woman Arrested as White Slave Agent."

24. "Woman Arrested as White Slave Agent."

25. "Woman Arrested as White Slave Agent."

26. Daniel Hogan, Clerk. The President of the United States, To the Marshal of the Eastern District of Illinois, *The United States v. Hazel France*, Case no. 2051, General Record 6, p. 409, Complete Record 7, pp. 425, 435, 436, United States Court, Eastern District of Illinois, National Archives at Chicago, National Archives and Records Administration.

27. United States of America: SS. Eastern District of Illinois, *The United*

States v. Hattie Black, Case no. 2048, General Record 6, p. 408, 434, Complete Record 7, p. 413, United States Court, Eastern District of Illinois, National Archives at Chicago, National Archives and Records Administration; "Hattie Black Is in County Jail," *Danville Commercial News,* February 20, 1912, 1.

28. "Women Slavers Sent to Prison," *Journal Gazette* (Mattoon, IL), March 12, 1912, 1.

29. Laura María Agustín, "Helping Women Who Sell Sex: The Construction of Benevolent Identities," *Rhizomes* 10 (Spring 2005), www.rhizomes.net/issue10/agustin.htm.

30. Agustín.

10: "Feeble-Minded" Women at Harper's Lodge

1. Alexandra Minna Stern, " 'We Cannot Make a Silk Purse Out of a Sow's Ear': Eugenics in the Hoosier Heartland," *Indiana Magazine of History* (2007): 3–38.

2. Robert L. Osgood, "The Menace of the Feebleminded: George Bliss, Amos Butler, and the Indiana Committee on Mental Defectives," *Indiana Magazine of History* (2001): 253–77; Jason S. Lantzer and Alexandra Minna Stern, "Building a Fit Society: Indiana's Eugenics Crusaders," *Traces of Indiana and Midwestern History* (2007): 4–11; Paul A. Lombardo, ed., *A Century of Eugenics in America: From the Indiana Experiment to the Human Genome Era* (Bloomington: Indiana University Press, 2011).

3. James W. Trent, *Inventing the Feeble Mind: A History of Mental Retardation in the United States* (Oakland: University of California Press, 1994).

4. Stern, "Silk Purse," 27–28.

5. Lisa Pasko, "Damaged Daughters: The History of Girls' Sexuality and the Juvenile Justice System," *Journal of Criminal Law and Criminology* 100, no. 3 (Summer 2010): 1099–1130, 1101.

6. Martin S. Pernick, *The Black Stork: Eugenics and the Death of "Defective" Babies in American Medicine and Motion Pictures Since 1915* (New York: Oxford University Press, 1996), 15.

7. "Custodial Care of Feeble-Minded Women," *Fifth Report of the Board of State Charities Made to the Legislature of Indiana* (Indianapolis: Wm. B. Burford, 1894), 50–51.

8. Pasko, "Damaged Daughters," 1101.

9. Nicole Hahn Rafter, *Partial Justice: Women, Prisons, and Social Control,* 2nd ed. (New Brunswick: Northeastern University Press, 1997), 159.

10. "General Report of the Board," *Fifth Annual Report of the Board of State Charities and Corrections* (1894), 7.

11. Osgood, "The Menace of the Feebleminded," 263–64.

12. See also Scott W. Stern, *The Trials of Nina McCall: Sex, Surveillance, and the Decades-Long Government Plan to Imprison "Promiscuous" Women* (Boston: Beacon, 2018).

13. *Laws of the State of Indiana* (Indianapolis: Wm. B. Burford, 1901), 156–59.

14. "Table No. 2. Inmates by Counties," *Twenty-Fourth Annual Report of the Indiana School for Feeble-Minded Youth* (Indianapolis: Wm. B. Burford, 1903), 27.

15. "Feeble-Minded Women," *Fourteenth Annual Report of the Board of State Charities of Indiana* (Indianapolis: Wm. B. Burford, 1904), 68.

16. "Report of Superintendent," *Twenty-Ninth Annual Report of the Indiana School for Feeble-Minded Youth* (Indianapolis: Wm. B. Burford, 1908), 12.

17. "Report of Superintendent," *Twenty-Fifth Annual Report of the Indiana School for Feeble-Minded Youth* (Indianapolis: Wm. B. Burford, 1904), 12.

18. "Report of Board of Trustees," *Thirty-First Annual Report of the Indiana School for Feeble-Minded Youth* (Indianapolis: Wm. B. Burford, 1910), 7.

19. "Report of Board of Trustees," *Thirty-Third Annual Report of the Indiana School for Feeble-Minded Youth* (Indianapolis: Wm. B. Burford, 1912), 8–9.

20. "Report of Board of Trustees," *Thirty-Fourth Annual Report of the Indiana School for Feeble-Minded Youth* (Indianapolis: Wm. B. Burford, 1913), 7–8.

21. "Report of Board of Trustees," *Twenty-Fourth Annual Report of the Indiana School for Feeble-Minded Youth* (Indianapolis: Wm. B. Burford,1902), 12–15.

22. *Twenty-Fourth Annual Report*, 15.

23. Alexander Johnson, "Manual Training for Feebleminded Women," *Indiana Bulletin of Charities and Corrections* (June 1906): 25–29, 25.

24. Johnson, "Manual Training for Feebleminded Women."

25. Given allowances for misinterpreted names.

26. "Place of Birth": Alabama (1), Arkansas (3), California (1), Canada (1), Germany (1), Illegible (4), Illinois (28), Indiana (1,127), Iowa (2), Kansas (11), Kentucky (31), Maryland (1), Massachusetts (1), Michigan (13), Mississippi (9), Montana (1), Nebraska (3), New Mexico (1), New York (5), North Carolina (1), Ohio (29), Oklahoma (2), Pennsylvania (5), Wales (1), Tennessee (9), Indian Territory (2), Texas (1), United States (50), Unknown (27), Utah (1), Virginia (1), Washington (2), West Virginia (2), Wisconsin (2).

27. "Report of the Committee on Institutions for Defectives (Blind, Deaf and Feeble-Minded) and Soldiers' and Sailors' Orphans' Home,"

Fourth Report of the Board of State Charities Made to the Legislature of Indiana (Indianapolis: Wm. B. Burford, 1893), 66.

28. "Industries," *Thirty-First Annual Report of the Indiana School for Feeble-Minded Youth* (Indianapolis: Wm. B. Burford, 1910), 71.

29. Stern, "Silk Purse," 4.

30. Lombardo, *Century of Eugenics in America*, 29.

31. "An Act Entitled to Prevent Procreation of Confirmed Criminals, Idiots, Imbeciles, and Rapists," *Laws of the State of Indiana* (Indianapolis: Wm. B. Burford, 1907), 377–78.

32. Stern, "Silk Purse," 11–13.

33. "An Act to Provide for the Sexual Sterilization of Inmates of State Institutions in Certain Cases," *Laws of the State of Indiana* (Indianapolis: Wm. B. Burford, 1927), 713–17.

34. Stern, "Silk Purse," 28.

11: Sisters

1. "Sisters to Close Home for Girls," *Terre Haute Tribune*, July 19, 1967, 12.

2. Michelle Jones and Lori Record, "Magdalene Laundries: The First Prisons for Women in the United States," *Journal of the Indiana Academy of the Social Sciences* 17 (2014): 166–79. Their article won the 2015 George C. Roberts award for the best article published by the journal during the preceding year.

3. Jones and Record, "Magdalene Laundries," 174.

4. U.S. Bureau of the Census, *Benevolent Institutions, 1904* (Washington, DC: Government Printing Office, 1905).

5. U.S. Bureau of the Census, *Benevolent Institutions*, 270 (Indiana) and 272 (Kentucky).

6. James H. Madison, *Hoosiers: A New History of Indiana* (Bloomington: Indiana University Press, 2014), 97.

7. James H. Madison, *The Indiana Way: A State History* (Bloomington: Indiana University Press, 1986), 185; Vincent N. Parrillo, *Strangers to These Shores* (Boston: Allyn and Bacon, 1997). See Michael Katz's *Poverty and Policy in American History* (New York: Academic Press, 1983).

8. See Daniel A. Cohen, "The Respectability of Rebecca Reed: Genteel Womanhood and Sectarian Conflict in Antebellum America," *Journal of the Early Republic* 16, no. 3 (1996): 419–61. Here elite Protestant whites sent their children to Catholic schools.

9. William Robeson Holloway, *Indianapolis: A Historical and Statistical Sketch of the Railroad City, a Chronicle of Its Social, Municipal, Commercial and*

Manufacturing Progress, with Full Statistical Tables (Indianapolis: Indianapolis Journal Print, 1870), 104.

10. Holloway, *Historical and Statistical Sketch.*

11. Holloway.

12. Holloway, 194.

13. Holloway, 104.

14. Holloway, 126.

15. Holloway, 126.

16. Jacob Piatt Dunn, *Greater Indianapolis: The History, the Industries, the Institutions, and the People of a City of Homes,* illustrated (Chicago: Lewis, 1910), 648. Dunn notes that Fletcher later served as president of the Board of Trustees of the Indiana Reformatory Institution for Women and Girls.

17. "Council Proceedings," *Indianapolis Journal,* August 3, 1869.

18. Holloway, 126.

19. Holloway, 126.

20. "Council Proceedings," *Indianapolis Daily Journal,* February 3, 1866.

21. Holloway, 104.

22. "City Council," *Indianapolis Daily Journal,* April 17, 1866.

23. "City Council."

24. "City Council."

25. "The Council Difficulty," *Indianapolis Daily Journal,* April 17, 1866.

26. "Council Proceedings," *Indianapolis Journal,* August 3, 1869.

27. "Council Proceedings," *Indianapolis Journal,* August 3, 1869.

28. "Council Proceedings," *Indianapolis Journal,* August 3, 1869.

29. August Bessonies, VG, letter to the editor, *Evening News,* February 25, 1875, 4.

30. "Council Proceedings," *Indianapolis Journal,* August 10, 1869.

31. "Council Proceedings," *Indianapolis Journal,* August 10, 1869.

32. "Council Proceedings," *Indianapolis Journal,* August 10, 1869.

12: Billy

1. "Good Shepherd Sisters," *Indianapolis News,* March 23, 1898, 9.

2. According to a deed dated July 25, 1864, "Stoughton A. Fletcher Sr and Julia A. Fletcher, his wife, of Marion County, Indiana, conveyed and warranted to the city of Indianapolis for the nominal sum of one dollar the following real estate." See "This Indenture" (July 25, 1864), Good Shepherd Sisters Indianapolis, Marydale School/Correspondence/ Sacramental Records/Entrance Records/Transcripts, Archdiocesan Archives, Archdiocese of Indianapolis.

3. Typewritten copy of the *Annals of the Indianapolis, Indiana House,*

March 19, 1873–March 19, 1923, Good Shepherd Sisters Indianapolis, Box 2, Archdiocesan Archives, Archdiocese of Indianapolis, 1873, pp. 3–5.

4. *Annals,* 3.

5. *Annals,* 20; Weltha M. Kelley, "Survey, House of the Good Shepherd, prepared for Most Reverend Joseph E Ritter, Bishop of Indianapolis," Indianapolis, Indiana, 1935, Good Shepherd Sisters Indianapolis, Marydale School/Correspondence/Sacramental Records/Entrance Records/Transcripts, Archdiocesan Archives, Archdiocese of Indianapolis, p. 9; Rev. Dorman, "The Convent of the Good Shepherd, Indianapolis, Indiana, 1873–1949," Good Shepherd Sisters Indianapolis, Marydale School/Correspondence/Sacramental Records/Entrance Records/Transcripts, Archdiocesan Archives, Archdiocese of Indianapolis, p. 21; "City News," *Indianapolis News,* October 5, 1875, 4.

6. [No title], *Richmond Item,* January 24, 1883, 1.

7. "Town Brevities," *Noblesville Ledger,* May 30, 1879, 4.

8. "A Subject for Philanthropists," *Indianapolis Journal,* December 14, 1889, 7.

9. "City News," *Indianapolis News,* May 13, 1880, 4.

10. "Transformation Scene," *Indianapolis News,* November 28, 1877, 4.

11. "Transformation Scene"; *Annals,* 48.

12. *Annals,* 48.

13. "Fighting for Her Child," *Indianapolis Sentinel,* May 22, 1889, 8.

14. *Annals,* 26.

15. *Annals,* 99–100.

16. *Annals,* 83, 113.

17. *Annals,* 48.

18. "Additional City News. Can It Be True? A Young Girl Kidnapped Turns Upon Her Imprisoners—Lively Times Ahead," *Indianapolis News,* July 7, 1873, 1.

19. "The Alleged Kidnapping Case," *Indianapolis News,* July 12, 1873, 4.

20. "City News," *Indianapolis News,* May 10, 1897, 5.

21. "Prisoners Admitted from City Court," Good Shepherd Sisters Indianapolis, Box 1, Archdiocesan Archives, Archdiocese of Indianapolis.

22. *Annals,* 49.

23. "City News," *Indianapolis News,* November 16, 1880, 3.

24. "City News," *Indianapolis News,* August 22, 1877, 3.

25. "Prisoners Admitted from City Court."

26. *Annals,* 49.

27. *Annals,* 49–1.

28. *Annals,* 49.

29. "Prisoners Admitted from City Court."

30. Dorman, "Convent of the Good Shepherd," 22; August Bessonies, V.E, "The Social Evil," *Indianapolis News,* June 13, 1873, 2.

31. *Annals,* 17.

32. *Annals,* 29.

33. "Two Runaway Girls," *Indianapolis News,* February 17, 1894, 6.

34. Lee R. Finehout, "The Case of Miss Noon," *Indianapolis News,* May 10, 1897, 10.

35. Dorman, "Convent of the Good Shepherd," 28.

36. Eleanor Conlin Casella, *The Archaeology of Institutional Confinement* (Gainesville: University Press of Florida, 2007), 24–25.

37. *Annals,* 55.

38. Jennifer Cote, " 'Habits of Vice': The House of the Good Shepherd and Competing Narratives of Female Delinquency in Early Twentieth Century Hartford," *American Catholic Studies* 122, no. 4 (Winter 2011): 23–45, 31.

39. Cote, 31ff.

40. Jennie Batchelor, " 'Industry in Distress': Reconfiguring Femininity and Labor in the Magdalen House," *Eighteenth-Century Life* 28, no. 1 (Winter 2004): 1–20.

41. Bessonies, "Social Evil."

42. *Annals,* 48–48a.

13: "Poor Stray Sheep"

1. Typewritten copy of the *Annals of the Indianapolis, Indiana House, March 19, 1873–March 19, 1923,* Good Shepherd Sisters Indianapolis, Box 2, Archdiocesan Archives, Archdiocese of Indianapolis, 1873, p. 15.

2. *Annals,* 27.

3. *Annals,* 24, 27, 28, 36, 37, 38.

4. *Annals,* 15, 18, 38.

5. *Annals,* 24, 6.

6. *Annals,* 39.

7. *Book of Benefactors. Convent of the Good Shepherd, Indianapolis, Indiana.* Good Shepherd Sisters Indianapolis, Box 1, Archdiocesan Archives, Archdiocese of Indianapolis; Miscellaneous financial documents, Good Shepherd Sisters Indianapolis, Marydale School/Correspondence/Sacramental Records/Entrance Records/Transcripts, Archdiocesan Archives, Archdiocese of Indianapolis.

8. *Annals,* 16–20; *Book of Benefactors,* 2.

9. *Annals,* 14; *Book of Benefactors,* 2.

10. *Annals,* 44.

11. *Annals,* 14.

12. *Annals,* 14; Rev. Dorman, "The Convent of the Good Shepherd, Indianapolis, Indiana, 1873–1949," Good Shepherd Sisters Indianapolis, Marydale School/Correspondence/Sacramental Records/Entrance Records/Transcripts, Archdiocesan Archives, Archdiocese of Indianapolis, p. 23.

13. *Annals,* 40.

14. *Annals,* 63.

15. *Annals,* 15.

16. *Annals,* 106.

17. *Annals,* 77; Dorman, "Convent of the Good Shepherd," 19.

18. Dorman, "Convent of the Good Shepherd," 19.

19. *Annals,* 11.

20. *Annals,* 14.

21. *Annals,* 21, 26, 27.

22. *Annals,* 27.

23. *Annals,* 60.

24. *Annals,* 72.

25. *Annals,* 77.

26. Dorman, "Convent of the Good Shepherd," 22.

27. *Annals,* 88.

28. *Annals,* 25.

29. *Annals,* 25.

30. "Cloistered Life Led Here in Indianapolis by the Sisters of the Good Shepherd, Who Never Leave the Six Acres Within Their Convent Walls," *Indianapolis News,* October 10, 1903, 14.

31. To demonstrate the relationship they thought proper, the sisters referred to all women and girls in their care as "children" regardless of their age and expected all to refer to each sister as "Mother." The sisters thought this would show the "children" the interest the sisters had in their charges. *Annals,* 3.

32. "Redeem Wayward Girls in Convent," *Indianapolis Star,* January 24, 1909, 29.

33. *Annals,* 3–4.

34. *Annals,* 85, 88, 99, 106, 116, 163, 176, 195, 215, 221, 305, 327.

35. "Dedicating a Convent," *Indianapolis News,* February 26 ,1889, 1; *Annals,* 215.

36. "Cloistered Life."

37. *Annals,* 305.

38. *Annals,* 295.

39. *Annals*, 85.

40. "Growth of a Good Mission," *Indianapolis Journal*, February 27, 1889, 7.

41. "Growth of a Good Mission"; "Preparing for More Work," *Indianapolis Journal*, June 6, 1887, 5.

42. *Annals*, 92, 99.

43. *Annals*, 98, 99, 107.

44. "Cloistered Life."

45. "Dedicating a Convent"; *Annals*, 88.

46. "Redeem Wayward Girls in Convent."

47. "Cloistered Life."

48. "Dedicating a Convent."

49. *Annals*, 83.

50. "The Greatest Charity of Charities," *Indianapolis News*, September 26, 1887, 3.

51. Dorman, "Convent of the Good Shepherd," 34.

52. *Annals*, 83; "The Greatest Charity of Charities."

53. *Annals*, 71; "This Indenture" (May 4, 1887), Miscellaneous financial documents, Good Shepherd Sisters Indianapolis, Marydale School/Correspondence/ Sacramental Records/Entrance Records/ Transcripts, Archdiocesan Archives, Archdiocese of Indianapolis. They borrowed this sum from Stoughton J. Fletcher, the second son of Stoughton A. Fletcher, who had donated the land. The Fletchers would prove a crucial family in the order's financial health.

54. *Annals*, 78, 80–83, 89; "Preparing for More Work."

55. *Annals*, 164

56. *Annals*, 77, 80, 88–89.

57. *Annals*, 78.

58. *Annals*, 77. This loan was from the bank of Allen M. Fletcher, eldest son of Stoughton A. Fletcher and brother of Stoughton J. Fletcher.

59. *Annals*, 77.

60. *Annals*, 77.

61. *Annals*, 83–85. "City Matters in General. Laying of a Corner Stone," *Indianapolis Journal*, June 5, 1887, 10.

62. "A Home for Wayward Girls," *Indianapolis Journal*, November 20, 1887, 7; "A Slice for the Sisters," *Indianapolis News*, November 21, 1887, 3; "Death of J.A. Reaume," *Indianapolis Journal*, April 22, 1894, 8.

63. The $25 was donated in response to an application prepared by Father Bessonies and Sister Mary. "A Home for Wayward Girls"; "A Slice for the Sisters."

64. *Annals*, 81.

65. *Annals*, 82.

66. *Annals*, 78, 81.

67. *Annals*, 89–90.

68. "A Sale of Needle Work," *Indianapolis Journal*, May 11, 1889, 7.

69. "Miscellaneous Wanted," *Indianapolis News*, December 3, 1914, 16.

70. *Annals*, 129, 148.

71. *Annals*, 149.

72. *Annals*, 151, 165.

73. *Annals*, 154.

74. *Annals*, 168.

75. *Annals*, 170.

76. "Activity in Building," *Indianapolis News*, October 10, 1908, 3.

77. *Annals*, 181.

78. *Annals*, 188.

79. *Annals*, 187.

80. "A Laundryman's Defense," *Indianapolis News*, August 30, 1899, 6.

81. *Annals*, 6.

82. *Annals*, 26.

83. *Annals*, 54.

84. *Annals*, 61.

85. *Annals*, 126.

86. *Annals*, 344.

87. *Annals*, 39.

88. *Annals*, 128.

89. *Annals*, 46.

90. *Annals*, 83.

91. *Annals*, 177–78.

92. *Annals*, 83; Weltha M. Kelley, "Survey, House of the Good Shepherd, Prepared for Most Reverend Joseph E Ritter, Bishop of Indianapolis," Indianapolis, Indiana, 1935, Good Shepherd Sisters Indianapolis, Marydale School/Correspondence/Sacramental Records/Entrance Records/Transcripts, Archdiocesan Archives, Archdiocese of Indianapolis, p. 8.

14: Minnie and Mamie

1. "Statement in Regard to the Suit of Mamie Smith Against the HGS, Indianapolis, Good Shepherd Sisters Indianapolis, Marydale School/Correspondence/ Sacramental Records/Entrance Records/Transcripts, Archdiocesan Archives, Archdiocese of Indianapolis [hereafter "GSSI, Marydale"]; "Mamie Sullivan," *Bedford Weekly Mail* (Bedford, IN), February 15, 1901, 3.

2. "Forced to Stay in a Convent," clipping from unknown newspaper dated April 18 (no year), GSSI Marydale; *Mamie Smith née Sullivan v. The Good Shepherd Society*, the Marion Circuit Court, Case no. 15979, document dated June 10, 1907, GSSI, Marydale.

3. "Mamie Sullivan," *Bedford Weekly Mail*, 3.

4. Minnie Morrison, *Life Story of Mrs. Minnie Morrison: Awful Revelations of Life in Convent of Good Shepherd, Indianapolis, Ind. (A True Story)* (Toledo, OH: Helen Jackson, 1925), preface.

5. Morrison, 3.

6. Morrison, 4.

7. Morrison, 9

8. Morrison, 7–8.

9. Justin Nordstrom, *Danger on the Doorstep: Anti?Catholicism and American Print Culture in the Progressive Era* (Notre Dame, IN: University of Notre Dame, 2006), 107–8.

10. Stephen J. Taylor, " 'Escaped Nuns Are Myths': The Roots of a Forgotten Riot," *Historic Indianapolis*, historicindianapolis.com/misc-monday-escaped-nuns-are-myths.

11. Nordstrom, *Danger on the Doorstep*, 107–8. For parallels abroad, see Rene Kollar, *A Foreign and Wicked Institution?: The Campaign Against Convents in Victorian England* (Eugene, OR: Pickwick, 2011).

12. Justin Nordstrom, "A War of Words: Childhood and Masculinity in American Anti-Catholicism, 1911–1919," *U.S. Catholic Historian* 20, no. 1 (Winter 2002): 57.

13. Nordstrom, "A War of Words," 57.

14. James H. Madison, *The Ku Klux Klan in the Heartland* (Bloomington, IN: Indiana University Press, 2020), 87.

15. Maeve O'Rourke, "Justice for Magdalenes Research: NGO Submission to the UN Committee Against Torture in Respect of Ireland," Justice for Magdalenes Research, 2017, aran.library.nuigalway.ie/handle/10379/15312.

16. James M. Smith, *Ireland's Magdalen Laundries and the Nation's Architecture of Containment* (Manchester, UK: Manchester University Press, 2008); Rie Croll, *Shaped by Silence: Stories from Inmates of the Good Shepherd Laundries and Reformatories* (St. John's, NL, CA: ISER Books, 2019). See also Rene Kollar, "Magdalenes and Nuns: Convent Laundries in Late Victorian England," *Anglican and Episcopal History* 73, no. 3 (September 2004): 309–34; Jennifer Cote, " 'Habits of Vice': The House of the Good Shepherd and Competing Narratives of Female Delinquency in Early Twentieth Century Hartford," *American Catholic Studies* 122, no. 4 (Winter 2011): 23–45.

17. Morrison, *Life Story of Mrs. Minnie Morrison*, 12.

18. Morrison, 22–24.

19. Morrison, 78–28.

20. Morrison, 24–25.

21. Morrison, 16–21.

22. Typewritten copy of the *Annals of the Indianapolis, Indiana House, March 19, 1873–March 19, 1923*, Good Shepherd Sisters Indianapolis, Box 2, Archdiocesan Archives, Archdiocese of Indianapolis, 1873, 264.

23. Morrison, *Life Story of Mrs. Minnie Morrison*, 20.

24. Morrison, 28–29.

25. "Two Runaway Girls," *Indianapolis News*, February 17, 1894, 6.

26. "Verdict in the Noon Case," *Indianapolis News*, May 10, 1897, 5.

27. "Verdict in the Noon Case."

28. "Outbreak at a Convent," *Logansport Pharos-Tribune*, May 10, 1897, 2.

29. "Girl Leaps for Liberty," *Indianapolis Star*, October 13, 1906, 1.

30. "Escaped from School," *Muncie Evening Press*, October 21, 1907, 6.

31. "Girl's Miraculous Escape," *Hamilton County Times*, April 3, 1908, 6.

32. [No title], *Noblesville Ledger*, May 30, 1918, 5; "Returned to Good Shepherd Home," *Indianapolis News*, July 2, 1926, 23.

33. "Denies She Wrote Letter Expressing Her Pleasure," *Indianapolis News*, May 12, 1910, 8; "Statement in Regard to the Suit of Mamie Smith Against the HGS."

34. Letter from S.B. Davis to Gavisk, Terre Haute, IN, March 29, 1907, GSSI, Marydale.

35. Correspondence records, GSSI, Marydale.

36. Letter "From Our Convent of Detroit," April 16, 1908, GSSI, Marydale.

37. Letter from William Allen Kinney to Francis H. Gavisk, February 13, 1909, GSSI, Marydale.

38. *Annals*, 186.

39. *Annals*, 199.

40. *Annals*, 200.

41. *Annals*, 186.

42. "Convent Letters Denied by Woman," *Indianapolis Star*, May 12, 1910, 14.

43. Brickert to Harris, May 29, 1907, GSSI, Marydale.

44. "Convent Letters Denied by Woman."

45. "Convent Letters Denied by Woman."

46. "Both Sides Score in Smith Contest," *Indianapolis Star*, May 19, 1910, 22.

47. *Annals*, 186–87.

48. *Annals*, 167.

49. "Convent Letters Denied by Woman," *Indianapolis Star.*

50. Letters from Mamie Sullivan to W. Sullivan, October 5, 1902, December 3, 1905, and December 31, 1905, GSSI, Marydale.

51. "Contradicts His Daughter," *Indianapolis News*, May 17, 1910, 14.

52. Letters allegedly from Mamie Sullivan to parents, October 5, 1902, December 7, 1902, and December 3, 1903, GSSI, Marydale.

53. "Denies She Wrote Letter Expressing Her Pleasure"; "Convent Letters Denied by Woman."

54. "Convent Defends Suit," *Indianapolis Star*, May 11, 1910, 3.

55. "Convent Defends Suit."

56. "Says Convent Girl Made No Objection," *Indianapolis Star*, May 14, 1910, 14.

57. "Woman Gets Damages," *South Bend Tribune*, May 24, 1910, 1.

58. *Annals*, 200.

59. *Annals*, 200.

60. "Good Shepherd Society Wins," *Indianapolis Star*, April 26, 1911, 6; *Mamie Smith v. The Good Shepherd Society*, On Motion for New Trial, GSSI, Marydale.

61. E.W. Brickert, letters dated June 23, 1910, and June 29, 1910, GSSI, Marydale.

62. "Good Shepherd Society Wins."

63. Letter from Ms. Morrissey to Mother Superior of HGS, April 12, 1911. GSSI, Marydale.

64. "Twice Clears Courtroom," *Indianapolis Star*, April 20, 1911, p. 6.

65. "Good Shepherd Society Wins."

66. *Annals*, 200–201.

Conclusion

1. Avery F. Gordon and Janice Radway, *Ghostly Matters: Haunting and the Sociological Imagination* (Minnesota: University of Minnesota Press, 2008), 3.

2. David Rothman, *The Discovery of the Asylum: Social Order and Disorder in the New Republic*, rev. ed. (Boston: Little, Brown, 1990), 62.

3. Rothman, 62.

4. Rothman, 79.

5. Chandan Reddy, *Freedom with Violence: Race, Sexuality, and the U.S. State* (Durham, NC: Duke University Press, 2011), 226; Michel Foucault, *The History of Sexuality: An Introduction* (New York: Vintage Books, 1978),

1:141; Kai Erikson, *Wayward Puritans: A Study in the Sociology of Deviance* (New York: John Wiley and Sons, 1966), 8.

6. Amy Halliday, Chelsea Miller, and Julie Peterson. "What Are Women's Prisons For?" Gendered States of Incarceration and History as an Agent for Social Change, *Museums and Social Issues* 12, no. 1:55–56, dx .doi.org/10.1080/15596893.2017.1292104.

7. Beth E. Richie, *Arrested Justice: Black Women, Violence, and America's Prison Nation* (New York: New York University Press, 2012), 131–32.

8. Ruth Wilson Gilmore, *Abolition Geography: Essay Towards Liberation* (London: Verso Books, 2022).

9. "Indiana Prison Incarceration Rates: Women," Prison Policy Initiative, www.prisonpolicy.org/graphs/IN_Women_Rates_1978_2015.html.

10. "Indiana," A Compendium of the Ninth Census (June 1, 1870), Population with Race.

11. "Indiana Reformatory Institution for Women and Girls Registry." The record keepers did not capture race and ethnicity in each record; however, blanks were likely white women, as the record keepers showed intent to record African American women each year.

12. A Compendium of the Ninth Census (June 1, 1870). (97.15% white men.)

13. Thomas W. Cowger, "Custodians of Social Justice: The Indianapolis Asylum for Friendless Colored Children, 1870–1922," *Indiana Magazine of History* 87 (June 1992): 105–8.

14. Cowger, 104.

15. See also Anne Gray Fischer's work on women and policing: *The Streets Belong to Us: Sex, Race, and Police Power from Segregation to Gentrification* (Chapel Hill: University of North Carolina Press, 2022).

16. Wendy Sawyer, "The Gender Divide: Tracking Women's State Prison Growth," Prison Policy Initiative, www.prisonpolicy.org/reports /women_overtime.html#statelevel.

Image Credits

page 8: *First Biennial Report of the Board of Managers of the Indiana Reformatory it being from November 1, 1896, to October 31, 1898, inclusive* (Jeffersonville: Reformatory Printing Trade-School, 1898). Photo courtesy of the Indiana State Library, Indiana Collection, Indianapolis.

page 14: Harrie J. Banka, "State Prison Life: By One Who Has Been There" Cincinnati: C. F. Vent, 1871.

page 21: "Sarah J. Smith," *American Friend* 7, no. 2. Harvard College Library out of Harvard Gift of Haverford College Library, May 2, 1935. Originally published 1900; Friends Publication Board, Five Years Friends' Meeting (Society of Friends: US).

page 22: *Studio Portrait, 32, Rhoda Coffin*, Mary Anne Thorne Chadeayne Collection, Historic Huguenot Street. Photo courtesy of New York Heritage Digital Collections.

page 34: *Report of the Indianapolis Home for Friendless Women, 1893* (Indianapolis: Baker-Randolph Litho and Eng., 1894). Photo courtesy of Indiana State Library, Indiana Collection, Indianapolis.

page 41: Richmond Home for the Friendless, South Seventh [Tenth] Street, 1869. *Indiana Historical Society*. Source: Michael A. Tomlan, 1982.

page 57: *Twenty-Eighth Report of the Managers of the Indiana Industrial School for Girls and the Indiana Woman's Prison for the Year Ending October 31, 1899* (Indianapolis: Wm. B. Burford, 1900). Photo courtesy of Indiana State Library, Indiana Collection, Indianapolis.

page 58: Bass Photo Company, #46276, *Indiana Women's Prison, Cleaning Lawn [Clearing?]*, April 24, 1916. Photo courtesy of the Indiana Historical Society, Bass Photo Collection, Indianapolis.

page 64: Bass Photo Company, #46278, *Women Feeding Chickens at the Indiana Women's Prison*, April 24, 1916. Photo courtesy of the Indiana Historical Society, Bass Photo Collection, Indianapolis.

page 66: Bass Photo Company, #46315, *Indiana Women's Prison, Work Room*, April 24, 1916. Photo courtesy of the Indiana Historical Society, Bass Photo Collection, Indianapolis.

page 67: Photo courtesy of Indiana State Library, Indianapolis.

page 69: Bass Photo Company, P0130, #36674, *Indiana Women's Prison Interior.* Photo courtesy of the Indiana Historical Society, Bass Photo Collection, Indianapolis.

page 82: *Workhouse on Blackwell's Island: The Dark Cell,* 1866, Miriam and Ira D. Wallach Division of Art, Prints, and Photographs: Picture Collection, New York Public Library, New York Public Library Digital Collections, digitalcollections.nypl.org/items/510d47e1-0714-a3d9-e040-e00 a18064a99.

page 90: Rhoda Moorman Johnson Coffin and Mary Coffin Johnson, eds. *Rhoda M. Coffin: Her Reminiscences, Addresses, Papers and Ancestry* (New York: Grafton, 1915).

page 95: Bass Photo Company, #46271, *Indiana Women's Prison, Ball Game [Basketball],* April 24, 1916. Photo courtesy of the Indiana Historical Society, Bass Photo Collection, Indianapolis.

page 101: Bass Photo Company, circa 1916. Photo courtesy of the Indiana Historical Society, Bass Photo Collection, Indianapolis.

page 101: Bass Photo Company, circa 1916. Photo courtesy of the Indiana Historical Society, Bass Photo Collection, Indianapolis.

page 107: Bass Photo Company, #46314, *Indiana Women's Prison, Interior,* April 26, 1916. Photo courtesy of the Indiana Historical Society, Bass Photo Collection, Indianapolis.

page 118: General Photograph Collection, Rare Books and Manuscripts, Indiana State Library. Photo courtesy of Indiana State Library, Indianapolis.

page 124: General Photograph Collection, Rare Books and Manuscripts, Indiana State Library. Photo courtesy of Indiana State Library, Indianapolis.

page 131: Bass Photo Company, #36690. Photo courtesy of the Indiana Historical Society, Bass Photo Collection, Indianapolis.

page 135: Brandy Schillace, "Of Manikins and Machines: The Evolution of Obstetrical Phantoms," Dittrick Museum blog, October 15, 2013.

page 139: P0069_P_FOLDER16_PARADE_MEN_WITH_SASHES, Indiana Historical Society.

page 141: Photo credit Elizabeth Nelson.

page 177: File name: PCC_SCH0027, #7983, American News Company, circa 1900–1909. Indiana Postcard Collection, Indianapolis Special Collections Room, Indianapolis Public Library. Photo courtesy of Indianapolis Public Library.

page 182: "Woman Arrested as White Slave Agent," *Indianapolis Star,* January 31, 1912.

page 231: "Girl Loses Arm in Wringer," *Indianapolis Star,* May 8, 1951.

About the Authors

The Indiana Women's Prison History Project was founded by a group of incarcerated scholars at the Indiana Women's Prison. The group has garnered national acclaim in the media and among scholarly organizations and was awarded the Indiana History Outstanding Project for 2016 by the Indiana Historical Society.

Publishing in the Public Interest

Thank you for reading this book published by The New Press; we hope you enjoyed it. New Press books and authors play a crucial role in sparking conversations about the key political and social issues of our day.

We hope that you will stay in touch with us. Here are a few ways to keep up to date with our books, events, and the issues we cover:

- Sign up at www.thenewpress.com/subscribe to receive updates on New Press authors and issues and to be notified about local events
- www.facebook.com/newpressbooks
- www.twitter.com/thenewpress
- www.instagram.com/thenewpress

Please consider buying New Press books not only for yourself, but also for friends and family and to donate to schools, libraries, community centers, prison libraries, and other organizations involved with the issues our authors write about.

The New Press is a 501(c)(3) nonprofit organization; if you wish to support our work with a tax-deductible gift please visit www.thenewpress.com/donate or use the QR code below.

WITHDRAWN